FORGOTTEN SACRIFICE

Dedicated to

Absent Friends

FORGOTTEN SACRIFICE

THE ARCTIC CONVOYS OF WORLD WAR II

MICHAEL G. WALLING

OSPREY
PUBLISHING

First published in Great Britain in 2012 by Osprey Publishing, Midland House, West Way, Botley, Oxford, OX2 0PH, UK
44-02 23rd Street, Suite 219, Long Island City, NY 11101, USA

E-mail: info@ospreypublishing.com

© 2012 Michael G. Walling

A CIP catalogue record for this book is available from the British Library.

Unless otherwise indicated, all images are in the public domain.

ISBN: 978 1 84908 718 6
Cover design by Gino Cieslik
Index by Sandra Shotter
Typeset in Minion Pro, American Typewriter and Palatino
Originated by PDQ Media, Bungay, UK
Printed in China through Worldprint Ltd

Cover photo © Topham/AP
Back cover image © IWM (A 27518)

12 13 14 15 16   10 9 8 7 6 5 4 3 2 1

Osprey Publishing is supporting the Woodland Trust, the UK's leading woodland conservation charity, by funding the
dedication of trees. To celebrate the Queen's Diamond Jubilee we are proud to support the Woodland Trust's Jubilee
Woods Project.

www.ospreypublishing.com

Acknowledgements

I am indebted to many people from many countries who gave their unstinting support for this most unusual project. First among these is my friend and mentor, Anatoly G. Uvarov in St. Petersburg, Russia. He arranged an exceptional itinerary for my research trip to that wonderful city, access to the Russian Naval Archives and State Library, and arranged for the excellent services of Maxim D. Melnikov as guide and interpreter. Maxim, a student at Herzen State Pedagogical University of Russia, effectively acted as my aide-de-camp, ensuring all went smoothly with interviews and getting around his city. A. Uvarov also arranged interviews with two remarkable veterans, Konstantin Sergeev and Israel Levinson.

Yelena V. Smirnova and Eric Johnson at the U.S. Consulate were very helpful and supportive during my visit. I am grateful for their support and assistance.

While in St. Petersburg, the members of the Polar Convoy Club, Juri Alexandrov, Anatoly L. Lifshits, Valentine V. Dremlyuga, V. V. Shehedrolosev, and Igor Kozyr graciously provided access to their remarkable collection of material and personal memories. Lifshits and Dremlyuga presented me with copies of their autobiographies, which have been a great help. Ludmilla V. Poljakova provided copies of the material as needed and also presented me with a signed copy of the Polar Convoy Club book *Polar Convoys in Photos and Statistics*.

My three-week Russia trip also included four days in Murmansk. There, Natalya K. Galeeva and Ekaterina V. "Kate" Yermolina of Gymnasium 9 were my hosts. Kate was my guide and interpreter, taking time off from her teaching duties to do so. These two remarkable women arranged for me to meet with Valentina I. Karepova, director of the Murmansk Shipping Company Museum. Karepova told me of Murmansk Shipping Company's history during the Great Patriotic War. While at the museum, I had the opportunity to interview three veterans: Alexander N. Kurganov, Vilen I. Astashin, and Yevgraf Y. Yakovlev. Each one served as a Ship's Boy during the Great Patriot War when they were in their early teens.

Also from Russia is Michael Suprun, who helped me with Russian sources about Lend-Lease and contacts with Russian authors.

Tony Cooper in the United Kingdom sent copies of thousands of documents from the British Naval Archives and, in many long conversations, helped me identify the most valuable ones for my research. Alan Blyth shared the letters from British veterans he corresponded with over the years regarding their experiences in the convoys. Nick Hewitt was kind enough to allow me to use material from his terrific paper *"Guns in the Night"* HMS Belfast and the Battle of North Cape, 26 December 1943.

From New Zealand, Chris King, president of the Russian Convoy Club of New Zealand, sent me his personal recollections of the convoys and granted permission to use articles from the club's newsletter.

Closer to home, George H. Evans in Canada sent me an autographed copy of his book *Through the Corridors of Hell* along with permission to use material from it. My good friend Dave Campbell in Nova Scotia spent hours with me on Skype evaluating my approach to the project, which helped me to avoid losing my focus. He also provided reassurance that I would get through this.

In the United States, John L. Haynes, a U.S. Naval Armed Guard veteran, autographed and sent me a copy of his book *Frozen Fury, the Murmansk Run of Convoy PQ-13* with his permission to use his memories as part of my work. Charles A. Lloyd, chairman and secretary treasurer of the U.S. Naval Armed Guard Association, assisted in locating information about U.S. Naval Armed Guard veterans and allowed me to use information and stories from the Association's magazine *The Pointer*.

The project would never have been conceived or written without my terrific Osprey editor Kelli Christiansen. It was her interest, great editing skills, and insights that helped make the project great fun.

I owe the most to my wife Mary, who has been my major supporter and cheerleader for yet another book. I don't have the words to express how deeply I love her.

Contents

CHAPTER 1

BRIEFING

The words "Murmansk Run" conjure visions of ice-laden ships and thoughts of freezing to death in minutes. Formally this was the Arctic Convoy run, fought primarily between three countries: Britain, the Soviet Union, and Germany. Numerous other forces also joined the convoys, including those from the United States, Canada, France, Holland, and Norway, and even as far away as Panama and India.

For five years, thousands of men and women from these countries and their allies battled ferociously in the coldest corner of hell on earth. Some fought for survival and some to help others survive, while many fought to crush their enemies. It was war without mercy. If manmade death didn't get you, the Arctic's weapons of ice and cold would. These natural weapons killed regardless of whose side you were on or how just was your cause. No one escaped unscathed the conflict's bitter essence—an essence distilled from fear, anger, killing lust, courage, self-sacrifice, and agonizing death, mixed with blood-stained, oil-tainted water.

Before we start this voyage into the heart of terror, death, and heroism, we'll first take a look at convoys, convoy escorts, the threats to the convoys, intelligence, the geopolitical landscape, and other related information.

CONVOYS

A "convoy" is two or more naval auxiliary vessels, merchant vessels, or both, assembled and organized for an operation or passage together; or a single naval auxiliary vessel or merchant vessel under escort of one or more warships.

Ships are the only way to move large amounts of material across an ocean. In peacetime, they sail alone and follow well-established routes between ports. The best way to protect merchant ships during war is to travel in a convoy with a screen of escorting warships for protection.

Going to sea any time is dangerous. Storms, ice, and fog, along with the risks of fire, mechanical breakdown, or collision await a ship. Crippling or fatal injuries are the penalties for a moment's inattention. War brings the added dangers of being torpedoed, bombed, or attacked by gunfire, or destroyed by a mine.

The best way to protect merchant ships is to gather them into a convoy. This way, fewer escorts can protect more ships at one time. However, convoys draw submarines, predatory aircraft, and enemy warships, increasing the danger. An analogy is a herd of sheep protected by sheep dogs. Trouble comes when there are too many predators and not enough sheep dogs—unless you're one of the predators.

History

The concept of convoying merchant ships in wartime dates back to the First Punic War between Carthage and Rome during the third century B.C. In England, convoys under the command of a naval officer were first employed by Edward III in the mid-1340s. During the following centuries, merchant convoys were employed during war or to protect against attacks by pirates in the Mediterranean Sea. When the threat was gone, the convoy system was abandoned. This was the case for England from the end of the Napoleonic Wars until well into World War I.

From August 1914 to November 1918, the first generation of German U-boats (*Unterseebooten*) sank 5,798 merchant ships. The losses threatened to starve Britain into submission. It wasn't until 1918, almost at the war's end, that the British Admiralty established convoys. That bitter lesson wasn't forgotten when World War II began in September 1939 and the Royal Navy immediately instituted a wide-ranging system of convoys.

Each convoy route was designated by a two- or three-letter code followed by the sequential convoy number. Initially, the Arctic convoys were assigned the letters "PQ" for the eastward voyage and "QP" for the return voyage to the west. The code PQ was chosen from the initials of Commander Phillip Quellyn Roberts, an operations officer in the British Admiralty. Later, the designations were randomly changed to "JW" for the eastbound and "RA" for the westbound convoys.

Convoy speed was governed by the slowest ship. In general, the Arctic convoys traveled at 8 knots. The distance from Reykjavik, Iceland, to Murmansk, Russia, is approximately 1,500 nautical miles (nm) and an additional 374 nm to Arkhangelsk. Thus, under ideal conditions, the voyage took roughly eight days to Murmansk and ten days to Arkhangelsk. Conditions were never ideal, however. Ice, storms, and German attacks forced diversions that often added days to each trip.

Organization

Convoys varied in size from as few as three to more than a hundred ships. The ships were positioned in columns 1,000 yards apart (one half of a nautical mile), and each ship in the column was positioned 500 yards astern of the ship in front of it. Each ship was identified not by name, but by a pennant flag number. The first was the column it was in, followed by the position in that column. For example, pennant number 64 was the fourth ship in the sixth column.

A medium-sized, 48-ship convoy arranged in 8 columns of 6 ships each covered an area almost 4 miles wide and 3.5 miles deep. Add the escort screen, and the convoy encompassed nearly 36 square miles of ocean.

Convoys were organized into two groups: the merchant ships under the direction of a civilian convoy commodore, in charge of the civilian ships when at sea, and the military escort commander, in charge of the accompanying warships.

The convoy commodore and a small staff of assistants rode on one of the merchant ships designated as the convoy's flagship. The military escort commander did not have authority over the commodore.

He could ask for, but not order, changes in the convoy operations or arrangement. The escort commander had the final say if there were any disagreements, however, and this command structure worked very well throughout World War II.

A major part of the commodore's responsibility was to retransmit any messages from the escort commander to the convoy at large directing evasive maneuvers. Because radio signals were easily picked up by the enemy, all messages were transmitted either by signal flags during clear weather or in Morse code by signal light when visibility was poor or at night. Traditionally, the only time a ship's captain was permitted to use his radio was to send a distress call if his ship had been torpedoed, attacked by a surface ship or aircraft, or if severely damaged by storms and in danger of sinking.

Before a convoy left port, a Navy officer held a briefing for all merchant ship captains. During the meeting, each master, as most merchant ship captains are called, was given copies of the convoy organization, the defensive zigzag patterns to be used, emergency communication instructions, and myriad other details needed to operate successfully in company with a city-sized flotilla of ships.

Rescue Ships

Before the addition of one or more rescue ships to a convoy in October 1941, the rear ship of each column was to serve as a rescue ship in the event of the sinking of one of the ships ahead of her. Although the rescue of survivors is an automatic reaction of any seaman, the task imposed considerable danger to the rescuer. In addition, the freeboard of a freighter or tanker in ballast and the unwieldy nature of merchant ships' boats made recovery of men in the water difficult.

With the increased sinkings of ships after mid-1940, the Admiralty sought to requisition certain small vessels for the specific duty of rescue ships. Principally small freighters with passenger accommodation, a good deal of work was required to fit them for their new role. To this end, they were equipped with special rescue boats (eventually one on either beam to guarantee a lee away from the wind), recovery equipment, cargo nets, and a properly equipped sickbay and operating theater staffed by a registered nurse surgeon officer and a sick berth attendant.

Within the ship, small, two-berth cabin accommodations were provided for officer survivors, while bunk-fitted messdecks were created in the tween decks for ratings. Additional, properly fitted washing and toilet facilities were provided for both sets of accommodations, and the original catering facilities of the ships were expanded. Staffing was increased to cope with the added numbers. Eventually, most rescue ships could accommodate some thirty officer survivors in cabins and in excess of 150 ratings in individual bunks.

Given that all survivors had only what they wore when rescued and all clothing was frequently fouled by oil fuel, replacement kits in rescue ships were essential. Every survivor received a set of underwear, socks, shoes, trousers, a jersey or cardigan, a raincoat or oilskin, a cap, and gloves. A toilet kit included razor, blades, soap, and toothpaste.

The completed vessels were allocated to convoys as specific rescue ships and usually were stationed at the rear of the center column of the convoy.

Unlike hospital ships, rescue ships were neither painted white nor identified with a Red Cross emblem on their sides or decks. Instead, painted gray and featuring the blue ensign of naval auxiliaries, they were targets like any other Allied ship. Another significant difference was that the rescue ships were heavily armed, including a 12-pounder, 40-mm Bofors, and 20-mm Oerlikons.

An additional benefit of the rescue ships was that almost all were eventually fitted with High Frequency Direction Finding equipment (see below), and three radio officers specially trained in its use were embarked in addition to the normal complement. These officers were able to take bearings on enemy radio transmissions and pass them to the senior officer escort (SOE) in order to provide a cross bearing in conjunction with his set. This facility added materially to the defense of the convoy and was of great value to the escort.

Arctic Convoy Bases

The primary Allied bases for the Arctic convoys were in Iceland at Faxaflói (Faxa Bay) off Reykjavik and at Hvalfjödur (Whale Bay) just north of Reykjavik, as well as secondary assembly and refueling bases at Seydhisfjordhurd on the east coast and Akureyri on the north coast; Loch Ewe and the River Clyde in Scotland; Scapa Flow in the Orkney Islands; and Murmansk and Arkhangelsk in the Soviet Union.

In the west, Reykjavik and Hvalfjödur were the primary assembly and destination bases from August 1941 through June 1942. After June 1942, operations were initially shifted to Loch Ewe and, later, south to the River Clyde.

At the eastern end of the route, convoys sailed to and from Arkhangelsk only in the short summer months since the Dvina River and the White Sea freeze during the winter. The Soviets strove to keep both Arkhangelsk and the neighboring unloading berths at Molotovsk, Ekonomiya, and Bakaritza open during the winter by the use of icebreakers, but during the first winters of the convoys, they couldn't accomplish the mission. Also, Arkhangelsk lies almost 400 miles further east from Reykjavik than Murmansk, which added several days to each voyage.

Murmansk is the only western Russian port to remain free of ice all year. The city is situated on the eastern side at the head of the Kola Inlet, 200 miles southeast of the North Cape of Norway. The facilities there were primitive. For example, there was no crane with a lift of more than 11 tons, which was needed for unloading tanks, so a crane ship had to be sent from Britain to do the job. The city itself was built largely of wood and, in consequence, suffered severely from the incendiary bombing raids by the Luftwaffe; only a few concrete buildings survived the bombing.

A few miles below Murmansk on the eastern shore of the inlet lies Vaenga Bay, where the oiler from which the British ships refueled was moored. It afforded a poor anchorage, the water being deep and the holding ground bad. At the time, the Soviets were unwilling to allow Allied warships other than submarines the use of their naval base at Polyarnoe, so the convoy escorts were obliged to anchor there. At the head of the bay was a pier, alongside which two destroyers could berth. Survivors from torpedoed ships were accommodated inside a hutted camp that had been constructed on shore.

The Soviet Northern Fleet naval base at Polyarnoe was a narrow, deep inlet off the Kola Inlet north of Murmansk. It afforded excellent shelter to the ships berthed at its wooden jetties. However, its facilities were not offered to the Allies for two years.

Convoy Routes

Three routes were available for getting supplies to the Soviet Union. The shortest but most dangerous was north around German-held Norway to Murmansk and Arkhangelsk. The second went south around Africa to the Persian Gulf, which seemed preferable, but there weren't the necessary rail lines or roads to move material quickly into Russia from the Persian ports. The third was into Vladivostok in Siberia. This was the longest and involved transiting Japanese-controlled waters. Also, from Vladivostok material had to be moved across thousands of miles by means of the Siberian Railway.

Almost all military deliveries went to the Soviet Union exclusively through Great Britain through the Barents Sea to Arkhangelsk and Murmansk. It took between ten and twelve days for each voyage.

The Arctic Convoy Route

Between the coasts of Greenland and Norway lies one of the most turbulent stretches of water in the world. Across it a never-ending succession of gales sweep northeastward, lashing the sea with their fury and pushing up waves to a tremendous height, which hurl themselves against the gnarled and rocky coast of Norway. Speeding round the North Cape, these storms enter the Barents Sea where, their destructive mission accomplished, the high barometric pressure over the polar icecap forces them into the upper atmosphere.

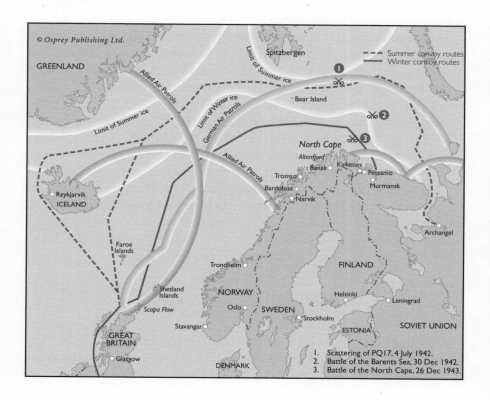

The warm waters of the Gulf Stream flow past the east coast of Iceland and on up the coast of Norway, where they divide: one stream turning north past Bear Island and along the west coast of Spitzbergen, the other flowing along the Murman coast and into the Barents Sea. The mingling of these comparatively warm waters with the colder and less saline waters of the polar region not only covers the region in frequent fog, but also provokes unusual variations in the thermal layers and the density of the sea, both of which are a great handicap to the operators of underwater sound detection apparatus searching for submarines that lie hidden in the depths. Furthermore, the temperature of the sea in these latitudes rarely exceeds 40 degrees Fahrenheit: A man unfortunate enough to find himself immersed in these icy waters has little chance of survival unless rescued within minutes.

The drift ice that forms the northern boundary of this tempestuous area advances and recedes with the seasons. During winter, the southern edge sometimes approaches to within 80 miles of Norway's North Cape, whereas in summer, clear water may be found around the shores of Spitzbergen, especially on the west coast, which, as already mentioned, is washed by an offshoot of the Gulf Stream.

An additional hazard of navigation in these latitudes arises from the freezing of the spray as it falls on a ship buffeting her way through the angry sea. If allowed to accumulate unchecked, the weight of ice thus formed can add so much weight to the superstructure and masts that a small ship becomes unstable and capsizes.

Finally, in time of war, when ships navigate without lights, the almost perpetual darkness which persists in latitude 77 degrees North, for instance, for 115 days in each year makes station-keeping in convoy or formation at these times one long nightmare throughout the voyage. And although concealing darkness for all its difficulties makes it harder for enemy aircraft to locate the ships which they are searching to destroy, the long summer days when the sun never sinks out of sight for the whole twenty-four hours enables them to attack "all round the clock" until defenders are worn out and ammunition runs low.

ESCORT OF CONVOY

The number and types of warships comprising the Escort of Convoy varied with the availability of warships as well as the convoy's destination. Arctic convoys were more heavily escorted compared to those sailing the North Atlantic routes or to those from England to the Mediterranean.

By February 1942, organization of the ocean escorts had been formalized into American, British, and Canadian groups, with each national group designated alpha-numerically. The British Royal Navy primarily covered the western approaches to England; the U.S. Navy protected the mid-Atlantic from its bases in Newfoundland and Iceland; and the Royal Canadian Navy protected the convoys as they departed or arrived off Newfoundland and Nova Scotia. Thus, the British Royal Navy was tasked to continue its role as the primary Arctic Convoy protector.

The Arctic convoy escort typically was divided into two forces. One was the close escort, initially composed of a cruiser accompanied by destroyers, corvettes, armed trawlers, and minesweepers. Later an escort carrier (see below for more information) was added to provide air support and extended antisubmarine warfare (ASW) coverage. The second was the covering force, positioned away from the convoy to counter attacks by German battleships, cruisers, and their accompanying destroyers. This second force was made up of battleships, heavy cruisers, and an accompanying screen of destroyers.

Providing ocean escort for the convoys fell to the Royal Navy. The Soviet Northern Fleet and Air Force were to provide local escort through the White Sea, and later when operations shifted to Murmansk, also along the Murman coast. The reason for this seemingly uneven distribution of responsibility was simple: the Soviet Northern Fleet did not have the resources or experience for long-range escort work.

At the beginning of the Great Patriotic War on June 22, 1941, the Northern Fleet, commanded by Rear Admiral Arseni G. Golovko, was a relatively small force. It consisted of eight destroyers, seven frigates, fifteen submarines, fifteen patrol boats, and several torpedo boats and minesweepers. There were 116 Northern Fleet Air Force aircraft, mostly older types.

The Northern Fleet's primary missions were to protect local Soviet convoys, interdict German convoys along the northern Norwegian and Finnish coasts, and provide support for the Soviet Army fighting on the Kola Peninsula. These missions were accomplished with great valor and sacrifice. As the war progressed, the fleet grew with the addition of aircraft, patrol boats, minesweepers, submarines, destroyers, a cruiser, and a battleship. Some of these were provided by the Allies or produced by the Soviets themselves.

CONVOY THREATS
U-boats

U-boats were the primary threat to convoys during World War II. A U-boat on the surface at night was virtually invisible. By keeping only its conning tower above water, it could get close to the flanks of a convoy or slip in between the columns without being detected. Because sonar and ASDIC (the British sound-detection system) only worked if a U-boat was submerged and until the escorts had radar, the night surface torpedo attack was perfect. To make the attacks more deadly, several U-boats would hit the convoy from different points in a coordinated action. This was the wolf pack.

The wolf pack concept (*die Rudeltakic*) was developed by Kapitän zur See (later Grossadmiral) Karl Dönitz in the late 1930s. Through radio communications, operations officers coordinated the attacks of multiple U-boats against a convoy. When information about a convoy's location, course, and speed was received from reconnaissance aircraft or by decoding radio signals at the shore-based operations center, messages were sent to selected boats directing them to locate the convoy precisely. The first U-boat to locate the convoy would transmit a homing signal for the others and then continue to shadow the convoy until the pack gathered. When the pack was gathered, the attack began.

The wolf pack's favored position was on the dark side of the convoy with a moon illuminating the ships, leaving the U-boat in the shadows. After attacking, the boats would pull away to regroup, rest, and report to headquarters. If contact with the convoy were maintained, they would surface out of visual range and trail behind or attempt to get ahead of the lumbering ships in order to gain a favorable position for the next night's work.

Aircraft

Arctic convoys faced the threat of two types of attacks not often encountered by their brethren in the Atlantic. The first was bomb- and torpedo-carrying aircraft. Luftwaffe bases in Norway enabled twin-engine Junkers Ju-88, Heinkel He-111, and Heinkel He-115 aircraft to reach the convoys throughout most of the voyage. In addition, Blohm & Voss BV-138 flying boats and four-engine Focke-Wulf FW-200 Condor long-range reconnaissance aircraft shadowed the convoys, providing the attackers with accurate location information. Both BV-138s and

Condors often carried bombs and were direct threats to ships. These aircraft would be joined by single-engine Ju-87 Stuka dive bombers when the convoys approached land.

He-111, He-115, and Ju-88 aircraft often teamed up for simultaneous high-altitude bombing and low-level torpedo attacks. While the bombers made their runs, the torpedo planes attacked from several different directions. This forced the convoy to split its anti-aircraft defensive fire power, which increased the chances of one or more ships being damaged or sunk.

Surface Ships

German *Kriegsmarine* (war navy) surface ships, including the battleship *Tirpitz* and battlecruisers *Scharnhorst* and *Gneisenau*, *Lützow*, and *Admiral Scheer* also operating from Norwegian bases, posed a significant threat to the convoys. German destroyers were more heavily armed than British destroyers, which gave them a significant advantage in ship-to-ship engagements. Although attacks by surface ships were rare, the threat was real for almost every convoy that sailed.

Surface ship tactics were fairly simple: Get past the escorting warships and destroy merchant ships with gunfire and torpedoes. Executing these tactics was more complex, however. First, the ships had to sortie from their Norwegian bases without being spotted either by reconnaissance aircraft or submarines. Often, word of these sorties was obtained by radio interception of coded signals (see "Intelligence" below).

After getting to open water, the ships needed accurate information as to the convoy's course and speed. This information had to be updated regularly in case of any significant change in the convoy's course or speed. Even then, though, interception wasn't guaranteed.

CONVOY DEFENSE

In addition to the escorting force of warships, merchant ships were fitted with guns of various quantities and sizes. When war broke out, the British Admiralty began arming merchantmen (Defensively Equipped Merchant Ships [DEMS]).

The Admiralty had laid aside surplus weapons and equipment that had survived the disarmament process at the end of World War I. The initial supply of weapons being very limited, many small ships in coastal waters received only machine guns, even then frequently on a loan basis, the guns withdrawn when the ships moved to less dangerous areas.

On British and Allied ships, these guns were manned either by merchant seamen or by crews from the Royal Navy or Regiment of Royal Artillery.

At first Soviet ships' gunnery crews were made up of soldiers from elite Red Army Guards units because they were the most reliable in the political sense and because Soviet authorities feared that ordinary seamen would desert as soon as they got to England. However, the Guards' lack of preparedness for sea service was quickly revealed, and they had to be replaced by ordinary sailors. Gun crew training was conducted by the Commissariat of the Navy.

When the United States entered the war in December 1941 after the attack on Pearl Harbor, her merchant ships were armed with a variety of weapons manned by teams of U.S. Navy Armed Guard. The teams, comprised of gunners, signalmen, and radiomen, served on both U.S. and Allied merchant ships.

No matter if they were British, American, or Soviet, the gunnery teams suffered higher percentages of casualties than their comrades assigned to warships since they were in combat situations during convoys more frequently.

Antisubmarine Warfare (ASW)

Depending on the size of the escort force and the convoy, two or more escorts typically swept across the front of the convoy, one or more on each side and at least one astern. If weather permitted, one or more escorts would be detached from the screen to range far ahead or to the sides during the day as much as 20 miles from the convoy, looking for ships that had either pulled ahead of the convoy (rompers) or lagged behind (stragglers). Additional sweeps would be made in hopes of surprising a surfaced U-boat. The key was to find the U-boat and at least prevent it from attacking the convoy, and the tactics to accomplish this varied with the number and experience of the escorts assigned to the convoy.

If the U-boat was on the surface, gunfire and ramming were used to destroy her. Ramming almost always disabled the escort, but the trade-off was deemed worth it. It was a different story, however, if a submarine was submerged.

ASDIC and sonar were the only means of detecting a submerged U-boat. Once contact was made, the escort went to full speed for the attack. Sonar could determine the range but not the depth, and, as the escort approached, contact would be lost as the vessel passed over the object. To counter the lack of depth information, a pattern of depth charges would be dropped, set to explode at different depths. Until the introduction of the forward-firing mouse-trap and, later, the Hedge-hog, whose charges only exploded if they hit a submarine, nothing could be done by a single escort to avoid losing the contact as it passed over the target. If there was the luxury of two escorts working a contact, one could feed range and bearing information to the second as the other swept in for the attack. No matter which approach was used, the exploding charges created a wall of bubbles that was impenetrable by sonar. This complicated follow-up attacks.

Sometimes when an escort got a doubtful contact, she would drop what were called "embarrassing" charges on the chance it was a U-boat and that the charges would either cause damage or at least keep it away from the convoy. A depth charge was lethal for a radius of less than 100 feet. Usually it was the accumulated pressure of several charges that cracked the U-boat's pressure hull.

The British began equipping their escorts with radar in 1941, but the sets weren't reliable and had a limited range. Even in moderate seas, a U-boat's conning tower was too small a target to be detected. Until a reliable surface search radar set was developed, there was no way to detect a surfaced U-boat at night except by eye. The best hope was to keep them far enough away during daylight so an attack could not be mounted at night.

During night attacks, specially designed ammunition-carrying magnesium flares attached to parachutes, known as "Star Shells" or "Snowflakes," were fired to illuminate the area and, with luck, a surfaced U-boat. Often, however, the only result was to give the U-boat better visibility for its attack.

Anti-aircraft, Antiship, and Countermine Measures

Massive firepower is the only effective means of defeating an air attack. As the threat from aircraft escalated, so did the number of anti-aircraft guns mounted on both navy and merchant ships.

Also, as air attacks increased, the British outfitted anti-aircraft ships equipped with the latest air search radars and guns designed to fire at high angles. In addition, these ships had more than the normal number of 20-mm Oerlikon and 40-mm Bofors anti-aircraft weapons. Two anti-aircraft cruisers, the HMS *Scylla* and HMS *Charybdis*, were outfitted in 1942 to counter the increasing number of air attacks on the convoys.

Early in the war, strictly defensive items supplied were kite balloons and kites, designed to be flown as a barrage to deter low-flying aircraft; "wiping" and "degaussing," the former a temporary and the latter a permanent defense against magnetic mines; and the Admiralty Net Defence fitted to certain vessels as a partial protection against torpedoes. Paravane gear, which streamed out on both sides of a ship, was fitted to many merchant ships as a defense against moored contact mines also.

In the early days of the convoys, several devices were provided, whose principal purpose was the maintenance of morale; however, danger from the devices was more likely to strike the user than the intended recipient. These included the Holman Projector, with which a primed hand grenade would be ejected by steam pressure from a metal tube aimed at an aircraft; PAC (parachute and cable), a rocket-propelled device that ejected a small parachute with a dependent wire into the track of an approaching aircraft; and "Pigtrough," which, both trainable and with variable elevation, launched a series of small rockets at a target.

Ship-borne fighter aircraft also were used. Initially these were carried on modified merchant ships known as Catapult Aircraft Merchant (CAM) ships. CAM ships were equipped with a rocket-propelled catapult launching a single Hawker Mark 1 Hurricane mounted on the forecastle (fo'c'sle) and carried their normal cargoes after conversion. The catapult could be moved from ship to ship as needed. The Royal Air Force pilot who flew the Hurricane could not land back on board, so he had to either bail out or ditch his plane when his mission was accomplished. In both cases he had to survive in the Arctic water, buoyed by his parachute and lifejacket, until rescued by the nearest escort vessel. CAM ships carried one Hurricane mounted and ready to launch as well as a second crated one stowed in the hold to be mounted when the ship reached its destination. As escort carriers became available, CAM ships were phased out.

In mid-1943, an escort carrier was usually assigned to each Arctic convoy. The escort aircraft carrier or escort carrier, also called a "jeep carrier" or "baby flattop" in the U.S. Navy or "Woolworth Carrier" (referring to the then-famous five-and-dime stores) by the Royal Navy, was a small and slow type of aircraft carrier built using merchant ship hulls and typically half the length and one third the displacement of the larger fleet carriers. Although they were slower, less armed and armored, and carried fewer planes, they were less expensive and could be built in less time. This was their principal advantage, as escort carriers could be completed in greater numbers as a stop-gap when fleet carriers were scarce. However, the lack of protection made escort carriers particularly vulnerable and several were sunk with great loss of life.

For Arctic convoy escort duty, the escort carriers usually carried between fifteen and twenty aircraft, typically a mixture of Hawker Sea Hurricanes, Grumman F4F Wildcats (referred to as "Martlets" by the British), or biwing Fairey Swordfish, or Albacore torpedo/reconnaissance/dive bombers. The escort carriers were used for close support of the convoy while larger fleet carriers accompanied the covering force.

Attacks by surface warships needed to be countered by opposing warships with their greater firepower. Although this is another ideal situation, on several occasions, merchant ships fought gun duels with enemy warships. Rarely did the merchant ship survive these encounters.

Impact of Convoy Loses

The following summary from a 1943 U.S. Naval Air Training Manual sheds some light on the significance of the loss of just three ships. Although it mentions U-boats, the impact also applies to losses caused by aircraft and surface ships:

> *If a submarine sinks two 6000-ton ships and one 3000-ton tanker here is a typical account of what we have totally lost: 42 tanks, 8 six-inch howitzers, 88 twenty-five-pound guns, 40 two-pound guns, 24 armored cars, 50 Bren [weapons] carriers, 5210 tons of ammunition, 600 rifles, 428 tons of tank supplies, 2000 tons of stores, and 1000 tanks of gasoline. In order to knock out the same amount of equipment by air bombing, the enemy would have to make three thousand successful bombing sorties.*

INTELLIGENCE

Knowing what your enemy plans to do and where his forces are is a crucial part of warfare. There are many ways of gathering this information, but four types formed the intelligence backbone for the Arctic convoys: spies, radio direction finding, crypto analysis, and visual observation.

Probably the oldest way to get information is by using spies. During World War II, both the Allies and the Axis powers had agents who either passed along information when convoys were leaving port or when a U-boat was about to go out on patrol. Once ships began carrying radios, it became possible to locate them through radio direction finding. RDF enables users to locate a target by taking a bearing on the direction the signal is coming from. If multiple receivers can get a bearing on the enemy's radio, a fairly accurate fix can be determined. The more bearings and/or the closer to the source, the more accurate the location.

A refinement on RDF was High Frequency Direction Finding (HF/DF), nicknamed "Huff-Duff." This type of intelligence was of significant value for the escorts. Using Huff-Duff, an escort could obtain a bearing on a U-boat that was transmitting, even if the U-boat was over the horizon. Using this information, the escorting force could take evasive action and/or send an escort to attack the U-boat. Because its range wasn't limited to line-of-sight as was radar, Huff-Duff proved more valuable in deterring attacks.

Crypto analysis is the ability to decode the enemy's radio messages. The most famous of these in World War II was Enigma, used by the Germans, which the British were able to break. British code-breaking operations were located mainly at Bletchley Park.

Decrypted German naval signals were referred to as "Z" intelligence or "Special Intelligence" and classified as "Ultra" for security purposes. Knowledge of the existence of the fact that decryption was being achieved was restricted to a very few senior officers and the staff actually engaged in the interception and processing of signals. Until May 1941, it was impossible to break any German Trident naval code. From May 1941 until January 1942, most signals could be read; then there was a blank until the end of 1942 so far as Atlantic submarine traffic was concerned. Thereafter, most German naval signal traffic could be read with increasing ease until the end of the war.

After intercepting an Allied signal regarding ship movements, *Beobachtungsdienst* (B-Dienst or BdU), the German naval code-breaking organization, would form a line of submarines across the probable line of advance of a convoy so that one boat would make contact and report, then issue the necessary orders. In order to use knowledge of an opponent's intentions, it is essential that:

1   The information is received in time to study it and act thereon.
2   The means with which to act are available.

3 There is sufficient time in which to act effectively, i.e., deploy assets, reroute convoys, etc.

Before the U-boats could attack, a convoy had to be located and its position, course, and speed signaled to a command station. BdU would then decide the action to take, bearing in mind the location of other U-boats, and signal accordingly to effect a concentration of several U-boats around the convoy to make a concerted attack.

If the Allies intercepted and deciphered a German order to form a U-boat patrol line, then the Admiralty could divert the convoy around the line to pass undetected. However, the speed of advance of a convoy was about 8 knots, somewhat less than 10 miles per hour (mph), so that the patrol line of the warning that had been received must have been sufficiently far ahead of the convoy for effective alteration of course to be made to carry the convoy clear of the line. Even in the best circumstances, the interception of the signal, its decoding, transmission to Admiralty, and plotting of the positions likely would have taken several hours.

But code breaking went both ways, and the British by no means had a corner on the market. BdU was successful in reading the Royal Navy's secure communications for most of the war. The Finnish Intelligence Service was successful not only in compromising Soviet secure communications, but it also was able to compromise the classified transmissions of other, non-Axis nations as well.

Lastly, visual intelligence consisted of reconnaissance flights and stationing submarines along the enemy's projected track or at key access points to his bases. As it pertains to the Arctic convoys, this method was extremely successful for the German forces. Luftwaffe long-range BV-138 flying boats and FW-200 Condors routinely spotted the convoys and maintained contact throughout most of the passage. U-boats also were effective, but convoys could avoid them by changing course or holding a U-boat down with depth charges until the convoy was out of range.

The Allies had less success with visual intelligence for several reasons. Among these were the range reconnaissance aircraft had to fly to their search areas, weather over the search areas, multiple exit points from fjords for the Kriegsmarine, and limited Allied resources for conducting the reconnaissance. The exception was the Norwegian Resistance, which radioed information about German ship movements. This was done at the risk of capture, torture, imprisonment, and death.

GEOPOLITICAL OVERVIEW
Northern Europe, Britain, and the United States

August 1939–August 1941
Setting the Stage

By mid-summer 1939, the threat of another cataclysmic war hung over Europe like the Sword of Damocles.

Germany had invaded Czechoslovakia on March 15, 1939. In response to Germany's aggression, Britain and France pledged their support to guarantee the independence of Poland, Belgium, Romania, Greece, and Turkey. During the first week of April, Poland and Britain agreed to formalize the guarantee as a military alliance, pending negotiations.

Ten weeks after invading Czechoslovakia, Germany and Italy signed the Pact of Friendship and Alliance, which secured Germany's southern flank from attack. This still left the possibility of war on two fronts: France and Britain in the west and the Soviet Union in the east.

Fueled by the opposing political ideologies of Communism and National Socialism, as well as being led by two of the world's most ruthless leaders, western governments believed there was no chance that Germany and the Soviet Union would ever form an alliance. This belief was rudely shattered when, on August 24, the two countries announced the signing of a nonaggression pact. Publicly the agreement stated that the two countries would not attack each other. The pact was intended to last for ten years.

A secret protocol was included in the pact: in exchange for the Soviets agreeing not to join the possible future war, Germany would give the Baltic States (Estonia, Latvia, and Lithuania) to the USSR. Poland was to be divided between Germany and the USSR. The new territories gave the Soviet Union the land buffer it wanted as surety from an invasion by the West. It also freed Hitler of the threat from the east.

On August 25, two days after the German–Soviet nonaggression pact was signed, Britain and Poland signed a Mutual Assistance Pact. These pacts were the death knells for continued peace in Europe.

War Begins

Germany invaded Poland shortly after midnight on September 1, 1939. Reaction from the rest of Europe was swift at least as far possible. France, Britain, New Zealand, and Australia declared war on Germany on September 3. This day also heralded the beginning of the sea war.

Without warning, *U-30* (Kapitänleutnant Fritz-Julius Lemp) torpedoed British passenger liner *Athenia* south of Rockall Bank in the Irish Sea. The liner was carrying 1,103 passengers; 118 men, women, and children were killed, including 28 Americans.

Lemp torpedoed *Athenia* in the belief that she was an armed merchant cruiser despite having been given strict orders that all merchant vessels were to be treated in accordance with Naval Prize Law (i.e., giving a warning before attacking). The attack gave the British the erroneous impression that Germany had commenced unrestricted submarine warfare.

Following Lemp's sinking of *Athenia*, the Royal Navy was heavily engaged in antisubmarine warfare against the U-boats, with losses on both sides. One early decision was to institute the convoy system starting on September 16.

Poland's fate was sealed when Soviet troops invaded Poland on September 17. Ten days later, Poland surrendered. The subsequent partitioning of that country was complete within a mere forty-eight hours.

At this point, the strongly isolationist United States was doing all it could do to stay out of the conflict. President Franklin D. Roosevelt issued a Neutrality Proclamation on September 5, as required by the Neutrality Act of 1937, which, among other provisions, forbade the shipment of arms and munitions to belligerents. This meant American arms could not be shipped to the Allies as was done in World War I. The President also ordered the U.S. Navy to establish a Neutrality Patrol. The purpose was to track any belligerent air, surface, or underwater naval forces approaching within a three hundred-mile zone off the U.S. Atlantic coast or the West Indies.

Norway and Denmark: April 9–June 10, 1940

As the war progressed, Britain and France became increasingly concerned about securing Norway and Denmark against German aggression and blockading shipments of Swedish iron ore, which were vital to Germany's economy. Much of the ore was transported by ship through Narvik and the Norwegian Leads.

Control of Norway by Germany would give the Kriegsmarine unhindered access to the North Atlantic, Baltic Sea, and the Arctic Ocean, as well as the approaches to the Soviet Union from the far north.

Winston Churchill, at the time the First Lord of the Admiralty, proposed a preemptive strike at Norway before Germany could do the same. However, the British government refused to take action on this proposal. All Churchill could achieve by April 8 was the mining of Norwegian coastal waters to deter German transports. It was a flagrant violation of Norwegian neutrality, but Churchill justified it by noting it would hurt Germany far greater than it would Norway. The move was too little too late.

In the early morning of April 9, Germany invaded Denmark and Norway (Operation *Weserübung*), ostensibly as preventive maneuvers against a planned Franco–British occupation of Norway. After the invasions started, German envoys informed the Danish and Norwegian governments that the *Wehrmacht* had come to protect the countries' neutrality against Franco–British aggression.

The invasion of Denmark lasted less than six hours before the Danes surrendered, making it the shortest military campaign conducted by the Germans during the war.

Norway was a more costly and prolonged battle, although the German attack was a stunning operational success. Kriegsmarine operations were conducted against strong British Royal Navy opposition. This opposition proved more costly to the Germans than to the British.

Britain and France moved quickly to reinforce the Norwegians. However, there was no coherent tactical or strategic plan for using these reinforcements, and they were defeated piecemeal by the better-coordinated Wehrmacht. The retreating Allied forces were evacuated on June 9. Norway capitulated to Germany the next day.

Western Europe: May–June 1940

As the Allies poured men and material into the Norwegian cauldron throughout the spring, Germany invaded the Netherlands, Belgium, and Luxembourg on May 10, and four days later struck France directly.

By May 26, the combined French and British forces were destroyed as effective offensive fighting units. Evacuation of the remaining troops began at Dunkirk and other French ports in Operation *Dynamo*, which lasted until June 4. The French sued for an armistice on June 17, which ended active combat in Europe.

Although fighting on land ended, the war at sea intensified. Kriegsmarine warship, armed commerce raider, and U-boat operations extended from the North Sea to the South Atlantic and into the Pacific. The number of Allied merchant ships sunk mounted monthly with no relief in sight.

Harking back to May 10, two other events occurred which would have a significant impact on the war. First, British Prime Minister

Neville Chamberlain resigned and was replaced by Winston Churchill. Second, British forces occupied Iceland without warning.

Iceland: May 1940

Winston Churchill wrote that, "It has been said 'Whoever possesses Iceland holds a pistol firmly pointed at England, America, and Canada.'"

At the time, the "pointed pistol" threatened the northern convoy route between Britain and the western hemisphere, upon which the island kingdom was dependent for delivery of most of the materials required to sustain its war effort, as well as much of what was needed for its very subsistence. Iceland was perched on the flank of these shipping lanes, which were under heavy attack by U-boats and Kriegsmarine surface warships. German air and naval bases on the island would almost certainly render the northern route unusable and put pressure on the longer and more vulnerable southern Atlantic route.

After the preemptive German invasion of Denmark and Norway, the British government grew concerned that Iceland would be next. Diplomatic attempts to persuade the Icelandic government to join the Allies and become a cobelligerent against the Axis forces failed. After diplomatic efforts failed, Winston Churchill, First Lord of the Admiralty, initiated planning for the occupation of Iceland. Code named Operation *Fork*, the invasion force consisting of 815 officers and men plus a small intelligence detachment was commanded by Colonel Robert Sturges. Departing Greenock, Scotland, on May 8 aboard two cruisers (HMS *Berwick* and HMS *Glasgow*) and two destroyers, the expedition entered Reykjavik Bay two days later.

Meeting no resistance, the troops moved quickly to disable communication networks, secure strategic locations, and arrest German citizens. Requisitioning local means of transportation, the troops moved to Hvalfjödur, south to Kaldaðarnes and Akranes, and east to Sandskeiði, thus securing landing areas against the possibility of a German counterattack. In the following days, air defense equipment was deployed in Reykjavik, and a detachment of troops was sent to Akureyri.

The Icelandic government issued a protest, charging that the neutrality of Iceland had been "flagrantly violated" and "its independence infringed" and noting that compensation would be expected for all damage done. In an effort to placate Iceland, the British promised not only compensation, but also noninterference in Icelandic affairs, favorable business agreements, and the withdrawal of all forces at the end of the war. Resigned to the situation, the Icelandic authorities provided the invasion force with *de facto* cooperation, though formally maintaining a policy of neutrality.

On May 17, 4,000 troops of the British Army arrived in Iceland to relieve the Marines. The British Army garrison was reinforced by Canadian Army units in early June.

Construction of naval facilities at Hvalfjödur began soon after the occupation, and these gradually grew into a large and important military complex. RAF presence likewise grew. Eventually there were five Sunderland flying boats and six Lockheed Hudson bombers for antisubmarine patrol and about a dozen Fairey-Battle seaplanes. However, after German reconnaissance planes overflew the island with impunity and strafed military camps at least once, Hurricane fighters were consequently dispatched in June 1941 to deal with the threat.

The United States: August 1939–July 1941

The United States was strongly isolationist when the war broke out and remained so through mid-1941. The Navy-enforced Neutrality Zone off the east coast was the outward sign of this. With Germany's increasing military success, President Roosevelt realized that neither a policy of isolation nor the vast Atlantic Ocean would safeguard the United States. However, under the neutrality legislation passed at the end of World War I, his options to assist Britain, and, initially, France, were severely limited.

A significant change in policy occurred on November 4 when the Neutrality Act of 1939 became law. It repealed the arms embargo and substituted a policy of "cash and carry," prohibited U.S. vessels and citizens from entering combat zones, and established the National Munitions Control Board, comprised of the secretaries of State, Treasury, War, Navy, and Commerce. The act was blatantly pro-Allies since German merchant ships couldn't successfully penetrate the British blockade and neutral ships carrying war materials to Germany were subject to seizure by British warships for carrying contraband.

Throughout 1940, the United States, under Roosevelt's leadership, continued to expand its role in the war. On May 3, Greenland, a crown colony of Denmark, sought U.S. protection so that Danish sovereignty could be maintained during the German occupation of Denmark.

It was on September 4 that Secretary of State Cordell Hull and British Ambassador Lord Lothian, Philip Henry Kerr, concluded an agreement to trade destroyers for bases; the United States provided fifty overage (built under World War I Emergency Program) destroyers in return for ninety-nine-year leases on bases in the Bahamas, Antigua, St. Lucia, Trinidad, Jamaica, and British Guiana. The British provided bases at Newfoundland and Bermuda as outright gifts.

Britain was running out of money to pay for food, weapons, and other materials. President Roosevelt's solution was unique, and he proposed it in a radio address on December 17, 1940:

It is possible—I will put it that way—for the United States to take over British orders and, because they are essentially the same kind of munitions that we use ourselves, turn them into American orders. We have enough money to do it. And there-upon, as to such portion of them as the military events of the future determine to be right and proper for us to allow to go to the other side, either lease or sell the materials, subject to mortgage, to the people on the other side. That would be on the general theory that it may still prove true that the best defense of Great Britain is the best defense of the United States, and therefore that these materials would be more useful to the defense of the United States if they were used in Great Britain than if they were kept in storage here.

Now, what I am trying to do is to eliminate the dollar sign. That is something brand new in the thoughts of practically everybody in this room, I think—get rid of the silly, foolish old dollar sign. Well, let me give you an illustration: Suppose my neighbor's home catches fire, and I have a length of garden hose 400 or 500 feet away. If he can take my garden hose and connect it up with his hydrant, I may help him to put out his fire. Now, what do I do? I don't say to him before that operation, "Neighbor, my garden hose cost me $15; you have to pay me $15 for it." What is the transaction that goes on? I don't want $15 —I want my garden hose back after the fire is over. All right. If it goes through the fire all right, intact, without any damage to it, he gives it back to me and thanks me very much for the use of it. But suppose it gets smashed up—holes in it—during the fire; we don't have to have too much formality about it, but I say to him, "I was glad to lend you that hose; I see I can't use it any more, it's all smashed up." He says, "How many feet of it were there?" I tell him, "There were 150 feet of it." He says, "All right, I will replace it." Now, if I get a nice garden hose back, I am in pretty good shape.

In other words, if you lend certain munitions and get the munitions back at the end of the war, if they are intact—haven't been hurt—you are all right; if they have been damaged or have deteriorated or have been lost completely, it seems to me you come out pretty well if you have them replaced by the fellow to whom you have lent them.

The "Lend-Lease" concept was brilliant but flawed: most of the material was either consumable or likely to be destroyed in combat. Congress passed the Lend-Lease Act (Public Law 77-11) on March 11, 1941. It permitted Roosevelt to sell, transfer title to, exchange, lease, lend, or otherwise dispose of any defense article.

Capping the events of 1940 was President Roosevelt's December 29 radio address during which he called for America to become a great "Arsenal of Democracy."

Lend-Lease and establishing the United States as an "Arsenal of Democracy" ended the charade of America's neutrality.

By early spring 1941, the British position in the Mediterranean had become untenable. Weakened by the withdrawal of some 50,000 troops to Greece and surprised by greatly reinforced German and Italian forces, Britain's Army of the Nile was driven back, with serious losses, across the African deserts to the Egyptian border. They seriously needed the roughly 20,000 British troops tied down in Iceland. Meanwhile, the Battle of the Atlantic had taken a critical turn when, in March, U-boats moved westward from their hunting grounds off England and the Irish Sea into the unprotected gap between Canadian and British escort areas due to the lack of long-range escorts at this point in the war. Shipping losses mounted steeply. Although the Royal Navy immediately established a patrol and escort staging base in Iceland, a dangerous gap in air coverage in the ocean defenses remained.

The Icelandic government took a pessimistic view of England's chances of survival, and had, as early as mid-July 1940, approached the U.S. Department of State concerning the possibility of Iceland's coming under the aegis of the Monroe Doctrine, which viewed efforts by European countries to colonize land or interfere with states in the Americas, Europe, or Africa as acts of aggression requiring U.S. intervention. If a garrison was required, it was thought that American troops, being those of a neutral power, would not draw German attacks.

American concern in the protection of the North Atlantic sea lanes and in the defense of Iceland as well, had been acknowledged in the recently concluded Anglo-American staff conversations. On June 4, President Roosevelt ordered the Army to prepare a plan for the immediate relief of British troops in Iceland. The question of where the troops were going to come from arose immediately. Although the

U.S. Army had reached strength of nearly 1.5 million men, the great bulk of its soldiers were raw recruits gathered in by selective service and recently called up National Guardsmen. By law, these men could not be sent beyond the Western Hemisphere unless they volunteered.

The only legal alternative was to send the Marines, who were all volunteers and, unlike the draftee-encumbered Army, could be ordered overseas. Moreover, the 1st Marine Brigade (Provisional), under Brigadier General John Marston, was already at sea prepared for expeditionary duty. On June 5, Roosevelt directed the chief of Naval Operations, Admiral Harold R. Stark, to have a Marine brigade ready to sail in fifteen days' time.

On July 7, President Roosevelt announced to Congress that an executive agreement had been made with Iceland for U.S. troops to occupy that country and that the Navy had been ordered to take all steps necessary to maintain communications between the United States and Iceland. Task Force 19 landed 1st Marine Brigade (Provisional) at Reykjavik.

Early that morning, as TF 19 approached Reykjavik, the sea was glassy calm; the sun was well up and bright, as it never set in July in northern lands. As the convoy approached the coast of Iceland, the pilots of the U.S. Army Air Force 33d Pursuit Squadron flew their P-40 Warhawk fighter planes off the deck of the aircraft carrier *Wasp* in what was, for Army Air Corps pilots, a most unusual performance. The same day, VP-73, another squadron of six PBYs as well as VP-74, a squadron of long-range five PBM Mariners arrived at Skerjafjördur (Camp SNAFU) from Argentia. The primary mission of the Navy aircraft was to patrol the Denmark Strait between Iceland and Greenland and fly Neutrality patrols over the transatlantic convoys up to 500 miles away.

On August 12, 1941, a secret conference concluded between President Roosevelt and Prime Minister Churchill on board the heavy cruiser *Augusta* (CA-31) in Argentia, Newfoundland. It was in Argentia that Roosevelt privately reassured Churchill that when the United States entered the war, it would accord the defeat of Germany first priority.

Out of this conference came a joint statement of principles called the Atlantic Charter. It endorsed the rights of all people to choose their own leaders, regain lands lost to them through force, trade freely with one another, have access to raw materials on equal terms, improve the lot of backward countries, disarm aggressors, and create freedom from want, freedom from fear, and "such a peace should enable all men to traverse the high seas and oceans without hindrance." This last phrase was directed at Hitler's U-boat campaign and served as justification for the United States to take part in the battle. Roosevelt also pledged that U.S. warships would escort British merchant ships between the United States and Iceland.

Following the conference, a directive from U.S. General Headquarters established the joint Army and Navy tasks and specifically interpreted the approach of Axis forces within 50 miles of Iceland to be "conclusive evidence of hostile intent" which would "justify" attack by the defending U.S. forces. President Roosevelt expressed his views as follows: "… I think it should be made clear that the joint Task … *requires* attack on Axis planes approaching or flying over Iceland for reconnaissance purposes." Simply stated, it was a "shoot on sight" order six days before the *Greer* incident took place on September 4.

On that day, the USS *Greer* (DD-145), while tracking *U-652* 175 miles southwest of Iceland, was attacked but not damaged. Soon thereafter, *Greer* counterattacked with depth charges. Although no damage was done to either ship, the shots blew away the last vestiges of U.S. neutrality in the North Atlantic.

As of September 1, the U.S. Navy assumed the responsibility for trans-Atlantic convoys from a point off Argentia, Newfoundland to longitude meridian off Iceland on September 1. Admiral Ernest J. King, commander in chief, Atlantic Fleet, also designated a task group as a Denmark Strait patrol to operate in waters between Iceland and Greenland.

President Roosevelt's approval to search for and destroy German warships carried consequences that were not long in coming. USS *Kearny* was one of five destroyers escorting convoy ON-24 westbound from the United Kingdom to North America when the group was diverted to help a Canadian and British force defend the fully laden, fifty-two ship eastbound convoy SC-48. Two ships had been torpedoed on October 14, and a thirteen-boat wolf pack surrounded the convoy.

On the night of October 16/17, in the midst of the battle around that convoy, *U-568* laced a torpedo into *Kearny*'s starboard side, killing eleven men and injuring twenty-two. Surviving crewmembers stopped the flooding and regained power, and *Kearny* limped to Iceland. The Navy repair ship, USS *Vulcan*, provided timely and effective assistance to the destroyer.

The next encounter took place only two weeks later, when the Navy oil tanker, USS *Salinas*, was torpedoed south of Iceland on October 30 by *U-106*. While the crew worked to repair the damage, the U-boat surfaced and fired three more torpedoes. They missed. *Salinas* returned fire, forcing the attacker to dive. Escorting destroyers attacked with depth charges and reported sinking the U-boat. They hadn't.

USS *Reuben James* and four other U.S. destroyers were escorting the eastbound convoy HX-156 also on October 30. At 0539 hours on October 31, *Reuben James* was hunting down a U-boat contact when *U-552* fired a torpedo into the destroyer's magazines. The explosion broke *Reuben James* in two. As she sank, her depth charges exploded amongst the survivors; there had not been time to disarm them before the ship went down. Of the 159-man crew, 115 were killed.

Thus, the United States engaged in combat operations and sustained casualties more than a month before officially entering the war against Germany on December 11.

The Soviet Union: June–July 1941

On June 22, Germany invaded the Soviet Union. Code named Operation *Barbarossa*, it consisted of more than 4.5 million troops along a 1,800-mile front stretching from the Baltic Sea in the north to the Black Sea in the south. By the end of the first week, the Germans had achieved their major campaign objectives and continued toward Leningrad and Moscow.

Stalin made an effort to rally his demoralized nation on July 3. Calling on them as "brothers and sisters," something he had never done before and would never do again, he exhorted them to fight a "great patriotic war" against the treacherous fascist invader. Stalin asked them to fight, to take everything away before the advance of the invader, and to destroy anything that couldn't be removed, leaving nothing but "scorched earth."

Most western military experts believed that the Soviets would be defeated within a month. Despite this prediction, Britain and the United States immediately offered assistance. Notwithstanding the willingness to help, there were formidable physical and logistical problems of getting aid to Russia.

Among logistical problems were moving supplies to embarkation ports, assigning ships to carry the supplies, and detailing the warships for escort duty. The opening and protection of a new convoy route which, unlike the transatlantic ones, was exposed for a great part of its length to enemy-held territory on its flank was added to the Royal Navy's tasks. Already stretched almost to the limit by worldwide responsibilities, this additional requirement drained resources from other critical areas. The merchant marine fleet also was stretched almost to the breaking point. The German forces of U-boats, surface raiders, and Focke-Wulf Condors were sinking ships faster than new ones could be built or damaged ones repaired.

The Soviets held on through the summer, disproving military experts. The first convoy sailed for Arkhangelsk on August 21.

CHAPTER 2

SKIRMISHING
August 1941–March 1942

HMS *Adventure*, a fast, mine-laying cruiser, was the first ship to arrive in Russia on August 1, 1941, with a consignment of war materials including mines and depth charges, bound for Arkhangelsk. Combat cooperation between the Soviet Northern Fleet and the British Royal Navy began on July 31 when the Soviet destroyer *Sokrushitelnyy* rendezvoused with *Adventure* near Gorodetski Lighthouse and escorted her to Arkhangelsk along the intricate fairways of the White Sea and Dvina River. To Admiral Arseni Golovko, head of the Soviet Northern Fleet, the British mines were worthless. However, worthless or not, four Russian destroyers laid the mines on the seabed off the Fisherman's Peninsula in two mine barrages.

Outside the Kola Inlet on August 8, *V. Kuibyshev*, a ship of the same division, met the British submarine *Tigris*, the first that came to reinforce the North Fleet Submarine Brigade, located in the Polyarnoe Naval Base north of Murmansk. Later, destroyer *Uritzkiy* escorted a second British submarine, *Trident*, to her new home at the naval base.

Although the Kriegsmarine were not concerned about British operations at this point, they had already sown mine fields along the White Sea coast. The first victim was the cargo passenger ship *Pomorie* (Captain S. V. Varakin) on August 22. She was carrying thirty-two crewmembers and thirty passengers. Only two crew survived, a grim toll and a foretaste of what was to come for all who sailed these waters.

On August 21, "Dervish" was the first Allied convoy to sail from Hvalfjödur to Arkhangelsk. The convoy consisted of the merchant ships *Lancastrian Prince, New Westminster City, Esneh, Trehata,* and *Llanstephan Castle* and the Dutch freighter *Alchiba*. The convoy delivered 10,000 tons of rubber, 3,800 depth charges and magnetic mines, 15 Hurricane fighters, 1,500 tons of army boots, and a great deal of other essential equipment, as well as 534 pilots and ground crew from Britain who were carried on the convoy ships and escort vessels for service in Russia.

Escort of Convoy consisted of the destroyers HMS *Electra, Active,* and *Impulsive*; the antisubmarine warfare Shakespearian-class trawlers *Hamlet, Macbeth,* and *Ophelia*; and the Halcyon-class minesweepers *Halcyon, Salamander,* and *Harrier*. The minesweepers and their crews would remain in Arkhangelsk supporting the convoys.

Distant cover was provided by the heavy cruiser HMS *Shropshire* and the destroyers *Matabele, Punjabi,* and *Somali*.

At the same time, the old aircraft carrier HMS *Argus* carried twenty-four Hawker Hurricane fighters of the Royal Air Force's 151 Aviation Wing consisting of the 134th and 81st squadrons. Nearing the Murman coast, RAF 81 Squadron aircraft were flown off and landed at Vaenga airfield, 25 miles north of Murmansk. Taking off from a carrier deck is a skill usually acquired through much practice and done with aircraft specifically designed for carrier operations. But the RAF pilots had no training in carrier flight operations, and Hurricanes are land-based aircraft. This was a one-time shot. Fortunately, all fifteen aircraft got off without significant damage.

The Hurricanes reinforced the Soviet Air Force, which had lost approximately 3,000 aircraft during the initial stages of the German invasion. One of their most pressing needs was for fighters to assist in the defense of Murmansk, which the Germans were determined to capture.

A Luftwaffe base was located less than 50 miles away at Petsamo, making the Kola Inlet too dangerous for the ship containing the crated aircraft to dock in Murmansk. So it continued on to Arkhangelsk, where the aircraft were assembled with Russian assistance, and rejoined the rest of the wing at Vaenga on September 12.

The convoy arrived in the White Sea without loss, primarily because the Luftwaffe had only a few aerial reconnaissance forces in the region at the time. The Soviet Northern Fleet destroyers *Groznyy*, *Oritskyy*, and *Kujbyshey* met the convoy west of Cape Kanin Nos in the White Sea on August 30, and on the following day sailed down the Dvina River, arriving safely in Arkhangelsk. This first run was a quiet one for the escorts and merchantmen.

Though this initial run over the icy seas went smoothly, the welcome on shore was almost as cool as the weather. Ken Allen, a seaman on board the British freighter S.S. *New Westminster City* was not impressed with the reception from the Russians in Arkhangelsk:

I was Ordinary Seaman and later Sailor on the SS New Westminster City, *having joined the ship on 10th July 1940 and several voyages later re-joined her in Ellesmere Port on the 29th July 1941 for an unknown destination although large crates which contained "Kittyhawks" and "Tomahawks", [fighter] planes from the U.S.A. were clearly stenciled "Goods for Russian" and "Murmansk or Arkhangelsk". We sailed from Scapa Flow on the 21 August l941, six Merchant ships and a large naval escort including the old aircraft carrier H.M.S.* Argus *with twenty-four Hurricanes of No. 151 R.A.F. Wing onboard.*

It was dark for most of the time and we saw no action during the whole round voyage, German intelligence seemed to have fallen down for once. One of the merchant ships was the Union Castle Liner Llanstephan Castle *with Commandos on board. The convoy laid off Spitzbergen early one morning for two or three hours and I understand the Commandos landed to blow up communication installations etc. but the event appears to have had little publicity.*

Despite us taking war supplies to Russia, at that time in the war there was very little cooperation from the Russians. We were to dock in Arkhangelsk but arriving off the quay there were no boatmen to take our ropes. Our Master wanted to lay alongside the quay and land crewmembers to take our ropes but armed guards stopped them because we did not have shore passes. Eventually officials came down and a few passes were issued but when the gangway was down the passes were collected and we were not allowed ashore for several days.

Little labour was available and we crew drove our steam winches and helped with the discharge of cargo. When we loaded a full cargo of sawn timber it was stacked by Russian women, we still drove the winches.

The first contact RAF officers had with the Russians in Arkhangelsk was very different, however, and left a deep impression on them. One of them later wrote about it:

> I saw a couple of old Russian lumber-men and a party of a dozen Russian girls sawing up and loading timber into lorries as they arrived at the dockside. After they had loaded up all the timber that was in sight, they moved off to the next railway-shed, and from the coming and going of lorries it was obvious that the sawing and loading up was still going forward. The party was under the command of a girl about twenty, a qualified engineer. They worked away for three hours like absolute fury, the engineer-girl working the hardest of the lot. No one was looking on or supervising—but the speed of the work was prodigious. Once a lorry was loaded up with sawn timber, the girls would sit down for a breather and start smoking and singing. And then, when another lorry would come up, they'd start in all over again.
>
> The whole thing was, on their part, a marvelous exhibition of enthusiasm, energy and concentration. When they had finished loading every piece of timber in sight, they got to and swept down the whole quay-side (including all the rubbish chucked off the transport), a task which took an hour, and then buzzed off home. One had at last seen Russians at work, unwatched. Or rather—certain Russians at work unwatched. If there is anybody in Russia among the "higher-ups" making mistakes and blunders—and by what the Russian army is doing there is no evidence that any higher-ups are making mistakes and blunders—there is evidently a terrific mine of enthusiasm and energy backing the war effort among the "lower-downs."

RAF 81 Squadron pilots and aircraft were welcomed with open arms by their Soviet counterparts. The British pilots were hesitant at first about letting the Soviets fly without extensive training, but the Soviets weren't ready to wait, as related by Soviet Air Force Officer Vasily Minakov:

> In the first meeting of allies, the commander of a squadron, Captain B. F. Safonov with the pilots has come on landing the Hurricanes. They were met by the commander of English squadron A. T. Miller. Safonov has asked Miller to show the aircraft. Miller answered that the Hurricane [was] difficult to handle and only skilled pilots could tame it. But Safonov repeated the request. Miller gave in. After Safonov was seated in the cockpit, Miller stood with the translator on a wing and explained [the] appointment of devices, action with the basic panels and sequence of inclusion of toggle-switches for motor start.

> *Safonov listened attentively. When Miller [had] finished explanations, Safonov addressed to the translator: "Tell, to the major that I ask it to check up, whether I have correctly understood all". Miller lifted his hands and has told to the translator: "Tell to Mr. Safonov I'm impressed."*

Two minutes later, Safonov was airborne and handled the Hurricane with consummate skill.

During the following month, the Royal Air Force provided air cover to Soviet troops trying to hold off German forces from Murmansk and the Murmansk railway. In particular, they provided fighter escorts to Soviet bomber aircraft operating along the front. The RAF pilots carried out their final operational flight on October 8. At that point, they started handing their aircraft and equipment (including the pilots' flying helmets) over to the Soviet Air Force, a task they completed by October 22. The personnel of 151 Wing returned by sea on British ships, and they started arriving back in Britain on December 7, 1941. During thirty-six days of direct participation in combat, they flew 365 combat sorties, destroying or damaging twelve German planes at a cost of two RAF pilots killed.

On September 29, PQ-1, consisting of 11 merchant ships loaded with raw materials, 20 tanks, and 193 crated Hurricane fighter planes, sailed from Hvalfjödur for Arkhangelsk. Making the trip as part of the escorting force were the minesweepers *Britomart, Swan, Gossamer,* and *Hussar,* which were sent to reinforce three other minesweepers that had arrived as part of Dervish.

The first returning convoy, QP-1, comprised of the returning Dervish ships, four Russian merchant ships, and the fleet oiler *Black Ranger,* left Arkhangelsk and arrived at Scapa Flow on October 9. Both convoys arrived safely, having enjoyed good weather and no encounters with the Germans.

Arctic convoy duty differed from that of the North Atlantic or runs to the Mediterranean. John Squires, a seaman on board the destroyer HMS *Impulsive,* described the differences:

> There was no real threat from the enemy at this stage of the war, which was fortunate really, as it was summer in the north and we had twenty-four hours of daylight, apart from the odd patch of fog in the Barents Sea.
>
> It was an unusual experience to go on watch at midnight until 4am and to have the sun still shining, plus the clock had to go which played

havoc with the watch keeping duties, and the meal times, still, it did not interfere with the Up Spirits or Nelson's Blood ration [the daily issue of grog to all hands].

Squires also recalled both the routine and the unexpected beauty he experienced:

These were the times during long days and nights, on convoy runs, when the ships companies' talents came to light such as model making, embroidery, sketching, rug making, you mention it.

To avoid the enemy we had to sail into the Greenland Sea between Bear Island and Spitzbergen and those Arctic waters are notorious for fog and it can be very scary in dense fog surrounded by many ships, straining one's eyes in case another ship got too close. But on a moonlight night the north can be quite pleasant. I remember one night, it was very misty and moonlight, and round the ship's bow was a white crescent, just like a miniature rainbow but pure white.

Also there was the beautiful spectacle (sometimes) of the northern lights, Aurora-Borealis. They are huge ribbons of fabulous colours, dancing and flickering against the black of the night, and as we approached our destination, we sailed through the sea of pack ice. Some of the ice flow had the odd seal or two on them who, I thought, looked at us reproachfully for disturbing their peace.

Minesweepers played an integral part in the Arctic convoy story. In September, the First Minesweeping Flotilla, comprised of *Bramble, Gossamer, Hussar, Leda, Seagull, Speedy*, and *Windermere*, was allocated to Arctic convoy duties with north Russia as its base. The flotilla joined the escort force for PQ-2 in Liverpool and sailed to Arkhangelsk without losses. John Douglas-Hiley on board *Bramble* remembered his arrival in Russia:

While waiting to enter the Dvina River for passage to Arkhangelsk itself, we were met by a small Russian icebreaker tug. Although it was only late September, we were all "rugged up" with thick clothing—two pairs of socks and a pair of oiled wool sea-boot stockings under leather sea-boots. The Russian Engineer Officer of the tug, a young woman, came on deck to look at us. She wore a short sleeved shirt, trousers and ordinary shoes and stood there for some time without a goose-pimple showing. We were amazed and impressed.

Our minesweepers followed the tug up to Brevennik Island, just opposite Arkhangelsk itself. On the island, there was a small dockyard at one end and what appeared to be a detention centre at the other. This was guarded by sentries, many of them women soldiers. We learned early on that when they called on you to halt, it meant just that. They were quite ready to shoot if in doubt. We were issued with Red Stars to wear in our caps to help identification.

Even when not escorting merchant ships, the British minesweepers were constantly employed, and their crews got a taste of the bitter Russian arctic weather. One of the first independent operations for them was to investigate "unknown objects" dropped from enemy aircraft in the strait at the entrance of the Kara Sea. One crewmember of this operation described it:

As we moved east from the mouth of the White Sea, the sea [became] frozen, which looked to one like a thick mixture of water and cellulose. When we reached the strait we observed that the shore was completely covered with ice, but in the middle of the gulf we could see separate ice floes. We made several tacks without results with the electromagnetic and acoustic sweeps and were coming to think that it was a false alarm when a very powerful explosion rang out ahead, throwing into the air a tangled mass of broken ice. Those on deck threw themselves into shelter from the ice rubble, crashing down on the ship.

This was a terrific introduction to minesweeping in the Arctic. But there was more to come shortly, as Douglas-Hiley related:

The minesweepers' task was to provide close cover, because the Germans concentrated their principal attacks at this point (the entrance to Kola Inlet). They knew that every convoy had to converge on this point, thus providing the maximum target.

During our early days at Polyarnyy, two of our ships were attacked by two large German destroyers, and one of them was hit by a 5.9-inch shell, but the Germans broke off the action for reasons no one could explain. The after 4-inch gun mounting was on the superstructure immediately above the wardroom where the Gunnery Officer was sleeping. When the alarm sounded, he dressed and put on his steel helmet. Just at that moment, the shell hit the gun mounting killing one man and severely wounding another. A splinter penetrated the deck and the Gunnery Officer's battle-

bowler [helmet]. It raced around the inside of his tin-hat till it fell down on his bald-head leaving him struggling like mad to get the helmet off. The severely wounded man was sent to a Russian hospital where a kidney wound was successfully operated on, but without anesthetic. They were short of medical supplies.

Douglas-Hiley got an unexpected insight to his Soviet allies one day, an insight that summed up why the Soviets were fighting so hard:

I learned to speak some Russian and was able to exchange our cigarettes for their awful papirossi, those smoke sticks with a cardboard tube at one end and tobacco at the other. The brand was called Nasha Marka [Our Brand]. Talking alone with one of them, I asked what he really thought of Communism. "You must be joking, Ivan," he said. "Don't you know that Communism is only for export?"
"What are you fighting for then, Sergei?"
"Two things—Rodina (the Motherland) and the hope that, maybe, my grandchildren will have a better life," he replied.

Initially the convoys were planned on a forty-day cycle. Prime Minister Winston Churchill insisted that the cycle be shortened to ten days, with Arkhangelsk handling the bulk of the deliveries. The protection of the convoys heading to north Russia was a responsibility of the Royal Navy Home Fleet based in Scapa Flow and commanded by Admiral Sir John C. Tovey.

The route, which was open to U-boat attack throughout its entire length, was limited to the west and north by ice and to the east and south by an enemy-occupied coast, well provided with anchorages whence surface forces could operate at will, and airfields from which aircraft could dominate 1,400 miles of its furthest east, and therefore most vulnerable, waters. The whole route, including the terminal ports at each end, lay within the range of enemy air reconnaissance and at two points was crossed by German routine meteorological flights. British shore-based air support was confined to what could be given from Iceland and Sullom Voe in the Shetland Islands.

The most critical logistical problem was refueling the escorts while at sea. Other problems included lack of facilities of any kind for both naval and merchant personnel at journey's end, which posed a serious threat to morale.

In Iceland, the U.S. Navy escort force primarily consisted of three 327-foot Secretary Class Coast Guard cutters (USS *Bibb* [WPG-31], USS *Duane* [WPG-33], and USS *Ingham* [WPG-35]) and four older Navy destroyers (USS *Babbitt* [DD-128], USS *Badger* [DD-126], USS *Leary* [DD-158], and USS *Scheck* [DD-159]). These ships ran shuttle service, escorting empty merchant ships to the Mid Ocean Meeting Point, where the British escort force was relieved by either an American or Canadian escort force, picking up fully loaded vessels from an eastbound convoy and returning to Iceland. If all went well, the round trip took about seven days. They also were called to reinforce besieged convoys fighting their way through the mid-Atlantic (known as "Torpedo Junction"), conduct search and rescue missions, assist in resupplying outlying garrisons, and conduct weather patrols. Despite their extensive operations, none of the escorts sank a U-boat during the war.

From Loch Ewe, additional ships for the Arctic convoys were sailed in a series of convoys designated "UR" (United Kingdom–Reykjavik) and "RU" (Reykjavik–United Kingdom). Although not routinely harassed by U-boats or the Luftwaffe, the ships were battered by lethal storms while their masters grew gray trying to navigate through impenetrable fog.

The Army Air Force wasn't idle in Iceland, either. The 342nd Composite Group was tasked with preventing Luftwaffe reconnaissance and bombing attacks. Army pilots flying P-38 Lightnings proved effective, shooting down a Focke-Wulf FW-200 Condor in August 1942. Although not tallying a significant number of kills, the pilots did prevent the Germans from obtaining accurate information on shipping.

Navy Patrol Squadron VP-73, VP-74, VP-84 flying Catalina PBYs and PBMs, and VB-128 flying Ventura PV-1s endured seemingly endless flights over thousands of square miles of barren ocean, often under appalling weather conditions. Winter in Iceland was the worst enemy of the patrol squadrons. The British withdrew their PBY squadron, feeling that the weather was too extreme for operation of the slow patrol aircraft. On January 15, 1942, gales reaching 133 mph struck the area, sinking three of VP-73's Catalinas and two of VP-74's PBMs.

The first victory over U-boats was long in coming. It wasn't until August 20, 1942, while on convoy escort in Skerja Fjord, near Reykjavik, that Lieutenant (JG) Robert B. Hopgood and his crew attacked and sank *U-464*, Korvettenkapitän Otto Harms commanding. Hopgood and his crew pressed home the attack even though the crew of the U-boat elected to remain on the surface and fight it out with the lightly armed Catalina. HMS *Castleton* rescued fifty-three survivors. Returning to base, Hopgood sent the following message: "Sank Sub Open Club" (Hopgood was awarded the Navy Cross for his heroic action).

Despite the hardships and boredom, these intrepid airmen sank five U-boats between August 1942 and October 1943.

For the men, Iceland was a bleak and often inhospitable place to live and work. Army and Marine garrison troops had little to do day to day, and there wasn't much in the way of entertainment.

As difficult as it was for the troops and flight crews, the escort sailors had it worse. The frequent shuttle runs strained the ships to the breaking point. Particularly hard hit were the destroyers, which literally began falling apart. Even the tough 327s weren't immune. Lieutenant (JG) Joe Matte on *Ingham* reported that, during a two-week period, the boot on the underwater sound gear was stove in by heavy weather, rendering that vital equipment almost useless; the ship was battered by various misadventures in coming alongside tankers in gale force winds; No. 1 boat was slightly damaged; No. 2 boat was stove in; the port gun sponson (aft) was partially broken; and the starboard gun sponson was completely smashed by a wave, broke adrift, and fell into the sea.

Hvalfjödur proved as dangerous as the open ocean. On January 15, 1942, a storm with wind velocity of more than 80 knots and gusts of more than 100 knots struck; heavy cruiser *Wichita* (CA-45) was damaged in collisions with U.S. freighter *West Nohno* and British trawler HMS *Ebor Wyke* and grounded near Hrafneyri lighthouse. Storm conditions lasted until January 19 and caused heavy damage among patrol planes based there and tended by seaplane tender *Albemarle* (AV-5).

The strain continued throughout the year. There was no peace on earth on Christmas 1942 for *Duane, Ingham,* or *Campbell*. At noon, a 100-knot gale struck from the mountains. *Duane* had both anchors down, but the wind blew so hard they dragged across the bottom. The harbor was in chaos as ships tried to save themselves, at times fouling each other's anchor chains, a move that hamstrung their chances of survival. *Ingham* and *Campbell* fought for their lives as winds pushed them toward the rocks, powerful engines and low slung hulls straining to hold clear, the crews on deck working the anchor windlasses, braced against the blow.

In-port time, usually anchored in the harbor in Hvalfjödur, was spent refueling, rearming, repairing equipment, chipping and painting, and standing anchor and radio watches. The rare shore liberty for the escorts' officers was in Reykjavik, which offered little in the way of night life, or for enlisted men, at the base canteen, which was limited to a few hours and two cans of beer per man. Coast Guard crews held boat drills every morning, regardless of the weather. Pulling boats were launched, and the men rowed for an hour or more before breakfast. They rowed not for fun or simply to provide exercise, but to gain proficiency in handling the boats in all types of weather, good practice for those times when they would be called to rescue survivors from torpedoed ships in the open ocean. On board there was no privacy, and even the rare quiet times were haunted by the knowledge that the men soon would have to go out to sea again.

Somehow through all this, the air crews and escort sailors from the United States and at least one Royal Canadian Navy minesweeper, HMCS *Canso*, kept their sense of humor. No one remembers how or when it started, but by the spring of 1943, they began to refer to themselves as members of the "Brotherhood of the FBI." This, in that more refined period of time, was a nice way of saying "Forgotten Bastards of Iceland."

Convoys PQ-1, 2, 3, 4, and 5, totaling twenty-nine ships, as well as the returning convoys QP-1, 2, 3, and 4, all made runs during autumn and early winter of 1941 without losing any ships. But they did suffer casualties in men and equipment.

PQ-3 ran into severe storms and patrolling Luftwaffe Ju-87 Stuka dive bombers. On this run in November 1941, Godfrey P. Hudson kept a diary, which tells the story:

November 16th. Leaving today. Stormy outside. Getting a bad buffeting by head seas which sweep over the fo'c'sle head and roar along foredeck.

November 20th. Full gale. Two ships turned back—one hit a small berg and the other had engine trouble. One of the tanks in our 'tween deck broke loose and charged into the ships side flattening the angle irons. Bosun and crew got aboard the charging monster and shored it up with baulks of timber. (Ship was eventually awarded the OBE for this act of bravery.)

November 22nd. Crossed Arctic Circle. Course for 75 North. I believe. Stukas dive bombed the convoy. The flutes under the wings gave a banshee wail and every seventh shell was a tracer so when one of the gunners on the port wing Oerlikon was hit by a tracer it cauterized the wound and he survived the rough handling when the skipper ordered "that corpse off the bridge" I put him in the shelter of the wheelhouse which was reinforced with concrete slabs and took over the gun for a few exciting seconds. We were in the vicinity of Jan Mayen Island at the extremity of the Stuka's range so it was a short lived raid. They lost two planes and the crews were dead when picked up. Temperature 40 below.

The British seamen and the first of the American merchant seamen learned bitterly in the winter of 1941–42 about Arctic weather. The gales blew across the 900-mile-wide space between Greenland and Norway and swept northeastward. The wind struck the slowly laboring columns of a convoy with an unbroken fury. The crews lived in almost perpetual darkness for 115 days during the dark winter when the sun barely rose. It was so dark that a lookout stationed on a ship's bridge could not even see the bow of his own vessel.

The positions of the ships ahead, on each side and astern were unknown; all were under complete blackout regulation. Convoy machine-gunners had orders to fire directly at any light shown. But another ship might be detected by a veering wind gust that held a tang of stack smoke, or her engine sounds, the thud of her propeller, the waves hammering her hull.

Men strained to hear and to smell as well as to see. They explored the caverns of the wind in the lulls between gusts with extremely sensitized perception. Buffeting wind blurred their vision, and the unwilled tears froze on their cheeks. Their eyebrows and eyelashes were frozen. Their lashes would fall off later, painfully, in the heated quarters of the ship. Breath was agony if taken fully before the wind; a man turned aside, breathed, swung back, and examined the reaching dark again.

Ships often were saved from collision, severe injury, and loss of life by a lookout's recognition at the last instant. The other ship appeared as a shape darker than night, marked by the pale run of the wake alongside in the somber sea. Then the shout to the helmsman was given: "Hard over!" The slick brass of the whistle handle was grasped and pulled down, and signals exchanged. The ships swerved apart from each other, back into the vastness of the night and the wind.

Mates and helmsmen stood breathing rapidly after such near-collisions. They sweated inside their layers of clothing. Shivering overcame them. When they tried to drink coffee, their teeth clacked on the rims of the mugs.

Winter was brutal for the men on the convoys, and summer was little better, bringing its own dangers. Ice was within 80 miles of the North Cape during the summer months. The Atlantic Drift, the last of the Gulf Stream, flowing northeastward, separated in two forks, and both brought fog. One went along the Norwegian coast and then the Murman coast of the continent, and kept Murmansk ice-free. The other went much higher north, past Bear Island, in 74°29′ North latitude and 19°10′ East longitude. Summer convoys found protection in the fog, but also wandered far off course due to poor visibility, and suffered badly from collision. Fog, some convoy shipmasters said, was worse than the winter darkness.

A British ship's captain who had experienced both brutal winters and summers remembered the dangers wrought by the weather.

From February onwards it is lighting up quickly. At the end of January there are four hours' daylight, end of February eight hours' daylight, end of April 20 hours', and July and August virtually twenty-four hours' daylight, with sun all the time, which works along the horizon. From April to August there's no really bad weather; conditions are ideal for enemy attack.

Winter starts in September, and from October to the end of December there's a lot of fog and heavy snowstorms, but not much wind. From the end of December you may get gales of hurricane strength which can last five days, but between gales the weather may be flat. In the winds, a big short sea is built up—seldom more than fifteen feet, even in bad weather, for the seas are comparatively shallow—but in those big short seas the ship rolls like hell.

Storm damage was in some instances so severe that ships were forced to leave convoy. The crews of the merchant ships worked with almost frantic haste to make repairs at sea and keep their vessels within the protective screen of the escort.

They took a very great chance of being sunk if they returned alone to Iceland. U-boats ranged across the straggler ship's course back to the Icelandic ports. The temperature of the water was less than forty degrees in summer. A man could live in it for about ten minutes. Chances of survival were small in a lifeboat, and death from exposure was slow, painful, and terrible.

Even just working outside on a ship's main deck in the Arctic night with a gale blowing and the spray freezing as it fell was very nearly impossible. Escort vessels, with a good deal more ease of maneuver than a heavily loaded cargo ship, lost boats, davits, and men on many occasions.

Deck cargo that had shifted during battering storms was the usual problem for a merchant ship. Tanks, planes, trucks, and locomotives were stowed fore and aft on the main decks in the loading ports. These were thick-coated with ice. During a gale, some ships accumulated as much as 150 tons of ice that covered all of their deck gear. Windlasses and winches were stubborn and sluggish, even though they had been kept running for days.

A ship's deck gang first tried to remove the thick ice with chipping hammers, mauls, picks, and axes to clear the gear. Ice clogged the block sheaves. Ice formed in the manila core of the wire rope and swelled the diameter; the rope would not lead through the blocks. Pins were frozen in shackles, and were beaten free with a broad-headed maul in the darkness. Blows missed the pins and hit the hands of the men who held the shackles. There was no use complaining; voices and shouts went unheard in the wind no matter how loudly the curses were uttered.

Wire and chain were shackled in place and hauled across the dimly seen pieces of cargo. New lashings were secured. Men groped their way, working without light. Their sea boots were full of water. The towels wrapped within their weather-coat collars had long since been soaked. Their hands, stripped of icy and useless gloves, were numb, clumsy, and bloody. Seas smashed over the deck, and the men were knocked headlong.

Each of them had been secured singly by the chief mate when they started work. Individual lifelines, strong manila, were attached to a main hawser stretched fore and aft. When the sea struck, they were swept only the length of the lifeline—rather than overboard—then fetched up, the bowline knot yanking at their chests as their backs, legs, and arms banged against the deck plates, seawater soaking them in a smacking torrent that made them gasp out in fear. Drowning was an ever-present danger.

Some ships were so badly damaged or their cargo so shifted that they sailed with as much as a 30-degree list. Speed was reduced to 3 or 4 knots. Steering was dangerous and kept to a minimum. A sudden change of rudder direction might send a ship beam-end under, never to right herself.

When the ships reached Iceland and went to anchor in the safety of the deep bay at Hvalfjödur, the men felt a giddy intoxication of relief. Shore leave was not allowed. Permission was asked to take ships' boats away, and the men went around the bay visiting various vessels.

Americans getting ready for their first Arctic convoy, who boarded British ships with veteran crews, were told that their luck was just a bit more than ordinary. The British gave accounts of conditions in the White and Barents Seas, where it easily took a ship sixteen days to move just 70 miles.

Coming out of Arkhangelsk in February, the men on bridge lookout had icicles on their eyebrows, noses, and beards. Icicles as thick as a man's arm hung from the rigging. The chief engineer turned over the propeller every ten minutes to keep it free from ice. Even inside the ship, ice formed on the bulkheads, and the portholes were frozen shut.

The British seamen at Hvalfjödur showed the Americans their Arctic clothing. They had been issued hooded duffle coats lined with lamb's wool and padded around the skirt. There was an extra hood for each man, with only slits for eyes and mouth. Standard-issue underclothing was as thick as a sweater and made of soft, white wool. So were the two pairs of seaboot socks, which reached high on a man's thighs. There were long, broad scarves, wristlets, and mittens with a separate thumb and first finger. Sea boots were made of leather, and were lighter, more compact, and easier on the feet than the rubber boots the Americans wore.

Gunners, coxswains, and signalmen, whose duties involved prolonged exposure, were issued knee-length sheepskin jerkins. These they wore leather-side out, with a leather duty belt holding the waist tight. The garments were sleeveless to allow full freedom of action. Under their helmet liners, the gunners wore balaclava hoods, knitted so that the bottoms protected a man's chest and back.

Men and ships alike were susceptible to the icy sea. One Russian merchant ship in QP-3, *Kuzbass*, was the first to be caught by the Arctic winter's fury. The convoy sailed from Arkhangelsk on November 27. K. A. Egorov, a Soviet Northern Fleet officer on board *Kuzbass*, told what happened after the convoy reached the White Sea and set course for Iceland:

> *As soon as the icebreaker left the mouth of the Northern Dvina River in the White Sea we [were] met by intense cold and a raging gale which lasted two days.*
>
> *In the Barents Sea, the convoy met another violent storm. The heavy seas smashed the ship's rudder and bent it ninety degrees to starboard. Kuzbass fell behind the convoy. The captain gathered the ship's officers in an attempt to reach a solution. Some suggestions were made including making a wooden rudder (luckily it was a lot of wood) and [making] our own way to England. Fortunately, in the twilight the steamer Arcos, a straggler from the convoy, hove into view. Her captain agreed to tow us to safety.*
>
> *Now began a desperate struggle with the seas. In twenty below zero temperature and the ships casting about like wood chips, a bad dressed team (not even enough mittens) filed with the tugs Arcos in the Kuzbass and vice versa. Tow-lines rushed like a thread, when one ship billowing like an*

elk on the ridge, and the other plunged into the abyss at the foot of the waves. Finally, Arcos broke down and towing became impossible.

When the storm died down, we tried to tow again, but there was [a] big swell and it did not happen and soon we were trapped in the ice.

On 10 December at 0900 hours the ice breaker Litke, rescue ship Squall, and SKR-19 found us. At 1100, the captain of Litke reported that the southern passage [was] clogged with ice and planned to go north of the island of Kolga. December 13, began a strong contraction of ice and the ship's hull cracked. The captain explained the situation and gave orders to prepare to leave the ship. Avoiding panic, we prepared clothes and food, but the ship wasn't crushed.

At last, on December 18, Kuzbass, towed by Litke, headed east to safety. Only on December 26 at 1400, again in a raging storm, did we enter the harbor Iokanka.

Winter's onset necessitated drastic changes in the convoy routing. In the middle of January 1942, navigation had been stopped in the White Sea and Dvina River due to heavy ice despite the concentration of icebreakers in the White Sea. From the war's beginning, Arkhangelsk accepted 52 vessels that delivered 699 planes, 466 tanks, and other cargo, accounting for 95 percent of all deliveries to Russia.

But the move to Murmansk did little to solve the convoys' problems. The condition of its port was even more pitiable than Arkhangelsk's. Not only was almost all valuable equipment evacuated when the war began, but there was no housing for the dock workers in Murmansk. Among these were 1,500 people who had been evacuated to the Kola Peninsula from territory threatened by the German invasion, another 2,000 mobilized in the Ryazan region east of Moscow, and 500 (mostly women) were sent from Arkhangelsk.

The work went on through the polar night in blackout conditions. The weather alternated between hard frosts and blizzards whipped by gale force winds. Regardless of the harsh conditions, 2,500 people worked every day to unload the transports, averaging one transport every ten to eighteen days.

In both Arkhangelsk and Murmansk, the civilians were on the verge of starvation. Evgraf Evlogievichu, a student at the Arkhangelsk School of Ship's Boys, remembered that bitter time:

All winter 1941–1942 Arkhangelsk was very hungry. Cut bread ration to 200 grams. Ate not only the skin and birch bark, spruce, even coats: removed

*the pile, cut the peel into strips and cooked. On the streets there were no cats,
no dogs, no pigeons. At school for breakfast we [ate] bread and butter.*

Up to this point, there had been no concerted effort by the Germans
to disrupt the convoys, except for occasional attacks by the Luftwaffe.
However, the military supplies being delivered were helping to stiffen
the defenses in the Kola Peninsula and around Leningrad. This was
noted by the German high command and great action against the
convoys began in early winter.

PQ-4 was attacked by a small group of Ju-88 bombers in an area to the
south of Jan Mayen Island. Single planes continued to attack the convoy
until it reached the White Sea. However, the attacks were not driven
home. At this stage of the war, Luftwaffe pilots, as a rule, approached
at a height of 12,000 feet, winged over into a dive, and dumped their
bombs out of anti-aircraft fire range.

PQ-6 was the first to have a run in with Kriegsmarine destroyers.
Minesweepers HMS *Hazard* and HMS *Speedy* were scheduled to meet
the convoy as it approached the Kola Inlet. But, at 1845 hours on
December 17, 30 miles north of Cape Gorodetski, they encountered the
German destroyers Z-23, Z-24, Z-25, and Z-27, which mistook them for
Russian destroyers and attacked. The action resulted only in four hits
on *Speedy*, which was damaged and forced to return to Murmansk.

The minesweepers cut their trawls and opened fire on the enemy,
but the forces were obviously unequal. *Speedy* received four direct hits
and lost two men killed, with damage to the after gun, damage to the
propeller, and a smashed top-mast, which forced her to leave the action
under cover of a smoke screen and return to base escorted by the Soviet
ship *Leda*. Although her sister ship was out of action, *Hazard* continued
on to meet the convoy. An attempt by the British cruiser *Kenya* and the
Soviet destroyers *Groznyy* and *Sokrushitelnyy* to cut out the German
warships failed and the Germans retreated unscathed.

Surprisingly, between the end of December 1941 and March 1942,
out of a total of 158 merchant ships in convoy, only one merchant ship
and one British destroyer were sunk; one other merchant ship was
damaged by the Germans.

On January 2, *U-134* sank the British freighter *Waziristan* from
PQ-7A. *Waziristan* had been stranded on the ice edge and was attacked
by Luftwaffe aircraft before being torpedoed and sunk by *U-134*. None
of her forty-seven man crew survived.

PQ-8 was hit next, and once again the minesweepers were part of the fight along with Northern Fleet units.

Reinforcing the escort of PQ-8 on January 17, 1942, the destroyers *Sokrushitelnyy* and *Gremyashchiy* were sent, together with six motor launches, six motor torpedo boats, and the minesweepers *Hazard*, *Sharpshooter*, and *Hebe*. That evening, about 20 miles from the Kola Inlet, the commodore's ship *Harmatris* was attacked and torpedoed by *U-454*. The torpedoes blew a hole in her stern and started a fire, which was quickly extinguished.

In a repeated torpedo attack, *U-454* fired her stern tubes at the British tanker *British Pride*. The torpedoes were heard running by the escorts on that side of the convoy and may have been aimed at the cruiser *Trinidad*. These found their target in the magazines of *Matabele*, sending a sheet of flame 700 feet high into the night sky—the destroyer had disintegrated, hurling her crew into the icy seas. Several of the destroyer's already-primed depth charges set to explode at various depths blew up beneath those who had not been killed. The survivors still on board had no option but to jump from the blazing portion of the hull still afloat into the icy sea, which also was in flames. *Matabele* sank in two minutes. Most of the crew abandoned ship safely, but when the minesweeper *Harrier* arrived on scene a few minutes later, she found the area covered with corpses gently bobbing in the swell. It was a grim reminder that survival time in Arctic waters is measured in seconds. Of *Matabele*'s complement of 238, only two survived.

Hazard and *Sharpshooter*, along with the patrol ship *Smerch* and four motor launches, escorted the damaged *Harmatris* while she was being towed by two tugs from the Kola Inlet.

During the tow, two German aircraft attempted to attack the convoy, but the motor launches opened a deadly anti-aircraft barrage, driving off the marauders. On January 25, the convoy with the damaged transport *Harmatris* reached the Kola Inlet.

Throughout fall and early winter, German forces stationed in Norway were still minimal, and the commitment to provide convoy escorts didn't strain British Home Fleet resources, a situation soon to change.

On the German side, Hitler was shaken by the British Commando raids on the Lofoten Islands in March, which played on his fear that Great Britain might invade Norway. In November 1941, Hitler decided to send the battleship *Tirpitz* to Trondheim rather than into the Atlantic. Hitler, "convinced that Norway is the 'zone of destiny' in this war," ordered a heavy reinforcement of land and air forces and demanded that "every available vessel be employed in Norway."

This was a major shift in German policy, and it was further reinforced by Hitler's decision that the cruisers *Scharnhorst* and *Gneisenau*, based at Brest, should join the *Tirpitz* in Norway. In an audacious operation in February 1942, the two battlecruisers with the heavy cruiser *Prinz Eugen* returned to German waters via the English Channel, causing considerable embarrassment to the Royal Navy and the RAF. Yet both *Scharnhorst* and *Gneisenau* received serious mine damage, while *Prinz Eugen* was torpedoed off Kristiansand and had to return to port. It was seven months before the *Scharnhorst* could rejoin the *Tirpitz* in Norway.

In addition, the heavy cruisers *Admiral Scheer*, *Lützow*, and *Hipper*, light cruiser *Köln*, two flotillas of destroyers, and fourteen U-boats were transferred to the north of Norway. To ensure that these ships were safe from attack, as well as to protect their communications, the Germans concentrated a significant number of minesweepers, patrol ships, and various support vessels in the area. They also intensified their coastal and air defenses.

Grossadmiral Erich Raeder, head of the Kriegsmarine, insisted that the heaviest concentration of ships in Norwegian waters would be ineffective unless the Luftwaffe strength was correspondingly increased. As a result, more airfields were constructed in Norway and Finland. Luftflotte 5 was reinforced with two specialized antishipping units, KG 26 and KG 30, which were transferred to the air bases at Bardufoss and Banak, as well as another squadron of FW-200 Condors bringing the total to five hundred aircraft.

The main concern of the British was that the German ships in Norway, particularly the *Tirpitz*, did not break out into the Atlantic to attack the convoys. Just after *Tirpitz* arrived in Norwegian waters, Winston Churchill described the destruction of *Tirpitz* as "the greatest event at sea at the present time. No other target is comparable to it." He asserted that the whole strategy of the war turned at this period on this ship, which was holding four times the number of British capital ships from other assignments to say nothing of the two new American battleships retained in the Atlantic.

By springtime 1942, the Arctic nights were shortening and daylight hours were growing long enough to allow German surface ships and aircraft a fair chance of attack since the ice barrier lies further south in March and April than at any other time of the year. The barrier forced convoys to pass south of Bear Island and within 250 miles of the Norwegian coast, approximately 100 miles farther south than in the summer months. In addition, a large increase in the scale of the convoys had been decided on, and the two scheduled to sail at the beginning of March—PQ-12 (sixteen ships) and QP-8 (fifteen ships)—were the largest to date. The escort force consisted of forty warships for PQ-12 and, initially, eight for QP-8.

For the British this meant that big ship cover would have to be provided for these and future convoys. It also meant an increased U-boat threat, which in turn demanded destroyers for screening the capital ships, whose radius of action, except in emergency, was thus limited by the endurance of the screen.

The British and Germans knew that the most obvious use for the *Tirpitz* was against the Arctic convoys, and she made her first sortie on March 6, 1942, against PQ-12, which had been spotted by a FW-200 Condor reconnaissance aircraft the previous day. In turn *Tirpitz* was spotted by the British submarine *Seawolf*, and Admiral Tovey, the British C-in-C Home Fleet, providing distant cover with three capital ships and the aircraft carrier HMS *Victorious*, turned toward PQ-12 and QP-8.

On March 8, bad weather prevented aerial reconnaissance. The two convoys, the British Home Fleet, and *Tirpitz* with *Friedrich Ihn*, *Paul Jacobi*, *Hermann Schoemann*, *Z-25*, *T-5*, and *T-12* as escorts, were all within 80 miles of each other. The two convoys passed each other at noon. Tovey, who unknowingly had approached to within some 75 miles of them, turned to the southwest, little knowing that at that moment his opponent was only 60 miles away to the southeast and steering toward him at high speed. At 1630 hours, when the *Tirpitz* had crossed to the north of the tracks of both convoys, having passed some 60 miles astern of PQ-12 and 50 miles ahead of QP-8, one of the German destroyers, the *Friedrich Ihn*, encountered *Izhora*, a Russian straggler from the homeward convoy QP-8, which she sank at about 1715 hours, but not before her victim had managed to get off a distress message, which was picked up by the battleship *King George V*.

Unfortunately, the position received was incomplete, but soon afterward radio bearings of a German ship which might possibly have been the *Tirpitz* were picked up by the flagship. So at 1750 hours, Tovey altered the course of his force to the east, the direction from which the bearing had come.

In the evening of March 8, Admiral Otto Ciliax, commander of the Kriegsmarine task force, decided to terminate the operation due to poor visibility, bad weather, lack of air reconnaissance, the vastness of the operational area, and complete ignorance of the enemy's position, all of which made success more than doubtful.

At 0640 hours the next day, several British scouting planes from *Victorious* located the German task force. Assuming that the carrier to which the enemy planes belonged would not have ventured so close to the Norwegian coast without the protection of other heavy fleet units, Ciliax ordered *Tirpitz* to proceed toward the Lofoten Islands at maximum speed.

At 0730, a dozen Albacore aircraft armed with torpedoes took off and headed for *Tirpitz*. An hour later, a questing Albacore located *Friedrich lhn* and *Tirpitz* proceeding south at high speed 80 miles east of the Home Fleet. A few minutes after the Albacore made contact, Chief Petty Officer Finselberger, at an after anti-aircraft position aboard *Tirpitz*, spotted the shadowing plane and all of the battleship's formidable array of anti-aircraft weaponry, sixteen twin 10.5-cm guns, and sixteen 3.7-cm twin flak cannon were made ready. Ciliax flew off an Arado seaplane in an attempt to gain a little local air cover and then turned for the coast with an alteration of course to east, which would, with *Tirpitz*'s superior speed, open out her distance from the Home Fleet. The observer in the trailing Albacore wrongly reported this alteration as being to the northeast, an error that, with the loss of surprise, now conspired to rob Admiral Tovey of any chance of victory.

At 0842, the torpedo-armed Albacores sighted their quarry to the southeast in the direction of the rising sun. The squadron commander ordered his aircraft to climb into cloud cover, hoping to get ahead of the *Tirpitz*, but as they overflew the battleship and the *Friedrich lhn*, a break in the clouds exposed them to flak. Nevertheless, the Albacores split into subflights, which attacked immediately.

The first subflight of Albacores released their torpedoes at long range on the *Tirpitz*'s port bow but at too fine an angle for them to hit the racing ship. With great skill and coolness, Captain Karl Topp on *Tirpitz* put his helm over to port and combed the approaching torpedo tracks. The second subflight attacked from the starboard quarter with the same lack of success. The third and fourth also approached on the starboard side, but were delayed due to the difficulties of maneuvering ahead of the speeding ship.

Topp applied counter helm, which reduced the angle of approach of their torpedoes, and *Tirpitz* succeeded in evading them all. The barrage of fire put up by the German ships, especially the *Tirpitz* herself, was terrific. Two of the Albacores were shot down and, though more were thought by the Germans to have been hit, so intense was their fire, these were the only losses. The British planes had themselves fired machine guns at the gray superstructure as they had roared past. It was a bitter disappointment. The attack, made from leeward and from astern, had robbed the Albacores of any tactical advantage to be gained from a high rate of speed of attack. As the biplanes headed back for the carrier, the unscathed *Tirpitz* was racing unopposed for Norway. *Tirpitz* and her escort made it back to Norway without loss, but also without finding the convoy they were sent out to destroy.

Izhora's sinking seems an incidental loss in this confrontation between giants. She was an old, slow, coal-burning freighter long past her prime captained by Vasily Belov with First Mate Nicholas Adayev. The thirty-one-person crew included three women: Anna Avdeeva was a former barmaid and the eldest at age fifty, Basov Agne had been a charwoman, and Raisa Mogutova was the youngest at just twenty years old. Among the men were nineteen-year-old Peter Panteleyev and two sixteen-year-old sailors: Yuri Shumkova and Lesha Makarycheva.

The battle began when the German destroyer *Friedrich Ihn* hove into view on that overcast afternoon. At 1645 hours on March 7, *Friedrich Ihn*'s log noted: "At full speed have gone in this direction. The pipe [smoke stack] and two masts of the steamship, following a course on the West becomes soon visible."

Ihn ordered *Izhora* to stop, lower the flag, and not use the radio. The log continues: "17hrs. 20min. the Steamship informs the identification data: 'Timber carrying vessel *Izhora*, the port of registry Leningrad. Displacement of 2815 tons, I go with cargo'."

If the Germans seized the ship, the crew's fate was obvious: capture by a boarding team from one of the destroyers, and then a short trip to Norway, ending in a concentration camp. There wasn't a ghost of a chance that any would survive. Failure to comply with the order to stop would automatically mean a death sentence.

Knowing they would die one way or another, Vasily Belov increased speed and Nikolai Gusarov, the radio operator, immediately broke radio silence to report contact with the German squadron and its exact location. This was heard by the Germans, and *Ihn* immediately opened fire and destroyed *Izhora*'s Radio Room, killing Gusarov.

The other destroyers and *Tirpitz* then opened fire on the unarmed freighter. Incredibly, *Izhora* remained afloat despite being pummeled by one of the strongest fighting ships in the world (eight guns in caliber 380 mm, and numerous smaller guns), and three destroyers (five guns in caliber 127 mm or 150 mm).

It should have ended quickly, for each warship was capable of sinking *Izhora* within minutes. *Izhora* couldn't fight back, and there was no chance of help from the escorts, which were miles away. However, though brutally beaten up by shells, the gallant ship refused to sink. Most of the crew suffered painful deaths, scalded by steam, burnt by fire, killed by shrapnel under hailstones of shells, or frozen to death after succumbing to hypothermia in the cold water. Naturally, nobody wanted to die, including those two sixteen-year-old boys who had taken the place of their lost fathers and that twenty-year-old girl who, possibly, had not yet tasted her first kiss.

But *Izhora* paid the Germans back for her crew's deaths as the smoke from the burning ship rose high into the sky and was visible from afar possibly alerting the British escorts to the German presence. The German commander, watching the protracted fight between three destroyers and one small transport, grew angry. What should have been an easy operation was turning into a big problem. The Germans lost their secrecy and had remained in one place for too long. Consumption of shells on the sinking of the transport was comparable to the cost of transport itself and its cargo. Therefore, the admiral asked Topp to have the destroyers attack *Izhora* with torpedoes.

Ihn fired a torpedo at close range, but the torpedo suddenly turned around and almost hit the destroyer. After that *Schoemann* attacked, but missed at point-blank range.

Failing in a simple torpedo attack, *Ihn* dropped depth charges set at a minimum depth of detonation. They broke the bottom of the Soviet ship, and it finally disappeared under the water at 1758 hours after a battle lasting for more than an hour and a half.

The Germans picked up the only survivor from the water: Nicholas Adayev. Neither fire nor ice water, neither hailstones of bullets nor large-caliber shells could destroy Adayev. But a year in the Shtutgof concentration camp was too much for him to endure. He died in captivity, thereby affirming the choice made by *Izhora*'s crew not to surrender even against overwhelming odds.

Summing up *Izhora*'s bravery Anatoly Lifshits, assistant navigation officer on the Soviet destroyer *Rattling*, wrote about the event in somewhat broken English:

I remember, how have met on March, 12th in water area Kola a gulf transports PQ-12. We already knew about tragedy which was played on March, 7th with Izhora. *Also it is necessary to tell that thanking a heroic act of a command of a steamship* Izhora*'s convoy has not been crushed, and has reached whole and safe ....*

The Feat of Izhora *which was lost, but not surrendered to the enemy, was not in vain. Its radio signal has been accepted by escort PQ-12 that has helped it to avoid a meeting with a battleship* Tirpitz *and has rescued an escort from defeat.*

It [PQ-12] delivered the largest party of strategic cargoes received by the USSR in one caravan: 200 planes, 160 tanks and 180 armoured cars, 24 guns, hundreds trucks, machine tools, thousand tons of the equipment, raw materials and the foodstuffs. Also that is important these cargoes basically were used in Stalingradsky [Stalingrad] fight that, undoubtedly, has approached Day of Victories.

By the life the Soviet seamen have prevented death of many and many seamen of allied escort PQ-12 and QP-8, and also destruction of the ships of these escorts. And, how many lives of our people the military technology on the fronts could save up, what loss planes, tanks, and shells have put to the enemy, torpedoes which carried the escort ships, it is impossible to tell.

Four merchant ships had straggled from PQ-12 during its passage: the *Bateau* early on, the *Kiev* on March 3, *El Occidente* on encountering the ice on March 6, and the *Sevaples* as they broke out of the ice on March 11. One of the escorting antisubmarine whalers, the *Stefa*, had lost contact on March 6. *Kiev* and *El Occidente* reached Iokanka unmolested on March 10, and *Sevaples* sighted and joined forces with the *Stefa*, which, on March 13, shot down an aircraft trying to bomb the merchant ship. Ironically, despite the presence of a German battle squadron and a wolf pack of four U-boats strung out across the route of PQ-12 between Jan Mayen and Bear Island, this was the only engagement directly connected with the passage of PQ-12. *Bateau* returned to Iceland and sailed with PQ-13.

PQ-12 suffered one loss, but to the sea, not to the Germans. HMS *Shera*, one of four former Norwegian whalers being transferred to the Soviet Navy, capsized and sank on March 9. The weather at the time was not usual, and, although some icing of the upper deck had occurred, it was not severe. It is believed that *Shera*'s stability was affected by the ice, made worse by a low level of oil fuel on board and the excessive amount of guns and equipment on her upper decks. Only three of her crew survived: Lieutenant Hansen RNR, Ordinary Seaman Harris, and Steward Phillips, to be rescued by her consort, *Svega*, which reached

Murmansk independently on March 11, unaware that PQ-12 had altered course far to the north.

On March 14, 1942, Hitler decided to make the Arctic convoys a strategic target of major importance linked directly to the campaign in Russia. The Anglo-American deliveries of war supplies were "sustaining Russian ability to hold out." He declared that, "it is necessary that maritime communications over the Arctic Ocean between the Anglo-Saxons and Russians, hitherto virtually unimpeded, should henceforth be impeded."

The skirmishing was over and the now battle began in earnest.

CHAPTER 3

ARCTIC SHOOTING GALLERY
March 1942

___

As winter warmed into spring, the Allies were fighting defensive battles—and losing. U-boats rampaged along the U.S. east coast, sinking ships in broad daylight, leaving funeral pyres of smoke visible to people on the beach 10 miles away. North Atlantic convoys fought east and west through an unremitting gauntlet of deadly wolf packs. In North Africa, British forces pushing west ran into a reinforced Afrika Corps under Field Marshal Erwin Rommel, which stopped the advance and forced a retreat toward Egypt. The Mediterranean Sea was closed to Allied shipping from Alexandria in the east to Gibraltar in the west. Japan's forces controlled the entire southwest Pacific, ruthlessly rolling over anyone who opposed them. After a brutal Russian winter, German forces were still within striking distance of Moscow, fighting house to house in Stalingrad and shelling Leningrad on a daily basis.

Although not in massive quantities, the supplies arriving in Russia via the convoys were enough to help the Soviet Union hold out through the winter. After assessing the reasons for the unexpected Soviet ability to resist defeat, the Wehrmacht and Hitler realized that the Arctic Convoys were making a difference and were a serious threat to defeating the Soviets. Although the Germans had been blocked in their attempts to capture Murmansk, they were determined to sink every ship at the docks and bomb the port into oblivion.

With the coming of spring, planning went on for more and larger convoys, which would have to sail during increasing hours of daylight, making them easier to find. Sailing of eastbound PQ convoys was synchronized with westbound QP convoys so that their courses would cross one another in the vicinity of Bear Island, where the cruiser covering force could cover both convoys in the most dangerous area.

Convoys still had to fight the Arctic's brutal weather, coupled with an ice pack pushing south ever closer to Norway, decreasing the maneuvering room to avoid attack. This narrowing gap meant the convoys were within range of Luftwaffe bases in Norway during most of the voyage. Long-range FW-200 Condors and BV-138 flying boat reconnaissance aircraft easily located the convoys in good weather and were impossible for the slow-moving ships to elude. Also, these planes were heavily armed and seemingly impervious to attack by the lightly armed British fighters accompanying the ships on the new escort aircraft carriers.

Eight convoys—PQ-13, 14, 15, and 16 and QP-9, 10, 11, and 12—totaling 163 ships sailed between March 21 and May 21. Only one, QP-9, made it through without loss to either the weather or the Germans.

There were nineteen ships in PQ-13, which sailed from Reykjavik on March 21. British Vice Admiral A. T. B. Curteis covered the western route on battleship *King George V* with a second battleship, *Duke of York*, the battlecruiser *Renown*, the carrier *Victorious*, and the cruisers *Edinburgh* and *Kent*, screened by eleven fleet destroyers. The cruiser *Trinidad* provided close cover together with two destroyers, *Fury* and *Eclipse*, which joined off Iceland. Destroyer *Lamerton* and the trawlers *Blackfly* and *Paynter* accompanied PQ-13 from Reykjavik, together with ex-Norwegian whalers *Sulla*, *Sumba*, and *Silja*, which were being transferred to the Soviet Navy in an attempt to beef up the local minesweeping force.

QP-9, also with nineteen ships, sailed from Murmansk on March 22. The convoy was covered west of Bear Island by the cruiser *Nigeria* and an ocean escort of the minesweepers *Sharpshooter* and *Britomart* and the destroyer *Offa*. Additional local support was given by five minesweepers led by *Harrier*, two Russian destroyers, *Gremyashchiy* and *Sokrushitelnyy*, and the British destroyer *Oribi*. These accompanied QP-9 two days into its homeward passage, until the early hours of March 23 when they turned back to Murmansk. Little more was achieved by the cruiser *Kenya*, intended to be performing the equivalent role of *Trinidad*, which left Kola on March 22 but failed to locate the convoy. She did, however, succeed in carrying home 10 tons of bullion.

On March 23, QP-9 ran into a severe southwesterly gale with heavy snowstorms, but the convoy managed to stay together. As the weather abated the next evening, lookouts aboard the minesweeper *Sharpshooter* spotted *U-655* 300 yards away. Lieutenant Commander David Lampen, *Sharpshooter*'s captain, immediately altered course to intercept, but his quarry submerged. *Sharpshooter* laid down a series of depth charges, which blew the U-boat to the surface, where she was rammed and sunk by *Sharpshooter* before she had time to dive again. None of the U-boat's forty-seven-man crew survived. *Sharpshooter*'s bow was damaged, but she stayed with the convoy.

During the course of its voyage, QP-9 endured additional attacks by U-boats and aircraft, all of which were beaten off by the escorts and intense fire from the merchant ships. The convoy reached Reykjavik on April 3 without loss.

PQ-13 was less fortunate, however. The convoy sailed from Iceland on March 21 and had four days of clear sailing before running into a savage storm.

"The Barents Sea became a fury of tumultuous water," said Ronald Adds, a stoker on board HMS *Fury*:

The waves reared up in enormous mountains of water sixty to eighty feet high. Then, there was the cold. Freezing spray formed into ice as soon as it hit superstructures, decks, and guard rails.

Imagine a destroyer climbing such waves at a slow speed and, leaving the quiet of the trough, meeting the full force of the tempest on the wave top. Then, there was the cold. At times there was so much ice—up to 3 inches thick—there was danger of capsizing.

To take over the watch in the engine-room of a destroyer dressed in a duffel coat, woolen socks and sea boots was an experience I had never had before. Beneath the duffel coat I wore full uniform, but with a roll-collar pullover instead of collar and tie. Beneath that were hand-knitted woolen long johns and a long sleeved vest. When I was issued with this kit in Scapa Flow,

I never imagined having to wear it. I had always worn cotton gloves on watch, but now I was wearing fur-lined mittens—and very happy to do so.

Every now and then flurries of snow would filter down through the air vents, whilst the three foot diameter copper pipes supplying cooling sea-water to the condensers under the turbines were inches thick in ice. The thermometer reading of the seawater showed 28 degrees Fahrenheit—way below the freezing temperature of fresh water. Due to this, the normal use of circulating pumps was considered unnecessary. I've never been so cold in my life.

We were all scared. There isn't a man who served on these convoys who would not admit to being scared. But I cannot recall any panic amongst Fury's ship's company, although some of them were at sea for the first time. Such was life in those days. Cigarettes were our main consolation, which, thank goodness, were duty-free. There was also the consoling effect of the daily ration of rum, all too often not drunk on the spot but illegally bottled for the provision of "Dutch Courage" at times of stress.

At times so much ice built up on decks, masts, guns, and superstructures that the ships were in danger of capsizing. This was the fate of *Sulla*, one of the whalers. Harold G. Neill, a crewman on *Sumba*, shared vivid memories of the storm and *Sulla*'s fate:

We all left on March twenty-second and as soon as we left the shelter of the fiord the weather was atrocious, gales with blizzards, it was impossible to see, the snow was so thick. We joined up with PQ-13 and lost them because of worsening conditions. I was personally involved in chopping ice as far as I could reach. I was on the engine room casing lashed to an iron stanchion, as fast as I cleared the ice it was back again.

This icing of the ship had to be experienced to believe it. I went into the C.O.'s cabin and there was a good inch thick of solid ice covering the whole of the bulkhead where he slept or was supposed to, I don't think any of us did much sleeping that trip.

The boxes which had been made to take the sweep on both Port and Starboard of the superstructure had been smashed to matchwood, iron stanchion had been bent and twisted, everything on the deck seemed to have disappeared such was the force of the sea and ice.

The Sulla was on a parallel course to us not too far away. One minute I looked over and she was there, the next time I looked she had gone, I assumed at the time that she had turned turtle and gone down with the weight of ice, there was no sound of an explosion just nothing, no debris visible or any sign of her; she had vanished.

Sulla sank on March 25, taking her entire crew of twenty-one men with her. The storm lasted three days and scattered the convoy across 150 miles. Because of the storm, Vice Admiral Curteis's ships ran short of fuel and returned to base, leaving only the close escort to cover the convoy.

On March 27, the senior officer of the escort force in HMS *Harrier* began trying to reassemble the convoy, but no ships were in sight. The Commodore's ship, the tanker *River Afton*, unable to steer within five points of the wind (roughly 55 degrees), had drifted toward the Lofoten Islands in northern Norway. The most easterly ship was the *Empire Ranger*, all alone and only about 80 miles north of the North Cape; 40 miles astern of her was a group of six merchant ships with an armed whaler in company; 35 miles further west was the SS *Harpalion* escorted by the destroyer *Fury*; while a further 65 miles astern was another group of six ships escorted by the destroyer *Eclipse*, the whaler *Sumba*, and the trawler *Paynter*. The cruisers *Trinidad* and *Nigeria* were searching for stragglers in an area 100 miles to the southwest of Bear Island.

March 28 dawned clear and sunny with occasional snow flurries, but the convoy was still dispersed, having been unable to reassemble since the storm that sank the *Sulla*. At 0700 hours that day, Kapitänleutnant Heinrich Brodda of *U-209* made the first contact after sighting the Polish steam merchant *Tobruk* escorted by the armed trawler HMS *Blackfly*. The encounter was inconclusive, as the U-boat missed the trawler with a stern torpedo and the depth charges dropped on her caused no damage. Soon thereafter the ships dropped out of sight in a snow squall.

Just after 1000 hours, *Trinidad* was spotted by a BV-138 flying boat. Two hours later, the Luftwaffe launched attacks by Ju-88 bombers, and for the rest of the day, gunners on the scattered ships tried to fight them off.

First blood was drawn by the bombers, sinking *Empire Ranger*, romping ahead of the convoy, and the *Raceland*, a straggler from the easternmost group of six ships. *Raceland* was attacked by two aircraft, two bombs hitting about 20 yards from the ship on the starboard side near No. 3 hatch. There were no direct hits, but the concussion of the bombs ripped a hole in the starboard side of the forward hull, breaking deck fittings and steam pipes and stopping the engines. The engine room flooded, and the ship took a 45-degree list to port.

Herman Torgersen, who was in the food storage room sorting potatoes on *Raceland* when the attacks began, said to the Canadian next to him: "Now it's getting serious." The aircraft came right above them, but disappeared again; a few shots were exchanged. The aircraft next came from behind. The alarm sounded again, and the men grabbed their lifebelts. Torgersen donned his tall sheepskin-lined boots—but not his socks, which he bitterly came to regret.

The *Raceland* was poorly equipped for taking defensive measures. German aircraft dropped two bombs from about 100 feet up; they exploded under the ship, destroying the plating in the engine room on the port side. The ship immediately started to list to starboard at a sharp angle.

Torgersen was assigned to the starboard lifeboat, which was difficult to launch because of the heavy coating of ice on the boat falls. Torgersen recalled that all forty-five crewmen got safely in the boats: the first mate had one boat with fifteen on board, the second mate one boat with eighteen men, and the captain and the boatswain a small boat with six men each. None of the boats had a motor. *Raceland* wasn't sinking, so the captain gave orders to wait, which they did—for twelve hours. During those long hours, Torgersen and Danish First Engineer Svend Svenningsen (who later died) went back on board to retrieve food, blankets, canned fruits, preserved milk, clothes, and anything else they might need. Years later, Torgersen could still remember how he had to break a lock in the food storage room in pitch dark: He put the lock in his pocket, and it's the one remaining souvenir he has of *Raceland*.

At 2230 hours, *Raceland* finally sank. A tall column of flames rushed toward the skies in the tremendous explosion that followed. In the middle of the fire, survivors could see the profile of a raft from the *Raceland* being flung to the skies. Now the lifeboats tried to set a course for Murmansk, about 600 miles away. All four were tied together. The second mate, who had a working compass, led the group.

That night, a terrible hurricane blew up, bringing with it indescribable cold. The boats became separated in the storm, and the men never saw each other again. The two smaller boats probably went down immediately.

Brutal weather lasted for the eleven days they were on the sea. Bitter cold and vicious storms constantly nagged the men. All the food was lost during the first day of the storm, and soon the real tragedy began. The first engineer, whom Torgersen remembered as a nice Danish fellow, suddenly stood up, snatched the precious compass, and flung it in the water. He then fell to his knees, wrapped his arms around his legs, and died. Torgersen struggled for hours to free the dead man's arms from his legs, but they were frozen stuck. The second mate gave the order to throw the body overboard, but no one wanted to do it. But the boat was overcrowded, and finally he was given to the sea.

After that, someone died every day, usually preceded by a period of varying degrees of insanity. One fellow from Bergen, Norway's second-largest city, suffered in pain from extraordinarily cold feet. He suddenly pulled off his tall, fur-lined boots, threw them into the sea, stuck his feet into the ice-cold water, and said, "This is lovely. Now I can get warm." His boat mates could see death creep over him from his feet to his heart. He was dead within five minutes. Another man threw himself overboard; they managed to get him on board again, but it was too late. Another mate wildly flung an ax, cutting the ropes while yelling and singing before falling silent and dying.

The second mate, Johansen, was the last of the eighteen men on the lifeboat to die. The young man from Bodø, a small town in north-central Norway, had proved himself a first class seaman. But he, too, lost his composure, sailing the lifeboat round and round in circles for days, which his boat mates all realized even though they were not navigators themselves. Eventually, he, too, was seized by a violent death cramp. Only five of the original eighteen men in the lifeboat were left alive when they reached the Norwegian coast and were taken prisoner by the Germans.

Air attacks continued as the opponents played a deadly game of hide-and-seek through snow squalls and low-hanging clouds. The freighter *Ballot* suffered bomb damage, and, although not in any danger of sinking, sixteen men demanded to leave the ship. The men in the lifeboat were picked up by *Silja* and later transferred to *Induna*. Both ships became stuck in ice the next day. Despite being short-handed, *Ballot*'s remaining crew stayed to repair the ship and brought her safely to Murmansk on March 30.

Based on the sighting report from the BV-138, the destroyers Z-24, Z-25, and Z-26, under the command of Captain Gottfried Pönitz, sortied from their Norwegian base at far northeastern Kirkenes to intercept the convoy. Adding to the forces arrayed against PQ-13 were U-209, U-376, U-378, and U-655, which were ordered by Rear Admiral Hubert Schmundt, Flag Officer Northern Waters (*Gruppe Nord*), to form a patrol line off the North Cape.

The destroyers spread in a line 3 miles apart, swept west along PQ-13's estimated track. At 2245 hours, Z-24 came across *Empire Ranger*'s lifeboats and rescued the sixty-one survivors. Then, just after midnight on March 29, *Z-26* encountered *Bateau* and sank the freighter with torpedoes and gunfire, killing thirty-seven men. At the time of the sinking, the weather was bitterly cold with a blizzard blowing.

Robert Taylor, one of the two Maritime Royal Artillery gunners, survived. The other, Bombardier Richard Hector Waddy, only lived for about ten minutes in the frigid water.

"I was just about to go on watch when we were hit by two torpedoes amidships," wrote Taylor years later.

> I grabbed a kapok coat and tried to help some of the crew, but they seemed to want to go down with the ship. An air pocket in my heavy coat kept me afloat as I swam away. After about an hour, a German destroyer came up and they threw me a wire hawser and I grabbed it with both hands and my teeth. Soon they had me aboard.

The trapped air pocket in his upper body area apparently prevented the intense cold from reaching his heart—at least that was the explanation given to him by the German naval doctor aboard the ship that rescued him. Taylor was one of only six *Bateau* survivors.

By the morning of March 29, the convoy was in two groups about 80 miles apart from one another; the whereabouts of four ships were unknown. The westerly group of eight ships was being escorted by HMS *Eclipse* and the trawler *Paynter*. At 0645, they were reinforced by HMS *Oribi* and the Soviet destroyers *Gremyashchiy* and *Sokrushitelnyy*. *Trinidad*, accompanied by *Fury*, was steaming east at 0843 hours to collect the easterly group of four ships and bring them back to the other group. The weather started to deteriorate, the visibility shortening as heavy snow squalls driven by a bitter wind swept down, when *Trinidad's* radar picked up a contact bearing 079 degrees at a range of 6.5 miles. Suddenly ahead at only 1.5 miles were the three destroyers, each carrying guns equal to the fire power of the British cruiser and much larger than British destroyers and at top speed.

Trinidad's commanding officer, Captain L. S. Sanders, gave the order to open fire with main guns, anti-aircraft weapons, and machine guns, sending a curtain of fire crashing into *Z-26*, the lead destroyer, immediately setting it on fire. Shells could be seen exploding amidships with flame and smoke. The German ship began to return fire, and two shells smashed into *Trinidad's* port side. The German destroyer then broke off the engagement and headed northwest into a snow cloud. Sanders recalled the action:

As I knew the rough positions of my own force, these could only be the Germans, so when three shapes appeared out of the murk only a mile or so distant, I was able to open fire immediately without waiting to signal the challenge. They were Germany's latest Z class destroyers. It was an exhilarating moment to hoist, in earnest, the signal "Enemy in sight" and to wireless to the Naval world a real enemy report.

The enemy returned our fire. Several shells fell close and two exploded in my day cabin aft, killing the one man of the damage control party there who thought it foolish to lie down. My immediate reaction, and of those others on the bridge, was to duck! Quite pointless and soon stopped.

When I judged the time right, I turned a complete circle away from the enemy to avoid the torpedoes they had undoubtedly fired—two passed close by our side—and also because I did not want to get too close, which might encourage the enemy to split up and press home an attack simultaneously from different directions. This would have spelled disaster. We could only engage effectively one ship at a time, so at least one destroyer could have got in to point blank range and put a salvo of torpedoes into me. Thank God this move did not appear to occur to them. They were intent on running away.

They disappeared into the murk during our turn, but our radar kept contact as I hoped it would. I wondered what to do next. I remembered Nelson's order—"No Captain can do very wrong if he lay his ship alongside that of the enemy." So I gave chase and in time sighted the rear destroyer. She had possibly had her speed reduced by our earlier shelling. We passed a few wretched German sailors in the water, but this was not the time to pick them up. Our salvoes continued to fall around her but with only an occasional outburst of flame indicating a hit.

In an attempt to finish off Z-26, *Trinidad* fired a torpedo, which in the intense cold ran erratically, and, reversing course, returned and hit the cruiser. It struck underneath the bridge, leaving a gaping hole 60 feet by 20 feet, which flooded the forward boiler room and killed thirty-one men, forcing the ship to break off the combat.

Meanwhile, *Eclipse* located the badly damaged Z-26 and began to chase her, scoring at least six hits until the enemy stopped. *Eclipse* was attacked by the two other German destroyers but escaped by taking cover in a snow squall, though not before she had been hit aft by two shells and holed above the waterline in the forward part of the ship by two others.

Attracted by the gunfire, *Oribi* and *Sokrushitelnyy* joined the action. *Sokrushitelnyy* fired six salvos at a German destroyer, claiming one hit until losing contact in a snow squall. *U-376* (Kapitänleutnant Friedrich-Karl Marks) had observed the gunfire but only once sighted a destroyer, which proved to be German.

After the battle, the U-boat sighted the German destroyers picking up survivors from the sinking *Z-26* and was ordered to participate in the rescue operation. The sinking vessel took 240 crewmembers into the deep with her; most of the men died in the freezing cold water. Although *Z-24* and *Z-25* rescued ninety-six men, only eight were still alive when *U-376* came to the rescue. Three of the men died of exposure during the next few hours and were buried at sea.

Escorted by *Fury*, *Trinidad* made her way toward Murmansk and safety. *Eclipse*, short of fuel and with nine seriously wounded men in need of urgent medical attention, also set course for Murmansk, which she reached the next morning.

After the warship fight and despite the casualties, the battle wasn't over yet. Sixteen merchant ships were still scattered across hundreds of square miles, each a target for the Luftwaffe above and the U-boats below. With *Trinidad*, *Fury*, and *Eclipse* out of the fight, few escorts remained, and those that did weren't always near the missing ships.

One of the missing ships was the freighter *El Estero*. Hoping to avoid detection, her master headed into the ice field at the first warning that the convoy had been discovered. He was only partially successful. Greg A. Novak, a crewman on board *El Estero*, told the tale:

> *Following our emergence from the storm the following relatively clement weather permitted a determined German attack upon the elements of our scattered convoy. We emerged from a stormy cloud-cover, heavily snow- and ice-clad, in nature's camouflage, dimming our presence near the iceberg-floes to be seen, closely north of us.*
>
> *At high altitudes, beyond the range of our AA Guns, bombers alone were to be seen. 50-foot geysers of sea-water shot upward where the dropping bombs hit the sea, generally of comfortable distances from our ship.*
>
> *The first mate, a seaman (names lost in memory) and I cast a heavy drum of smoke-screen material over the stem and into the sea as the ship headed into the ice-floes to minimize the Luftwaffe, warship long-range shell, and submarine activity.*
>
> *Once safely ensconced amidst the icebergs, difficult to get at, almost invisible to any other combatant within possible range, axe-wielding seamen*

beat off the ice, coating shrouds, deck, etc. to prevent cargo-shifting or to prevent a top-heavy ship from capsizing. The ship carefully was slowly threading its way among the icebergs.

We emerged from the ice-floes into a clear day only to enter a floating mine-field. A spined floating-mine was to be seen nearly in collision with our motionless ship on our Port side amidships. Our black-bearded Captain J. Beatovich, in a sonorous baritone voice barked out an order to me from the bridge to me amidships. I being the lone unfortunate within earshot, directing me, calmly, to fend off the mine from the ship's port side with a piece of timber, two by four inches and eight feet long, retrieved from a midship hatch.

No legendary figure of the Spanish Main, nor any cut-throat apparition ever depicted in Robert L. Stevenson's Treasure Island, or Boy's Own or Chums Annuals, avidly read, wide-eyed, some sixty years ago in my boyhood, ever could have inspired greater respect than this man, in his only recollectible [sic] verbal exchange with me, whose bellow, moreover, could carry from a coast-wise tramp in transit to a distant shore, no matter the intensity of a prevailing gale. His bark could shatter glass.

In any event, not daring to offend this stalwart controller of our collective destinies, I managed carefully to avoid the trigger spines of the floating mine and fend off the deadly six foot diameter sphere from contacting the ship's hull. However, there can be no doubt that my personal motivation was less than altruistically sparing a ship and crew from harm, but rather one of mere self-preservation, yet it seemed to me that, from that day forward, the crew showed me a little deference, forgiving me future faux-pas, as if they owed me something.

A few turns, slowly, of the starboard screw saw the ship's stern separate further from the ball, slowly drifting away in our wash astern of us. But the very motion of the ship exposed, off our port-bow, among the drift-floes a second floating mine, which fact I called out to the bridge and it was summarily acknowledged, after a moment's pause, by the captain, who had probably seen it earlier in any event. Nevertheless, it was easily avoided.

Within an hour we came within earshot of a heavily-armed minesweeping Russian trawler and a nearby destroyer [Gremyashchiy and Sokrushitelnyy]. The destroyer was shortly to leave us, but the trawler escorted the lone straggler into the Kola Inlet on, I believe, March 28, 1942, taking but a few hours.

While the *El Estero* fought for survival under German attack, the whaler *Sumba* was running out of fuel in her attempt to maneuver through ice fields. She needed help. Harold G. Neill, an officers' steward, recalled what was going on with *Sumba*:

> We were on our own and running out of fuel and wondering if we broke radio silence it would give our position away to the enemy. Our luck held and our signal was answered by the Fury who gave us a time when to expect them. Our spirits were uplifted when she turned up and began putting a fuel pipe over to replenish our tanks, they also sent over fresh bread etc. which was a godsend.
>
> All too quickly we were refueled and the Fury was on her way, without her assistance I wouldn't be sitting writing this today, we were all eternally grateful to her officers and crew. We felt happier having Paynter with us for company but it wasn't long before we heard the sound of planes that proceeded to attack. Their firing lacked precision and I thought at the time we were not worth the cost of a bomb, we made a very small target in a large expanse of water.
>
> At the start of the attack we manned our gun forward of the wheelhouse but as we tried to fire it the barrel blew off—it was full of ice. The explosion shattered the glass in the wheelhouse. We had twin Lewis guns set in armoured shields and they had also been made useless by the weight of ice.

Induna with *Silja* in tow tried to clear the ice field. It wasn't until the afternoon of March 29 that they finally freed themselves and set course for Murmansk. That night, the tow parted in heavy seas and they were unable to find the trawler in snow squalls. *Induna* proceeded on her way alone, only to be torpedoed and sunk by *U-376* the next morning, March 30.

Forty-one survivors abandoned ship in two lifeboats, but by the time they were picked up by a Russian minesweeper on April 2, only thirty were still alive; two later died of exposure in a hospital in Murmansk. The weather had been horrible with temperatures around 20 degrees below zero Fahrenheit and freezing winds. The survivors had been sprayed by ice-cold water, and most of them, including David, a fourteen year-old cabin boy, lost limbs. The master, twenty crewmembers, six gunners, and eleven men from *Ballot* were lost. Nineteen crewmembers and four gunners from *Induna* made it. Only five of the sixteen men who had abandoned *Ballot* survived.

Induna's Engineering Officer William P. "Bill" Shorts remembered what happened after their ship sank:

I was preparing to go on watch when the torpedo struck and I went immediately to my boat station. The lifeboat that I should have been in had already been launched. The weather was so bad, that the boat had to be cut adrift. I ran around to the other lifeboat, only to discover that it had, too, been launched with a full complement. I realized then that, if I were going to get off the sinking ship, I would have to jump into the Sea, which is mighty cold in the Arctic in March, plus the fact that I could not swim.

Eventually, the overcrowded lifeboat, which was damaged during the launching, picked me up, and it was leaking badly. With so many onboard, we were packed in like sardines in a tin can. There was no room to move, but there was hope of being picked up, as an SOS had been sent and perhaps a naval vessel would be sent to look for us. Hope for the first day was high, but, as the night fell, we realized that it would be a bitter cold night with sleet, snow and forty foot waves to contend with. Little did I realize at that moment, what an awful experience that was to follow. Could one's courage and endurance stand the ordeal?

There has always been the impression that a "tot" of rum will keep out the cold. There was wine and whiskey aboard the lifeboat and some indulged and drank too much. Those who did went to sleep and no matter how they were shook, they did not stir, as by now, they had hypothermia and when they went to sleep, they never awaken. Sadly, the first night, six died and all we could do was slide them overboard and commit their bodies to the deep.

This went on for four days. A "donkeyman", who had been badly burned in the engine room after a flashover, was lying in the bottom of the lifeboat and there was nothing we could do for his wounds. He eventually died; frozen to the bottom of the lifeboat and it was impossible to remove him. The water keg was frozen solid, so we were licking ice. Water had gotten into the wireless transmitter so we could not send another SOS. All the rations that were to sustain us were frozen solid, too.

At the end of the fourth day, out of thirty-four men to start with, only seventeen were alive. One man went mad. The sea spray was freezing on the gunwale and he started to lick the ice. His tongue became swollen; he then became deranged, and died from suffocation. We had given up hope of rescue and from time to time, we sighted land through the snow and whiteout, but it seemed so far away.

On the fifth day of their ill-fated voyage, when only four or five men remained alive, fate played an almost unbelievable last cruel trick. A swirling mist descended on them, fanned by a bitter breeze. As the fog thickened, it blanketed visibility and muffled just about every noise. Only the ceaseless lapping of water against the boat could be heard. Then suddenly they heard a whistle. The sound faded then rose again, louder and more constant. Hearts raced with excitement. Surely it was someone from a rescue boat trying to locate them.

With what little strength was left, they tried to shout. Despite their efforts, there was no answer. Still the whistle persisted. First it seemed to be ahead and then astern. The sound was eerie, almost supernatural. In their low state of mind, the mystery deepened every minute and became almost frightening. Desperate and frustrated, their eyes tried to pierce the fog bank but saw nothing.

Minutes later, their hopes came tumbling when the riddle was solved. On the thwart, gently rolling with the movement of the sea lay an empty bottle. As the wind swept through the boat, it played on the open end of the bottle, trilling the whistling sound. Hope turned to despair, optimism to despondency. It was the worst moment of their ordeal.

At dawn on April 1, aircraft of the Northern Fleet sighted boats with people 15 miles to the west of Tsyp-Navolok headland off the Murman coast and directed the minesweepers *T-882* and *KT-406* to the boats. *T-882* was on scene first and took on board twenty-eight survivors.

Bill Shorts finished the story:

A Russian minesweeper eventually picked us up. By now we were so weak; we had to be hauled aboard by ropes around our waist. I actually tried to walk, to get circulation going in my legs but it was impossible as my legs would not support me. When the Induna *was torpedoed, we were 175 miles from Murmansk, Russia. When we were picked up, we were told later that we were a scant 25 miles from Murmansk. So, in four days, we had drifted 150 miles.*

Four merchant ships and a warship in the convoy were sunk, and two warships and numerous merchant ships were damaged—all in just two days. The Germans lost a destroyer and several aircraft. But, for both sides, PQ-13's ordeal was not over yet. The fifth and last merchant ship lost was *Effingham* on March 30. A torpedo from *U-456* (Kapitänleutnant Max-Martin Teichert) struck amidships on the port side, and the crew of eight officers, twenty-six men, and nine armed guards immediately abandoned ship with two lifeboats in rough seas as the ship began to settle by the stern. Two men fell overboard and drowned. After about two hours, the survivors watched the *Effingham* explode after *U-435* (Korvettenkapitän Siegfried Strelow) torpedoed the ship again.

On March 31, the master, the chief mate, and fifteen men in one of the lifeboats were picked up by HMS *Harrier*, which was on patrol off Kola Inlet, looking for stragglers from the convoy. The *Harrier* landed them in Polyarnoe the next day, but not before six men in the lifeboat had died of exposure. Sixty-five hours after the attack, eleven men and three armed guards in the second boat were picked up by a Soviet patrol vessel, but four men in that boat also had died of exposure. All of the survivors were taken to Murmansk. John Guthrie, a member of the U.S. Naval Armed Guard detachment, wrote about the events:

> When the ship was hit they were only able to launch two lifeboats to the best of my recollection, I do remember the first two who froze to death and they were the warmest dressed two in our boat. After they died we took their heavy clothes and dumped them overboard. I don't recall how long we were in the boat but it was quite a few hours.
>
> I was quite excited when the H.M.S. Harrier came over the horizon. When they picked us up the 3rd mate believe who had been on the tiller the whole time hand had frozen to it so one of the crewman from the Harrier had to cut it off (tiller not his hand). After we were taken aboard they gave us some warm dry clothes and a couple of drinks of rum. Several of the crew didn't want theirs so I drank them so they wouldn't be wasted. I guess I must have passed out because they told me later we were again attacked by German torpedo boats going in.

Although the Germans had drawn first blood, they were to suffer the last loss by killing one of their own, *U-585* (Korvettenkapitän Ernst-Bernward Lohse). On March 30, the U-boat hit a German mine that had drifted from the Bantos-A minefield in the Barents Sea north of Murmansk. All forty-four crewmen died with their boat.

After escorting the wounded *Trinidad* safely to Murmansk, *Fury* immediately left again to patrol off Kola Inlet, where she was joined by *Speedwell*. Their tasks were antisubmarine patrol and to search for any remaining ships from PQ-13. They spotted the drifting *Silja*, which was towed by *Harrier* to the Polyarnoe Naval Base. *Fury*'s Ronald Adds recalled the event:

> What was left of Convoy PQ-13 arrived in Murmansk at about noon on 30th March, which was, incidentally, my second wedding anniversary. Five

merchant ships had been lost, the cruiser Trinidad *severely damaged and requiring considerable repair, and the destroyer* Eclipse *badly damaged by enemy gunfire. The survivors of this living hell now looked forward to a little respite in the calmer waters of a friendly harbour. We totally forgot that the German Air Force was only fifty miles away in Norway.*

Nineteen ships had started with PQ-13. Five were sunk. This was a loss of more than 20 percent, but the losses were deemed acceptable by the British Admiralty.

Because Murmansk suffered daily bombing raids, there was little rest for the convoy crews. In any event, the Russian city offered little in the way of recreation. Also, the wounded needed care, ships needed to be offloaded, repairs had to be made, and the convoy's dead still on board their crippled ships had to be laid to rest.

Of the ships to be repaired, *Trinidad* was the most seriously damaged, and she went into dry dock at Rosta, north of Murmansk on the Kola Inlet. Incessant bombing had put the electric power out of action, so the ship had to be pulled into dock manually by the weary and exhausted crew, following a recent harrowing experience of nearly being sunk by one of their own torpedoes.

Once in the dock, massive tree trunks had to be cut to size to shore the ship in place. As the water pumped out, the full extent of the damage could be seen: a gaping hole, three decks laid bare, and many bulkheads completely disintegrated. Steel plates were needed to repair the ruptured hull, but requests to the Russians for these plates were in vain. There were plates somewhere in the dockyard, but they were buried under tons of snow, making them impossible to find. An urgent signal was sent to the Admiralty for suitable plates to be sent in the next convoy, which was due to arrive in mid-April.

The crew, although safe, were stranded in Russia at Rosta with nothing around them except snow and ice, forced to gaze every day at their damaged, dry-docked ship, which they wouldn't be able to repair for weeks, a ship in which so many lives had been lost through enemy action and the malfunctioning of their own torpedo due to extremely cold weather. About all they could do was to undertake the grim task of removing the shipmates who had perished. "The next job was to collect and bury our dead," recalled Captain Sanders:

We had some sixty casualties, of whom thirty-two were dead or missing. The latter were scattered, many dismembered, in the compartments that had been flooded or damaged. This duty I gave to the splendid Royal Marines. It was a most unpleasant task that sickened everybody. I endeavoured to help them to face it by accompanying them and explaining that they must regard the remains as merely cast-off matter and that the souls had moved on to another plane.

We embarked the simple coffins, made by the Carpenters, in a minesweeper and buried them at sea at the mouth of the Kola Inlet, with the customary Naval Burial Service taken by our Chaplain. I wrote a personal letter to each of the next of kin.

In an attack on April 3, Luftwaffe bombers sank *Empire Starlight*, *New Westminster City*, and the Polish-manned freighter *Tobruk* and damaged the Soviet Survey ship *Ost* while the vessels were at docks in Murmansk. This raid is well remembered by crewmen who were there: Ted Starkey and Morris Mills on board *New Westminster City* and Greg Novak on *El Estero*.

The first account is from Greg Novak:

In Murmansk Harbor proper we tied up to a dock alongside a narrow-gauge railway spur connection that terminating in Leningrad and a grainery with an Army Field Hospital in its rear.

Despite numerous Air Attacks from nearby German-/Finnish-held Airfields, with low-flying planes generally coming from the west, flying low over the hills ringing Murmansk our ship, El Estero *came through completely unscathed. It's Anglicized name could well have been translated into "The (Lucky) Star." Shrapnel often fell like a light hail from the fiercely defensive Russian AA batteries ringing Murmansk harbor. We had endured everything from a 200-plane raid to nuisance raids of solitary dive-bombing Stukas, whose ominous wail was, to me, akin to the eerie night-cry of a lonely loon on some desolate Minnesotan lake.*

On one occasion, a stray bomb in a near-direct hit on a gun-turret aboard Empire Starlight *tied directly ahead of us and blown two brothers out of the turret. Miraculously, one survived intact but momentarily went mad, swinging a fire-axe at anyone near him until he was subdued.*

Ted Starkey and Morris Mills and *New Westminister City* weren't so lucky, as Starkey recalled:

We managed to get into Murmansk harbour and were all dismayed to see so many bits of ships, sticking up at odd angles. Several of our ships at that time were, like us, loaded with gunpowder in two of the holds. The Russians soon discharged the aircraft in crates from the 'tween decks, but before we could get the gunpowder off the big air raids started.

After about twenty minutes we were hit by three (I think) bombs, which all went through the decks before exploding. I was thrown violently onto the twin Oerlikons on the port bridge wing, where I had been assisting. The bombs set the ship ablaze, but luckily, did not set off the gunpowder.

As I lay on the bridge deck my left arm, especially my elbow, was a mess — but it didn't hurt to breathe! So, when asked, I said I was alright as we had several serious casualties which were taken off with difficulty, as the gangway was gone, and put into waiting ambulances. Not surprisingly, I seemed to have been forgotten — "sleeping" on the bridge deck. When I finally came to I was alone on the blazing ship — others were standing off about 600 yards away, waiting for the ship to explode as the flames neared the gunpowder.

There was no way I could get off so I returned to the gun, but as I swung it over to look through the cartwheel sight I saw not aircraft but Russian women, firing similar guns, on the roofs of the huge warehouses. The gun was in worse shape than I was — so no heroics for me!

I tried to slide down a mooring rope, but I was pitched off and in my dazed condition missed the quay as I fell into the icy water — which "sobered" me up. I was wearing a duffel coat, so my head was well above water. I watched the rivet heads in the ship's side and could tell that she wasn't sinking any further. I could hear noises inside the ship, which I thought must be the metal caps flying off the gunpowder cylinders.

Then a miracle happened! There was a lot of hissing steam, as the ship's fires became extinguished and the next thing I knew was a plain wide strop dangling in front of me. I wrapped the strop twice round my right hand, two little tugs and up I went. I must have weighed half a ton with all my sodden Arctic clothing, but everything held and I was soon shivering like hell on the quayside — courtesy of the Second Mate and four Russian firemen.

After some weeks I was discharged from hospital, left arm plastered from fingers to shoulder, and into the Hotel Arctica.

Morris Mills fared worse in the attack:

My recollections of the bombing are still vivid in my mind. That day we had been discharging cargo using the ship's derricks which were steam driven. The winches were driven by Russian Stevedores — mostly women — who were very inexperienced and tended to open the valves quickly, not taking the strain and resulting in many broken wires and strops. In one such incident a wire parted causing the load to slew round breaking the ship's Carpenter's leg.

After we had got the Carpenter ashore to hospital we continued with the backbreaking work of repairing and reeving cargo wires until we were knocked off at 1700 hours. After a meal I went ashore for approximately two hours and came back around 2000 hours and turned into my bunk and fell asleep.

I have no recollection of there being an Air Raid warning. I am convinced a single plane flew in undetected and bombed our ship prior to the main attack. The first bomb went straight through the bridge and exploded in No. 2 hold killing a large number of Russian dock workers. The explosion was immediately below my cabin and in a fraction of a second there was a vivid blue flash, a column of flame roared through the cabin and a bulkhead disintegrated revealing the occupant of the next cabin, and then darkness.

The detonation of a five hundred pound bomb within feet of one's self beggars description. A column of flame blasted through the accommodation, followed by a colossal roaring sound as the cabin disintegrated. The opposite bulkhead ripped apart like tissue paper revealing, for a split second, the horrified face of the Radio Officer. I was hurled into a corner and showered with burning debris.

The conflagration of flames, the hideous sounds of metal being torn apart, mixed with the cries and screams of the wounded, drove me to a mad desperation. Frantically I tore myself free of burning wreckage and hurled myself through a jagged hole where once the door had been. Out on the open deck, I ran blindly for several yards before collapsing in an alleyway. All around me the bridge was a blazing inferno and I could feel my skin scorching. I was quite rational and knew I had to get somewhere safer, so pulled myself upright only to fall down. "This is bloody stupid!" I thought. "What's wrong with me?"

Then I saw my left foot had been smashed to a bloody pulp and was only connected to my leg by strips of sinew, the white bone protruding at the bottom. Then the waves of agony raged through me in torrents. I may have screamed in my torment. If so, it was a silent scream, for I heard nothing. I was terrified the foot was going to drop off and sat cradling the bloody object in my hands, the hot blood pumping out through my fingers.

Put simply, I was a bloody mess and it was in this state that Captain Harris found me.

He realized that if I was to survive I must be got ashore as soon as possible however, this was no simple task because the explosions had blown *the ship several feet off the quay and brought down the gangway. It was decided to tie a heaving line around my body, lower me over the side and swing me like a pendulum until I gained sufficient momentum for those shore side to catch me.*

By this time the ship's side was glowing red hot and the ammunition exploding through the hull. Several times I was brought clashing against the ship's side until I was eventually caught and laid out on the wooden quay together with other wounded to await ambulances.

Whilst in this exposed position the ferocity of the raid grew with a large number of planes attacking ships. The Russians and naval ships were putting up tremendous ack ack fire but I saw the ship astern of us — Empire Starlight — receive several hits, and the New Westminster City was again hit. At this point I noticed our Arab engine room ratings who had been running around in a blind panic jumping off the ship onto the quayside and, even above the hellish din of guns and bombs, I heard their limbs breaking as they landed near to me.

At this point a plane came in low strafing the whole length of [the] quay and we were quickly dragged into a nearby warehouse. I remember some Russian women dock workers doing their best for us, trying to staunch the flow of blood, talking soothingly, stroking my hands and face, before a ramshackle ambulance arrived and conveyed me to hospital.

I must have lapsed into unconsciousness because my next memory is of coming to in a bare room with people grouped round me lying on a table and a Russian saying in broken English: "You very bad, must have blood, I give blood, you sleep."

They then put a mask over ray face for the gas, this was quite terrifying as I thought they were suffocating me and fought like mad to get the mask off before going under.

I was subsequently told that the Russian who had given blood was a Merchant Marine Officer who just happened to be in the hospital. Apparently he gave his blood direct, intravenously. Whether we were the same blood group — or not — I shall never know, but he certainly saved my life. Unfortunately, I never met him to thank him.

For some wounded survivors of lost ships, the agony suffered in open boats didn't end when they reached Murmansk. Bill Shorts, who survived *Induna*'s loss, tells a grim tale of his experience:

Murmansk had been heavily bombed and there were craters everywhere. All that was left standing were schools which were commandeered as military hospitals. Hospital, the conditions were unbelievable. The school had huge windows and the German bombers came over from Petsamo [Finland] every hour on the hour. Our hospital [was] also heavily bombed. One bomb exploded fifteen yards from the hospital, but the nurses did not pay attention to it.

We had no idea how hard it was for the Russians, until we saw the work of doctors and nurses. It seemed to us that they are working 24 hours a day.

In the hospital, I was covered with grease and bandaged from head to foot in an attempt to warm me up. A tube was put into my stomach. The tube had a filter on the end and tepid water was poured into my stomach to clear the ice that had formed inside my stomach. They managed to get the ice cleared out.

When the bandages were removed, it was found that gangrene had set in, in both of my legs. I was then taken to a makeshift operating theatre; a school classroom where there were six operations going on at the one time. Placed on an ordinary table, a white sheet was set to cover the front view I had and a voice told me, in broken English, "We're going to cut your legs off."

I was given no general anesthetic, no preparation, as medical supplies were non-existent. All I remember after that was excruciating pain in my legs prior to passing out. When I recovered consciousness, I was told that I had been delirious for three days.

When I became more aware of my surroundings, I discovered that both my legs had been chopped off, one below the knee and one above the knee and there were great incisions to the stumps in order to drain the gangrene away. It just flowed on the bed. No one was allowed near me for the real risk of infection. My legs had been literally chopped off just like chopping a roast of beef off. The bone was sticking out; the nerve endings exposed so when anyone [came] too close to me, the nerves reacted. It seemed very crude, but I would not be alive if the deceased parts had not been cut away, thus saving my life. Five months passed, my wounds were never stitched and bone still stuck out; nerves exposed.

Five of us had frostbite. Among them, two of them each had a leg amputated. Assistant Steward Jim Campbell, who was only 15 years old, lost a leg [and] all fingers of one hand. Food was not nourishing, for five months we had rice—stewed, fried, boiled and any other conceivable way. Some of the meat was supposed to be Yak meat.

My weight, I guess was about six stones [84 pounds], which was normally 12 stones. My leg bones were sticking out and I had close cropped *hair. Toilet facilities just did not exist and with no legs, my bowel, etc. were evacuated directly on the bed. I do not remember the sheets beings changed.*

There were very few nurses with too many patients. A very upsetting situation but we were all so weak that we couldn't do anything else. But, there was some humour. Dr. Opoprmenko sang "It's A Long Way to Tipperary" and "Pack up Your Troubles" he'd learned during the First World War. Natasha Mamonova, a translator, and Madame Wright of Leningrad [organized] competitions, where winners were rewarded with cigarettes. Then she discovered that some of us [could] sing and play musical instruments, and began holding concerts to support us.

Sailors, ships, and dock workers weren't the only ones who suffered from the air raids. Civilians also daily faced the risk of death, something Greg Novak witnessed firsthand:

In a log-topped earthen underground air raid shelter on one occasion I was denied refuge simply because it was overcrowded with peasants and their livestock. I then sought shelter from a low-flying, strafing Messerschmitt by diving into a ground-level coal bunker and buried myself below the remaining coal.

Subsequently I learned that some 300 peasants had perished in the overcrowded air raid shelter I had been denied entry. It took a direct hit and the majority of those inside had died from the concussion alone.

The ships and their crews at least could look forward to leaving with the next westbound convoy, even though it meant once more running the gauntlet of deadly weather and increasing German attacks. There was no escape for the civilians; all they could do was to pray for an early Allied–Soviet victory.

Because of massive German air raids on Murmansk, which cost men, ships, and equipment, British Naval Mission and officers of the Soviet Northern Fleet discussed the feasibility of having convoys once again go to Arkhangelsk.

In answer to this, according to Colonel V. V. Shehedrolosev and Captain of the First Rank Igor. V. Kozyr, the staff of the Northern Fleet, informed the British mission that before ships could use White Sea ports, the shipping fairways had to be swept for mines when the ice was breaking up. This would not occur until late April.

Northern Fleet staff officers repeatedly approached the senior British naval officer in January and February to request help in clearing the fairways. However, this help was slow in coming. Thus, the mine sweeping was only recommenced in June 1942, according to Shehedrolosev and Kozyr.

The representative of the British Mission declared that in the prevailing circumstances, they were forced to decline sending convoys to the USSR until the opening of navigation in the White Sea. The liaison officer attached to the staff of the Northern Fleet noted reasonably that the beginning of navigation in the White Sea coincided with the period of "white nights" (at the end of April, there are twenty hours of daylight, and from July through August it's light twenty-four hours a day), the most unfavorable period for the passage of convoys.

Despite the opinion of both Soviet Northern Fleet and British Admiralty officers, Churchill and Stalin insisted the convoys continue. On April 8, PQ-14, made up of twenty-four ships, left Reykjavik and headed east to Murmansk; westbound QP-10, comprised of sixteen ships, left from Murmansk on April 10. Both convoys were heavily escorted to contend with the growing German forces of aircraft, U-boats, and surface ships. And, there was still the Arctic Ocean to contend with.

CHAPTER 4

FATEFUL VOYAGES
April–June 1942

T he heavy attacks on Convoy PQ-13 left no doubt in the mind of Admiral Sir John Tovey, commander-in-chief, British Home Fleet, that the enemy was

determined to do everything in his power to stop this traffic. The U-boat and air forces in Northern Norway had been heavily reinforced, the three remaining destroyers were disposed offensively at Kirkenes and the heavy forces at Trondheim remained a constant, if reluctant, threat.

As a result of known threats, all convoys were heavily escorted to contend with the growing German forces of aircraft, U-boats, and surface ships. However, there was no protection against or escape from the Arctic Ocean.

On April 8, PQ-14 made up of twenty-four ships, left Reykjavik headed east to Murmansk, and westbound QP-10, comprised of sixteen ships, left from Murmansk on April 10.

PQ-14 had as initial local escort the minesweepers *Hebe* and *Speedy* with the antisubmarine trawlers *Chiltern* and *Northern Wave*, and the *Hunt Wilton.* The convoy made for the rendezvous 120 miles south-southwest of Jan Mayen, where HMS *Edinburgh* (which was carrying a large deck load of steel plates needed to repair *Trinidad*); the destroyers *Bulldog, Beagle, Beverley, Forester, Foresight,* and *Amazon*; the British corvettes *Campanula, Oxlip, Saxifrage,* and *Snowflake*; and the trawlers *Lord Austin* and *Lord Middleton* were to have joined them on April 11.

Heavy cover was provided by the *King George V,* wearing the flag of Commander-in-Chief Admiral Tovey, *Duke of York, Victorious, Kent,* and eight destroyers, while the *Norfolk* cruised in an area about 130 miles to the southwest of Bear Island, in a position where she could support either PQ-14 or QP-10 during part of their voyages.

However, PQ-14 ran into thick drifting ice during the night of April 10/11 and became scattered. Sixteen ships, damaged by the storm, turned back for Iceland. Only the cargo ships *Empire Howard, Briarwood, Trehata, Dan-y-Bryn, Yaka,* and *West Cheswald* and the tankers *Athel Templar* and *Hopemount* carried on.

The four trawlers, *Chiltern, Northern Wave, Lord Austin,* and *Lord Middleton,* were new additions to the escort forces. They were among the more than six hundred coal-burning fishing trawlers, drifters, and whalers requisitioned by the Royal Navy that had been converted for wartime use by converting their fishing holds into messdecks, installing communications and ASDIC equipment, and mounting guns, some dating from World War I or earlier, on the main decks. They were manned by fishermen, tugboat men, and bargemen, with officers drawn from fishing fleet skippers and mates. Communications ratings often came from a multitude of civilian jobs, many of whom had never been to sea. Added to this eclectic group were men from the Royal Navy and Royal Navy Reserve to provide some naval discipline. Although this was a rugged group, the Arctic proved a challenge.

Lord Austin should have gone through to Murmansk with *Lord Middleton,* but didn't make it. Through frequent snowstorms she steamed with the convoy steadily north around the snowbound Icelandic coast, fog and icy winds making it difficult for her crew to keep their eyes open, and frozen snow having to be scraped regularly from the bridge windows. Iceland behind her she forged on, but on the third morning she found herself in company with six large merchantmen. The rest of the convoy had vanished. Not knowing where the convoy was, *Lord Austin* took them back, out of stormy seas to the naval base of Akureyri on the north coast of Iceland.

In addition to *Lord Austin* and her six charges, another ten merchant ships that had been battered by the storm returned safely to Iceland.

On April 15, the convoy's remaining eight ships and their escorts were spotted by a BV-138 flying boat, which was relieved by an FW-200 Condor. Later that day, the first air attack by Ju-88 bombers arrived, and attacks continued throughout the rest of the day. Aircraft circled the convoy, making occasional attacks, which were beaten off. One plane that crossed the convoy was believed badly damaged by anti-aircraft fire from all the ships. After that, the rest of the day was quiet.

But things were different the next day when at least two U-boats reached the beleaguered convoy and escorts, adding deadly torpedo firepower to the bombs of their Luftwaffe brethren.

The chief officer on *Hopemount* recalled what happened:

Continuous high-level and dive-bombing attacks were made by Ju-88s and were combined with intense submarine attacks in a series of co-ordinated waves. It was a process of attrition as they tried to pick us off. Sometimes the bombers attacked so low that the escorts used to fire into the water hoping the shells exploding on the water would send up shock-waves and water to disrupt the attacks.

U-boat torpedoes were another matter for the men on the merchant ships as they plodded doggedly along the appointed tracks of the carefully formulated zigzag pattern, closed up in two short columns. The water was so gin-clear you could see the two red and white bands on the torpedoes. They passed right across the bow ... I can see them now.

An anonymous ship's master added his memories of the U-boat attacks on PQ-14:

I had 63 men on deck at the time—all the crew and gunners. Only two engineers and three stokers were down below.

Each man has a whistle and he blows it when he sees a torpedo. The torpedo is actually travelling 50 yards ahead of its wash, so if the wash hits the ship you know the torpedo is safely past. A man who doesn't know that may lose his nerve.

I put the helm hard a-port and squeezed her through between the torpedoes. This ship will do a full circle in four minutes; if on the swing, she'll turn with the swing enough to dodge in about 30 seconds; if against the swing, one and a half minutes.

The German method, he said, appeared to be to fire what is called a "Browning shot" (possibly derived from the old term of browning a covey of partridges, i.e., aiming at none in particular) from ahead and the flanks of the convoy, each submarine firing two or more torpedoes. Having done this, the U-boats withdraw out of range and lay in wait, so far as possible, for the convoy to reach them once more. On this occasion, the U-boat battle went on for four days.

Another master, asked to picture the action said:

> One would hear six short blasts on a siren. That meant torpedoes. Two blasts would be a warning from a ship that she was going to swing, perhaps out of control. The Commodore would give a long blast to draw our attention. During an air attack you might well see eight separate fights going on between ships and aircraft.

In his opinion, the air is colder than the sea, and so he advised his men, if they found themselves in the water, not to climb out on to a raft but to lash themselves to the raft with the fathom of line tied to the lifejacket and remain in the sea until picked up by a ship.

U-403, beating the sharpest lookouts and most adroit maneuvering, fired a salvo of five torpedoes into the convoy from starboard side. Two torpedoes hit the commodore's ship *Empire Howard* at 1245 hours, while *Dan-Y-Bryn* and *Briarwood* avoided the other three torpedoes by quick helm action.

The first torpedo struck Commodore E. Rees's ship *Empire Howard* in the boiler room, killing all on watch below. A few seconds later, another hit the after holds, where her cargo of ammunition exploded, instantly cutting the ship in two. Observers watched as her tween deck cargo of army trucks fell from her port side into the sea. She sank in forty seconds.

The American freighter *West Cheswald* was astern of her in the column. The explosion was so violent that the men of the engine-room watch thought their vessel was mortally injured. *West Cheswald* yawed and reeled from the concussion. Pumps shook on their base plates and almost stalled. Paint flaked from the bulkheads. The frightful clangor of the blast rang back and forth through the engine room and fire room, and men opened their mouths wide to relieve the eardrum pain.

Men on deck gazed at a pillar of fire several hundred feet high and nearly as broad. It rose from the sea where the British ship had been. Fragments of wood, steel, and bits of human bodies dropped from the pillar and rained into the roiling seas.

Of *Empire Howard*'s total complement of fifty-four, about forty men jumped overboard just at the moment that the counter-attacking trawler *Northern Wave* dropped depth charges in the vicinity. Many of those in the water died horribly of broken bones and ruptured organs as a result. The remainder were dragged semiconscious aboard the second trawler, the *Lord Middleton*.

Lord Middleton was steaming close to the *Empire Howard* when the torpedoes struck. Engineman Douglas Finney on *Lord Middleton* recalled what happened:

> *As I looked across I heard three explosions, saw her* [Empire Howard] *shudder, and in three minutes she had gone, taking the Commodore and many others down with her. We managed to pick up fourteen survivors. Among these was a young lad no more than fourteen years old and in a state of shock. He had probably lied about his age to make the voyage. He recovered, but four others died.*
>
> *The night before entering Murmansk we stopped ship in a howling gale to hold a burial service and put them overboard. During the service we heard enemy aircraft overhead, but luckily the storm screened us.*

Of the eighteen rescued, only nine lived, including Captain John MacDonald Downie, who afterward ascribed their survival in the freezing sea to the oil from the ship's ruptured bunker tanks, which covered them. Twenty-nine of *Empire Howard*'s crew were lost. Commodore Rees was last seen smoking a cheroot and hanging on to wreckage, but neither he nor any of his staff of convoy signalmen survived.

Captain W. H. Lawrence, vice-commodore and Master of the *Briarwood*, took over as commodore. Activity on Friday, April 17, 1942, began at 0430 hours with the arrival of the *Sokrushitelnyy* and *Gremyashchiy*, which, having escorted QP-10, transferred to PQ-14. Shortly before 0500, the first Ju-88s were overhead, and *Briarwood* shot down one of them. The air raid was unsuccessful and soon broken off due to low visibility. Finally, on April 19, the seven remaining ships of PQ-14 reached Murmansk.

German reconnaissance planes located QP-10 just as the convoy cleared the Kola Inlet on April 10. Providing protection for the vulnerable merchant ships were five destroyers; Commander John E. H. McBeath, in *Oribi* was the senior ship; also sailing were *Punjabi*,

Marne, Fury, and *Eclipse;* the minesweeper *Speedwell;* and two trawlers, *Blackfly* and *Paynter.* The cruiser HMS *Liverpool* provided close-cover anti-aircraft support.

Ju-88s attacked at first light the next day. Concentrated fire from the merchant ships shot down two aircraft and damaged several others. Among the convoy escort ships was the Soviet destroyer *Gremyashchiy* with Captain 3 Rank A. I. Gurin in command and Lieutenant B. Gavrilov as senior artillery officer, whose gunners shot down one of the Ju-88s.

During the attack, the merchant ship *Stone Street* was damaged, and *Empire Cowper* was sunk. *Stone Street* returned to Murmansk under her own power. *Empire Cowper* had straggled and was away from the anti-aircraft support of other ships in the convoy, making her a prime target for the bombers. One Ju-88 made it through *Cowper's* barrage and dropped three bombs—one was a near miss, but the other two struck home and the ship began sinking. T. H. Effington, one of the surviving engineering officers, recalled what happened on board when the bombs hit.

> I watched the dive bombers coming in on the starboard side and saw bombs leave the aircraft. One fell into the sea on the starboard side, another on the port side, but the one that did the damage fell directly down the coal bunkers and exploded in the bowels of the ship about ten feet in front of the boilers. One fireman died later because of lumps of coal buried in his face.
>
> After dropping its bombs, aircraft dived to about mast height and the pilot waved as he went past, but never regained height and crashed into the sea.

Effington reached his lifeboat station and started down the ladder to reach the boat. "At the bottom of the ladder I had to wait," he said.

> There was still some way on the ship and with the rough seas the boat was being dragged along [as] well as going up and down about fifteen feet from the bottom of the ladder.
>
> At this point a plane coming from the starboard side tried to machine gun the lifeboat below me. Fortunately, the boat was on its way down and the bullets struck the side of the ship between my feet and the boat.
>
> After drifting away from the ship, the Second Mate was in the bows praying to the Lord while a little Galley Boy, about sixteen years old, said "Let's all sing." I think he'd seen too many films.

The hero of the hour was Lieutenant R. Mossiter, commander of the trawler Paynter, *who placed just the trawler's bow against* Cowper's *hull of the sinking ship just below the foredeck so the men still on board could jump to safety.*

Nineteen men died with *Empire Cowper*.

The minesweeper *Speedwell* added to her score one aircraft shot down and another damaged on April 11. Two days later, she attacked a German submarine 60 miles to the south of Bear Island, but without success.

The British minesweepers of the local escort also took an active part in repulsing flights of aircraft, but when *Stone Street* was damaged, they were ordered to escort her to Kola Inlet.

The convoy was engulfed in a snowstorm before the German planes could attack again. For once the crews welcomed the bad weather and nearby ice flows, which hid them from prowling aircraft and U-boats. Such luck couldn't last. Less than forty-eight hours later, on April 13, clearing weather brought clear skies, good visibility, and U-boats.

U-435, commanded by Korvettenkapitän Siegfried Strelow, was first to arrive, at around 1300 hours. After missing an attack on HMS *Punjabi*, Strelow succeeded in slipping through the escort screen and torpedoing the Russian ship *Kiev*. The torpedo hit aft between Nos. 5 and 6 holds, blasting an enormous underwater hole and damaging the propeller shaft. *Kiev* plunged down sharply by the stern and sank within six minutes. *Kiev*'s captain, L. K. Silin remembered the attack:

> *At the moment of explosion I went from a cabin on the bridge and gave the order to abandon ship. The crew together with First Lieutenant launched the lifeboats and released two liferafts over the side. Boats number 3 and 4 have left filled with people. Having seen [the] hopelessness of Kiev's position I headed for Boat number 1, but after it was launched, the sinking ship carried [it] away aft and it capsized, throwing people into the sea. We swam to some nearby rafts and managed to pull ourselves on to them. The trawler HMS Blackfly approached about a half hour later and by that time our clothes began to become covered by ice. The trawler removed people from boats 3 and 4, then picked us off the rafts.*

Seventy-one people were on board *Kiev* when she was torpedoed: forty-nine crewmembers, eight passengers including two children, and fourteen military personnel. Nine of the seventy-one were killed, but the children survived.

After sinking *Kiev*, Strelow returned thirty minutes later and, again avoiding the escorts, hit the Panamanian freighter *El Occidente*. The attack killed twenty of *El Occidente*'s crew; there were twenty-one survivors.

Dense fog followed by a westerly gale later that day forced the enemy to withdraw once again, saving QP-10 from further attack. The ever-persistent FW-200 Condors regained contact at dawn the next day, April 14.

At 0600 hours, twenty Ju-88s arrived, diving out of the sun. Heavy fire from the convoy discouraged the planes from coming too close, and the bombers pulled off to regroup. Returning twenty minutes later, they again ran into a wall of ack-ack, which cost them four aircraft while the convoy escaped mostly unscathed. The freighter *Harpalion*'s rudder was blown off, making the ship impossible to steer. She could not continue in this condition, and the escorts were forced to sink her after taking off the crew.

The Russian freighter *Sevzaples* and her captain, I. S. Karasev, were in the thick of the attack. He recalled the attack and his crew's selfless devotion to their ship:

> *At five o'clock forty minutes, the convoy has undergone to an attack of four-motor bombers of type of Focke-Wolf and two-engine torpedo bombers Junkers-88 which went several waves of ten to twelve planes. On bombing they came in groups of three to four planes at once from different directions, at low height, to fifty meters.*
>
> *One plane has been lined (hit) by escort fire. The bomber has entered into a dive, has dumped bombs, but did not pull out and ran directly into water together with crew. The convoy has undergone to an attack from air the following wave, but without losses.*
>
> *Intensity of shooting by* Sevzaples *was such that barrels of 20-mm of guns of* Oerlikon *heated up so that they had to be cooled with water. Cooks, barmaids, and orderlies from the dining rooms recharged the ammunition for the guns and carried it to the combat positions. Hands and fingers were bloody with broken blisters, but there were no complaints from anyone.*
>
> *With a dawn it was possible to expect an attack of submarines. Pets of the wolf pack loved this maneuver when the sun shines on the horizon, accurately tracing a silhouette of steamships. It facilitated shooting, worked on unexpectedness, and suddenness attacks. Vigilance of watches,*

continuous supervision overseas, attentiveness to trifles, endurance, and patience were the unique weapons against it.

QP-10 arrived in Reykjavik on April 21, having lost four ships—25 percent of the convoy—in exchange for shooting down six German planes and damaging a seventh. For the Allies, this was a high price to pay. Replacing planes and aircrews is cheap compared to ships, the cargo they carry, and the large crews needed to man them.

On the Soviet side, the increasing German activity against the convoys and increasing attacks on Murmansk stretched the Northern Fleet's Air Force to the breaking point. So in March 1942, the Red Army Air Force 95th Fighter Aviation Regiment, consisting of two squadrons of Petlyakov Pe-3 twin-engine aircraft, reinforced the Northern Fleet Air Force. The 95th's missions included convoy escorts, attacks on German troops and airfields, and reconnaissance missions in support of the Fleet. The 95th Fighter Aviation Regiment had experienced hard fights in the German attack on Moscow and carried a rich tradition of excellence in combat. Two examples of the regiment's actions illustrate that tradition.

On April 23, the First Squadron of 95th Regiment, led by Captain S. S. Kiryanova, bombed the German airfield at Luostari in Finland. The raid was so unexpected that German anti-aircraft fire opened up only after the Soviets had released their bombs and were making strafing runs. One fighter, a Messerschmitt Me-109, took off in the midst of the attack. It was shot down by a Pe-3. Seventeen German aircraft were destroyed that day.

Three days later, Number Two Squadron of the 95th Regiment consisting of eight Pe-3s, headed by Major A. Sachkov, bombed the airfield at Heybukten, where the Luftwaffe sometimes concentrated hundreds of bombers, especially during periods when Allied convoys were on the Barents Sea. According to the testimony of a captured Luftwaffe pilot, X. Gunteya, six planes were destroyed, at least twenty aircraft were partially destroyed, two hangars and several barracks were burned, and fifteen soldiers and officers were killed. As the Soviets headed home, they were jumped by twenty-three Me-109 fighters, which shot down five Pe-3s. Only three of the eight Soviet aircraft made it back to base. It was a costly raid for the regiment, with the loss of five planes and ten men killed, but it guaranteed there were fewer German planes to go after convoys PQ-15 and QP-11.

PQ-15, the largest convoy yet, consisting of twenty-five ships and two ice breakers, sailed on April 25. QP-11, with thirteen ships, set out two days later. The Germans were waiting for both convoys with the Kriegsmarine heavy ships *Tirpitz*, *Hipper*, *Scheer*, and *Lützow*, destroyers, and twenty U-boats. The U-boats, organized into the Northern Waters Flotilla, were painted white, with polar bear insignia on the conning towers. The crews were tough, seasoned veterans from North Atlantic duty, where they enjoyed unparalleled success against thinly escorted convoys.

Luftwaffe squadrons had been reinforced with Heinkel He-111s and Ju-88s modified to carry torpedoes slung under their wings. Two distinguished Luftwaffe officers were responsible for the structure and organization of air operations in North Norway: Major Blordon, operating the Junkers 88 Squadron KG30, and Colonel Ernst Roth, the flight commander at Bardufoss conducting operations of the air torpedo group, flying Heinkel He-111s. The strength of the Luftwaffe in north Norway now totaled 103 Ju-88 long-range bombers, 42 He-111 torpedo bombers, 15 He-115 torpedo bombers, 30 Ju-87 Stuka dive bombers, and 74 long-range reconnaissance BV-138 and FW-200 Condors.

For the first time, U.S. Navy warships would be part of the escorting force. Task Force 39, commanded by Rear Admiral John W. Wilcox, Jr., in the battleship USS *Washington*, had departed Casco Bay, Maine, on March 25. In addition to the *Washington*, the task force was comprised of heavy cruisers *Wichita* and *Tuscaloosa*, aircraft carrier *Wasp*, and Destroyer Squadron 8, commanded by Captain D. P. Moon in *Wainright*. The task force ran into exceedingly thick and foul weather, so rough that *Wasp*'s flight deck, 57 feet above the waterline, shipped green water. In the midst of this, Admiral Wilcox was swept overboard and lost, and a plane launched by *Wasp* to search for him crashed and was lost. Rear Admiral R. C. Giffen in *Wichita* then assumed command. This was the first heavy unit of the Atlantic Fleet to reach British waters since the declaration of war four months earlier.

On April 28, this group, without the carrier *Wasp*, combined in one covering force with several British vessels: the aircraft carrier *Victorious*, light cruiser *Kenya*, five British destroyers, and battleship HMS *King George V* flying the flag of Admiral Sir Tovey. They departed Scapa in order to cover the North Russia convoys.

Commander J. Crombie in the minesweeper HMS *Bramble* led the close escort, which consisted of two other minesweepers and four trawlers, joined later by four destroyers. The convoy's defenses were beefed up with the inclusion of the CAM ship *Empire Morn* and the anti-aircraft cruiser HMS *Ulster Queen*, which was stationed in the body of the convoy to augment the anti-aircraft barrage of the merchant ships.

HMS *Ulster Queen* (Acting Captain C. K. Adam) was a former Irish Sea mail and passenger packet capable of 18 knots that had been requisitioned and commissioned under the Royal Navy white ensign as a fighting ship. She was fitted with six high-angle 4-inch guns, four twin 2-pounder anti-aircraft guns, and ten 20-mm Oerlikons.

The convoy also was covered by a patrol of four submarines, *Unison* (P43, British), *Minerve* (Free French), *Uredd* (Norwegian "Fearless"), and *Jastrzab* (P551, Polish "Hawk"), off Norway, guarding against a sortie by German warships.

PQ-15 enjoyed a quiet passage until just before midnight on April 30, when an FW-200 Condor spotted it about 250 miles to the southwestward of Bear Island. Luckily, poor visibility and frequent snow squalls gave considerable cover. It wasn't until 2200 hours on May 1 that six He-111s, each carrying two torpedoes, made the first German air torpedo attack of the Arctic war.

The planes appeared as little dots at first, low on the horizon. They swept in from the south, their shape and size becoming more clearly defined as they approached. Barely 20 feet above the water, they came in line ahead then swept in a wide circle around the convoy.

On the flank of the convoy and closest to the attackers was the corvette *Snowflake*. With her single 4-inch gun and two machine guns firing at maximum speed and efficiency, she raced toward the line of aircraft. The near shell blasts and accuracy of machine gun fire was so disconcerting that the planes were unable to concentrate on their target and, in an instant of confusion, loosed their torpedoes, which sped on ineffectually to run harmlessly among the ice floes. During the next thirty minutes, the bombers made repeated attempts to break through but without success, losing one of their number to the intense anti-aircraft fire from the convoy. With their torpedoes expended and thwarted in their endeavors, the Heinkels returned to base.

Also on May 1, the Distant Covering Force suffered two losses when *King George V* and the destroyer *Punjabi* collided in fog. A signal had been sent to *Punjabi* to watch out for a floating mine, and to avoid this, she had turned to starboard, and cut across the bows of *King George V*, unable to avoid collision. *Punjabi* was cut in half by the larger ship. As the two sections began to sink, and with the crew jumping into the water, more explosions sounded as the primed depth charges rolled off the stern into the water amongst the crew.

The two sections, sinking fast, were surrounded with blood, oil, debris, and bodies of the crew floating in the wash of the gray silhouette disappearing into the fog. Although realizing something awful had happened, no one was aware of the reason or result and assumed the battleship had been hit by a torpedo or mine.

Signalman Eric Whyte was in the communications mess waiting to go on watch on the flagdeck of the *King George V*:

Suddenly I felt the ship make a violent turn and seemed to heave out of the water. Soon after a loud explosion could be heard along with ship's side. "Hands to Mine" stations was piped. My station was amidships near the catapult, visibility was poor. Although there was plenty of activity on the signal deck we seemed to be proceeding as normal. A destroyer on port screen signaled intention to haul out of position to aid the now known crippled destroyer Punjabi *astern of us. We then learned our bows had cut her in half and as a result of the collision her primed depth charges had rolled off the stern and exploded near us and in the area of the doomed* Punjabi.

I was given to understand this tragic accident happened because the destroyer was out of position at the end of a maneuver and perhaps did not carry out the correct procedure. The sad fact remains that loss of life had been suffered and one of our own destroyers had been sunk and we felt for those lost and the thoughts of the Captain of this tragic accident.

Seaman Gerry Ricketts aboard *Punjabi* luckily survived the tragic sinking of his ship:

The sea was calm with frequent snow showers and dense fog patches, so the opening and closing of distance between the big ships and escorts was frequent and often frightening. As the fog closed in the escorts with fog buoys streamed formed port and starboard screens.

Punjabi *was second in the starboard column following the leader. As she turned towards the big ships to close the distance the fog buoy of the leader was lost. Within minutes* Punjabi *now blind crossed the line of advance of the 35,000 ton flagship* King George V, *who struck our port side aft of the engine room slicing through us like a knife through butter.*

The tremendous crash was heard, all power and lighting failed as the ship lurched violently to starboard with everything crashing around us. As the ship was slowly returning only temporarily to even keel we scrambled to the ladder and on to the upper deck when it was obvious that half had disappeared. We stood on deck the angle getting steeper every minute.

On the port side our stern could be seen vertical, some yards away and appeared to rise up out of the water as the depth charges exploded throwing up water and wreckage.

Looking aft, the battleship USS Washington *loomed out of the fog and altered course to starboard. Looking forward the huge hulk of the carrier* Victorious *swept across our bows. It became very obvious this was the time to leave so [I] went over to the starboard side. The ship's whaler was some distance and the water was rising fast up to my knees. Steadying myself on the boat davits I stood on the top guard rail when within seconds the water rose suddenly floating me off and away. I joined a messmate and shared his wooden staging where we could. I saw HMS* Martin *and HMS* Marne *coming towards us to pick us up as thankful survivors.*

Whilst in the water, oil, wreckage and other less fortunate bodies of our shipmates. Wichita *and* Tuscaloosa *passed close by before we were rescued by HMS* Martin.

For many of my shipmates the cold and oil fuel was too much and fifty-two of the crew of Punjabi *died that day.*

Stoker 1st Class George Stacey was aboard *Marne*, one of the rescue ships taking aboard survivors. He was on duty in the boiler room when the engine room rang for more steam:

We thought contact had been made with a U-boat. Then the buzz went round the ship, that one of the escorts had been sunk. We raced to the scene of disaster and then bridge rang down to stop engines. I came off watch and was standing on the upper deck. I have never seen such fog. Everything was deadly still, quiet and eerie.

As we drifted along silently, the sea became calm, all round was thick, black, oil fuel and trying to swim for their lives were the poor devils from the Punjabi. *Others that were past swimming just floated by looking terrible, just black oil covering their lifeless bodies amongst the wreckage.*

Again the silence was broken by further explosions from the depth charges rolling off the sinking stern of the doomed ship causing further havoc, injuries and death to the crew, before finally disappearing below the surface.

Norman Newton, a signalman on board HMS *Martin*, recalled the incident as well:

Upon entering any of the very dense fogs which prevail in the Arctic Ocean, the destroyers would form up in line ahead and drop astern of the capital ships. To assist station keeping, each destroyer towed a drogue astern. It was a nerve racking experience for those on the bridge, watching and following the spout of water created by the drogue, for very often the towing ship could not be seen.

It was during this hazardous manoeuvre that the destroyer ahead of Punjabi *must have made a slight turn; unfortunately the* Punjabi, *following the drogue, turned too much and sailed straight under the KGV's bows and was hit just aft of the bridge.* Martin, *which was following next in line and following* Punjabi, *also turned in towards the battleship, almost ramming her amidships. Fortunately our Captain (Commander C.R.P. Thompson, DSO., RN.) was able to do an emergency turn, which was followed by a nightmare journey travelling in the opposite direction through the oncoming capital ships.*

We saw these massive, ghostly shapes gliding past to port and starboard, accompanied by the noise of sirens signalling and foghorns wailing. After what felt like an eternity the fleet passed and, in the silence which followed, we turned to help Punjabi. *She was lying in two halves and the surrounding sea was covered in black oil fuel.*

We lowered every available boat and proceeded to pick up the poor souls struggling in the black mess. The stern soon sank, but the depth charges were all primed and, as soon as they reached the critical depth, they detonated causing a shock wave which stunned the men in the water, most of whom sank from sight. We managed to rescue quite a few survivors, including the Captain, from the forward section before it sank.

Our lads had great difficulty trying to haul survivors onboard, because it was almost impossible to hold them due to the fuel oil. Unfortunately several survivors died, due to inhaling fuel, and were buried at sea.

Punjabi's captain was on *Martin's* bridge when an Aldis lamp signal came from Admiral Tovey on board *King George V*, apologizing for the loss of his ship. Gus Brilton recalled that:

When asked if he wished to reply, Punjabi's *captain said "Yes, mate. It's a f—ing fine way to lose your shipmates". I wonder if* Martin's *Yeoman of Signals, Harry Plaice, remembers making that reply and if it is recorded in the enquiry report that must have been made after the collision.*

Of *Punjabi's* crew, 169 were rescued from the forward section and another forty were picked up from the sea by other escorts. Forty-nine crewmen lost their lives in the accident.

Punjabi sank directly in the path of the *Washington*, which had to sail between the halves of the sinking destroyer. *Washington* suffered slight damage from the detonation of the depth charges. *King George V* sustained serious damage to her bow and was forced to return to port for repairs.

Ill luck continued to dog the escorts on May 2 when the minesweeper *Seagull* (Lieutenant-Commander Pollock) and the Norwegian destroyer *St Albans* (Commander S. V. Storeheil) launched a depth-charge assault on an ASDIC contact which breached and revealed itself to be not a U-boat, but the Polish submarine *Jastrzab* commanded by Lieutenant Commander Bolesław Romanowski.

After a week of bad weather and only one U-boat contact, *Jastrzab*'s hydrophone operator detected warships approaching at about 1945 hours on May 2. Romanowski was able to see them through the periscope despite the fact it was snowing. After studying them for a few moments and consulting the ship recognition book, he announced they were friendly, but altered course and ordered the release of recognition flares to avoid being attacked. The flares broke from the casing and surfaced to release smoke signals.

These were not seen on either the *St Albans* or the *Seagull*, and there followed a chaotic few moments as the destroyer and minesweeper made a determined depth-charge attack, the consequences of which were serious. The main circuits were blown, and the submarine again lost trim. Seams burst and water soon was pouring into the pressure hull, contaminating the batteries and releasing chlorine. Romanowski blew his tanks and surfaced between the two attacking ships.

To surface ship crews, any and all submarines are enemies. As the *Jastrzab* broke the surface, she appeared to be heading toward the Norwegian destroyer, thus her identifying pendant numbers, P551, were invisible. However, her torpedo tubes also were laid upon the Norwegian ship, and a shot from a secondary 2.7-inch gun was fired at her as Romanowski, seconded by his British liaison officer and signalmen and the duty watch, scrambled up on to the conning tower, whereupon fire also was opened by machine guns from the bridges of both ships. Five people, including the two British ratings, were killed outright; six others, including Romanowski and his liaison officer, were wounded before it was realized aboard *Seagull* that an unfortunate error had occurred. This also had been realized aboard *St Albans* and both ships ceased fire and launched boats.

Commander Romanowski wrote in *Ice and Fire* about the attack from his perspective:

I saw ex-American destroyer [St. Albans] at angle of 120° running to my left and ship I did not recognize [Seagull] at 2000 meters distance. Snow falls. Due to a huge wave we lost depth control and broached. When we regained periscope depth, the destroyer attacked us. He was too close and I shot a yellow smoke identification signals then a series of depth charges exploded fairly close.

I shot another identification smoke flare—again, a series of five bombs, awfully close, and yet again just five more. All the bombs on the port side astern. I ran away as I could. The effect of explosions on the ship terrible: everything is broken off; the lights went out, stopped the motors, chlorine gas leaked from the batteries, short circuits, etc. I had to surface.

When I jumped on the bridge, the ship slowly twisted to the left [due to bombs]. I noticed the 200-meter trawler from us and destroyer at 800 meters. Both shot with machine guns. The English signaler, severely wounded, still tried to send the identification signals with the Aldis lamp, but killed on the spot. I got four bullets in the legs, I fell and could not afford, sat on the platform, holding the Polish flag over his head.

Seeing that the destroyer intends sink me, I ordered the crew go out of the boat. The destroyer passed astern of us then stood alongside the port side at a distance of fifty meters and opened fire. The trawler gave one burst from his pom-poms and stopped firing. Destroyer subsequently stopped the firing and from the bridge someone asked: "Are you German?"

In a strong voice I replied: "We are Polish submarine Hawk. *Cannot you see P 551, you bloody fool?"*

Romanowski, though hit by five bullets, brought his confidential codebooks off with him. *Jastrzab* was sunk by Seagull's 4-inch gun since there was no hope of saving her. Five crewmen, including the British liaison officer were killed and six injured, including Romanowski. The survivors were later transferred to the cruiser *London*.

PQ-15's luck finally ran out for good at 0127 hours on May 3, when six Heinkel He-111 torpedo planes attacked at wave-top height from the convoy's starboard side in the half light of the Arctic summer night. A wall of fire swept up toward the planes, blowing two of them out of the sky and damaging a third, which crashed.

Captain Julius Christoph Klepper, a veteran seaman of Finnish birth, was in command aboard *Expositor*. He handled her with immense care. Her cargo was 10,000 cases of TNT and 10,000 rounds of 75-mm and 37-mm ammunition.

There were only five men in her armed guard detachment, and at Tail o' the Bank in the River Clyde, extra guns had been mounted. Volunteer gunners from the ship's crew took over the two 20-mm Oerlikon pieces, the double-mount Hotchkiss machine guns, and a 50-caliber Browning machine gun. The merchant seamen were delighted with the Oerlikons, which delivered a shell about the size of an old-fashioned telephone shank. A few well-directed Oerlikon bursts could tear the leading edge off a Heinkel's wing and deflect her fast from her torpedo release point.

The volunteers remembered distinctly the famous warning given them in February 1942 by Hitler. The broadcast had been heard at sea and in all the sailor bars along America's East, West, and Gulf coasts. Hitler shouted hoarse-voiced into the microphone that American merchant seamen were fools. He warned that they should leave the ships and stay ashore. He promised those who sailed small chance of survival.

Now, having fired at the silver-painted Heinkels with the broad, black Iron Cross emblems on the wings and fuselages, the merchant gunners shouted, "F— you, Adolf! You and your sister!" They were not fully certain whether Hitler had a sister, but that was unimportant. They were shaken by rage and fear.

Three of the He-111s eluded the barrage, their torpedoes striking *Botavon*, *Jutland*, and *Cape Corso*, which was the first ship in the outboard starboard column. She carried an all-ammunition cargo. When the Heinkel torpedo found her, she was destroyed within seconds.

Leading Seaman Raymond Smith was aboard the trawler *Cape Palliser* when *Cape Corso* was hit. He recalled the incident:

> *Horrified, we saw one of the merchant ships go straight up and disappear in a purple flash. All that was left of her afterwards was a mass of floating debris of deck cargo, all else had gone to the bottom.*
>
> *Our four-inch was practically useless as the low-flying planes were on us before we knew it, and it was impossible to bring the gun to bear. As I was strongly built my action-station was on the stripped Lewis gun, a contraption which could be fired from the shoulder, like a rifle, instead of from the usual tripod. Only someone with a bit of weight could fire the monstrosity—if you didn't hold on tight you spun round with it.*
>
> *I was on the starboard side of the bridge near the wheel-house when a low-level bomber swept over us from the port beam. Its rear-gunner was "hosepipe firing" [strafing] and I could see him as clear as day working the gun in a figure of eight—and not too bad with his gunnery, either. I was told*

later that his shot fell just short of the starboard waterline—I don't think I'd time to look. I managed to get off somewhere near a pan-full, gradually spinning round and trying to keep the Lewis somewhere near the target; it was a hell of a thing to use. Our point-fives also got close to the target, but the two twin-Hotchkiss, one each side of the bridge, proved useless.

The survivors we picked up were mostly lascars, but among them was one Nigerian, whom they seemed to resent and wouldn't have in their presence, until after much trouble we told them they were all in the same boat—and lucky to be in it, too!

The escorts picked up 137 survivors from *Botavon* and *Jutland*. Seventy-three crewmen were killed in the attack, including twenty from *Botavon* and all fifty on board *Cape Corso*.

From about noon, May 2, to the afternoon of May 4, the convoy was shadowed by U-boats. The escorts made several attacks on what were believed to be U-boat contacts, but no U-boat was damaged or sunk.

A bombing attack took place at 2230 hours on May 3. Only *Cape Palliser* was slightly damaged by a near miss, and one Ju-88 was shot down during what was the last air attack PQ-15 had to face. The Soviet Air force helped divert the attack when a flight of Pe-3s, led by the commander of the 95th Regiment, Major A. Zhatkovym, found the convoy and jumped the low-flying Ju-88s. He recalled the incident:

The attack by our fighters in a remote area of the sea was a complete surprise to the enemy. The first volley [of] rockets created confusion in their ranks and they jettisoned their bombs then banked away from the convoy.

Our fighters circled over the convoy and several times enemy planes appeared on the horizon appeared, but dared to approach the ships.

Visibility deteriorated the evening of May 4, and a southeast gale sprang up, bringing with it heavy snow, which provided excellent cover for the remainder of the passage. Also on May 4, the destroyers *Sokrushitelnyy* and *Gremyashchiy* put to sea at 0100 hours to meet convoy PQ-15.

On May 5, Soviet Northern Fleet patrol ships *Rubin* and *Brilliant* and the British minesweepers *Harrier*, *Niger*, and *Gossamer* sailed from Polyarnoe to reinforce the convoy escort. At 2300 hours, the destroyers arrived at the convoy in the midst of the storm. The destroyer *Gremyashchiy* detected a U-boat with ASDIC and attacked her firing nineteen depth charges. The U-boat turned away and went deep.

The convoy arrived at Kola Inlet at 2100 hours on May 5.

Commander J. Crombie, commanding officer of the corvette HMS *Bramble* and escort commander, summed up the convoy's voyage to Murmansk in his report to the British Admiralty:

> The feeling of being shadowed day and night with such efficiency is uncomfortable and considering the efficiency of the shadowing I am surprised that more air attacks did not take place. It is possible that although the weather was fine at sea (except for the last day) the weather at the aerodromes may have been different. It is surprising also that there is only evidence that one submarine attack took place—that on the night of the torpedo aircraft attack.
>
> I should like to record the excellent conduct of the convoy, the majority of which were American ships unused to convoy work. Their steadiness when the torpedo attack took place and leading ships, including the Commodore and Rear Commodore's ships were sunk, their speed of opening fire and their excellent station keeping made the task of the escorts very much easier. It was largely due to the good conduct and discipline of the convoy that twenty two ships out of twenty five arrived at Murmansk undamaged.

Before leaving Murmansk, *Edinburgh* took on two large and unusual cargos. The first consisted of wounded merchant mariners from ships that had been bombed, torpedoed, or strafed in convoy or while in Murmansk as well as nearly two hundred passengers, including British Army and RAF personnel who had been training the Russians in the use of British tanks and aircraft, Poles released from Russian prisoner-of-war camps, and Czechs who had escaped from their country when Germany invaded in 1939.

As more casualties arrived aboard the cruiser, the vast hangar took on the appearance of a hospital ward and the small sickbay looked like an emergency operating theater. Day and night, Surgeon-Commander W. F. Lascelles, RNVR, Surgeon-Lieutenant D. C. Lillie, MB, ChB, RNVR, Surgeon-Lieutenant L. Cama, RNVR, and Surgeon-Lieutenant (D.) J. K. Donald, RNVR, worked ceaselessly, operating on the wounded seamen. In many cases, they found that wounds had become septic and amputations of feet and legs were necessary to save life. That section of the ship and those involved became caught up in a war apart. Surgically, it was a question of saving as much as possible of a man.

Among the casualties was Morris Mills who, after enduring having both legs amputated without anesthesia, was finally headed home to England:

Came the great day, the 27th April, and we were carried out into ambulances—in reality, battered old Army trucks with a canvas top and open back—they managed about six patients to a truck. We had not gone far before a ferocious air raid occurred. The vehicles came to a shuddering halt leaving us totally defenceless in the middle of the street. From the back of the truck we had a panoramic view of the raid. The air was full of bursting shells and shrapnel scythed through the air with a vicious whistling sound. From our grandstand view we saw buildings disintegrate in clouds of smoke and flames.

It was a miracle we survived that storm of shells and bombs, I can only liken it to being out in torrential rain and not getting wet. We had not gone much further when the next wave of bombers came in, again the ambulances screeched to a stop. In a mad haste we were rushed into a large building and laid in every conceivable space, corridors, hallways and tops of tables. To this day I have no idea what type of building it was—hotel, office block or barracks. I suspect the latter because it was crammed with soldiers destined for the Murman Battle Front, then only twenty miles away.

As we lay terrified, a Russian soldier came over and squatting down beside us, producing a balalaika (a stringed instrument), began singing haunting Russian songs, soon his comrades joined in. Before long, the mood changed as they broke out into rousing martial, marching songs, which they sang with such gusto they almost drowned out the dreadful din of battle. When it was time to leave my Russian placed the balalaika in my hands and said a few words, which I roughly translated as, "Good luck—this is a souvenir." I thanked him.

We arrived at the dockside and boarded a Fleet Minesweeper, I think it was HMS Gossamer, *and taken down river to Vaenga, where the cruiser HMS* Edinburgh *lay alongside the quay. I was in a bad way and cannot remember too much about it, but I had an impression of this magnificent 10,000-ton cruiser towering above me as I was carried on board. Here was the very pinnacle of British Naval power.*

There were some thirty to forty badly injured patients from Murmansk hospital. The ship's hanger had been turned into a temporary hospital, and most survivors were accommodated there. The most severe cases were taken into the ship's hospital, a small area with six cots, and as I found myself there it is reasonable to presume I was in a bad way. My verminous clothing was taken off and after being washed I was put into a clean cot.

Shortly afterwards, the ship's surgeon came down and said he wanted to have a look at my stump. He must have read the fear in my face for he said, "It's alright, lad, I'm going to give you a shot to kill the pain."

This was another world to what I had so recently left, everywhere efficiency, cleanliness, order, good food and medicine. Above all, the wonderful, cheerful, esprit de corps of the Royal Navy.

The second cargo arrived two days before *Edinburgh* sailed and was a rarity in the many tasks the Royal Navy was called upon to perform. Supply Petty Officer Arthur Start described in his own words what happened:

I had been asleep for about an hour when I was awakened by the bugler sounding off, "Both watches of the duty hands fall in, in the starboard waist". My messmate sat up with a start, looked at his watch and said — "What the 'ells going on — it's quarter to bloody midnight".

When we arrived on deck we could hardly believe our eyes. The scene was like something from a film. Secured along the starboard side were two barges and at vantage points aboard were about a score of Russian soldiers armed with "Tommy" guns held at the ready. On our own ship, stationed at regular intervals from the deck and up ladders to the flight deck were also our own Royal Marines keeping guard.

As we watched, a tarpaulin covering the barge's cargo was drawn back to reveal scores of ammunition boxes. The natural assumption at first was that these contained small arms ammunition — but why should there be such security for a routine job of work? And then in a matter of minutes the truth was out. The boxes contained not ammunition but gold — gold bullion. Over five tons of it to be stored in the cruiser and shipped to the United Kingdom.

The boxes, rope handled, were extremely heavy, each needing two men to lift them. In the dull grey daylight of the Arctic midnight we carried those boxes all the way up to the flight deck and there lowered them by ropes through a shaft trunking to the bomb room three decks below. All the time we were unloading the gold there seemed to be an aura of evil present. An uncomfortable feeling of impending disaster.

We all felt it — most expressed it. Superstition is a strong characteristic with sailors throughout the world. The ominous feeling persisted and when part way through the operation, sleet started falling and the heavy red stenciling on the boxes ran freely to drip a trail of scarlet along the snow-covered decks, apprehension redoubled.

One seaman expressed the thoughts of all of us when passing an officer he said, "It's going to be a bad trip, sir, this is Russian gold dripping with blood!"

More than 5 tons of pure gold was stacked in *Edinburgh*'s bomb room, a specially armored compartment deep in the bowels of the ship used for high-risk cargo, especially high-explosive ammunition. The value of the gold taken aboard *Edinburgh* was estimated then to be about £5 million and part of a deal between the Russian Government and the U.S. Treasury, a down-payment on thousands of tons of war equipment for the Soviet Army fighting the bitter war against the German invaders.

Convoy QP-11, consisting of thirteen ships, left Kola Inlet on April 28. Captain W. H. Lawrence, Master of SS *Briarwood*, was commodore. The close escort consisted of six destroyers, the *Bulldog* (Commander Richmond, senior officer) *Beverley*, *Beagle*, *Amazon*, *Foresight*, and *Forester*; four corvettes *Oxlip*, *Campanula*, *Snowflake*, and *Saxifrage*; and the trawler *Lord Middleton*. Close cover was provided by the cruiser HMS *Edinburgh* (Captain H. W. Faulkner), with Rear Admiral Sir Stuart Bonham-Carter commanding 18th Cruiser Squadron, on board.

Minesweepers *Gossamer*, *Harrier*, *Hussar*, and *Niger* accompanied the convoy until the evening of April 29, and the Russian destroyers *Sokrushitelnyy* and *Gremyashchiy* reinforced the escort through the Barents Sea.

Morris Mills recalled leaving Russia:

> *Lying in my cot, warm, fed, and partially sedated, I felt the ship dip her head into the seas, and felt a wonderful sense of suffocating joy surge through my body, such as almost made me fight for breath. I was going home on one of the most powerful warships in the British Navy. In my mind's eye I could see that dark, evil, shore receding into the distance.*
>
> *The following morning, Rear-Admiral Sir Stuart Bonham-Carter paid us a visit in the sickbay. A burly figure in a heavy naval coat without any insignia of rank—apart from his gold braided cap. The Admiral was full of bonhomie and confidence as he spoke with each of us. Before leaving he made a short speech. "Well, lads, you know we are escorting Convoy QP11 back to England. I don't think our German friends are going to let us pass without a fight, so you must prepare yourselves for action, but never fear, you are in the hands of the Royal Navy and we'll get you back safely." Stirring words.*

A German Ju-88 reconnaissance spotted the convoy on April 29, but there weren't any attacks that day. Everyone in the convoy knew attacks by German destroyers were inevitable and it was *Edinburgh*'s task to defeat them. Reports of U-boats kept the escorts alert and, instead of trailing the convoy at only 6 knots, *Edinburgh* was ordered to move 20 miles northwest and zigzag to avoid U-boat attacks. No destroyer escort was sent along to screen the cruiser from U-boat attacks.

The following afternoon, April 30, *U-456*, commanded by Kapitänleutnant Teichert, found *Edinburgh* steaming at a sedate 20 knots on a regular zigzag course, totally unescorted. Teichert's problem was that he only had two torpedoes left and could not afford to miss. He didn't.

The first torpedo, amidships, ploughed through to the region of the forward boiler room and below the stoker's messdeck, destroying compartments through to the port side, killing all personnel in the blast area and flooding other compartments in a deluge of oil and water.

The second struck aft, ripping off the stern, blowing the whole quarterdeck upward like a sheet of paper and wrapping itself around the guns of "Y" turret with the barrels protruding through the steel decking. With it went the rudder and two of the four propeller shafts. So great was the explosion that it blasted the bottom plates of the ship downward to form a distorted fin or rudder. With a noise of rending metal and the dreadful thunder of tons of seawater flooding through under enormous pressure, the cruiser shuddered to a stop, listing heavily to starboard. The proud warship, once the envy of cruiser squadrons, had in five seconds become a grotesque coffin of steel and smashed bodies, with two enormous gaping wounds lapped by the cold gray sea.

Within the cruiser, normal routine was being followed to the letter. The pipe had just sounded, "Fall out from action stations" and "Nonduty hands to tea." Most of the crew had been at "Stand by action stations" for the past forty-eight hours. This was the earliest opportunity for some to relax in the comparative comfort of their own messdecks. For the first time since the ship had left Murmansk, the pipe, heard throughout the ship including by those at their sea-going stations, seemed to dispense an atmosphere of relaxation. There was a natural buoyant air of optimism, a sense of security. It was in this unguarded moment that no one, not even the bridge lookouts, saw the torpedo wakes streaking toward the ship.

In compartments and gangways just above the explosion areas, men stumbled and staggered in the darkness, cannoning into one another as they made for the exits, cursing violently when they could not be found. The two torpedoes had destroyed all electrical power to the gun turrets. Only one of the forward turrets, "B" turret, could be operated at all.

Damage to the engine rooms and the stern was so extensive that only limited power could be applied to move the ship forward.

Below the cruiser's decks, conditions where the first torpedo had struck were chaotic. For the few who survived there it was a nightmare of living hell. Leading Stoker Leonard Bradley described the scene:

Just before the torpedo struck I happened to go into the stokers' messdeck which was fairly crowded at the time and was talking to a friend of mine, a young amateur boxer called Harrington. As we chatted, the torpedo exploded in the oil tank below us. The whole messdeck split in two and as the lights went out Harrington and I and at least another 50 men fell straight through into the storage tank which was partially filled.

The emergency lighting failed to come on and we were down there in complete darkness, floundering around in oil and water. In the blackness with men around screaming and shouting, I managed at last to get a footing and started to make my way towards where I thought the hatch might be.

As I moved, I heard Taff Harrington near me. I called out "Taff," and he grabbed me. The oil was now pouring in fast from burst pipes in adjoining tanks and rising up to our shoulders. Harrington tried to hold my hand but it slipped and he died in the oil. There was another boy called Harrison clinging to a stanchion. I tried to lift him above the level of the oil but he screamed blue murder for he had broken both collar bones and an ankle. All this time I was swallowing oil. Gradually the oil found its level and stopped rising. Everything went very quiet.

The hatch above us was sealed and we had no idea if the ship was afloat, partly submerged or at the bottom of the ocean. We must have been there nearly an hour when the miracle happened. The hatch was prized open and three stokers came down with ropes and pulled us to safety.

Above, on the fo'c'sle deck outside the galley, Engine Room Artificer Robert Sherriff was standing talking to the Chief Cook, "Dolly" Gray. The explosion split the deck open where they were standing and both fell through. Sherriff managed to cling to a projecting ledge and regain the deck but the Chief Cook was propelled on downward and was never seen again.

Supply Petty Officer Arthur Start, who, with his mate Petty Officer Bob Walkey, managed to save several trapped men, related his account:

I was in the Petty Officer's mess at the time the first torpedo hit. All the lights went out but fortunately I happened to have a torch in my pocket. Realising that the messdecks below might still contain trapped men, we lifted back the hatch cover of the vertical shaft down through which the gold had been lowered.

Sure enough within the compartment we could see men swimming around in oil and water. My mate ran to fetch ropes and ladders, but while he was away several of the men below managed to get into the shaft which was only two feet square. Within the trunking there were no ridges or ledges to provide a hold but in desperation those men somehow managed to come up through by working their knees and backs against the sides. Eventually the hatch was sealed. There were several men down there but they were dead anyway.

When the torpedoes hit, Morris Mills was in sickbay, propped up sipping tea while watching the ice-flecked seas racing past a porthole when the torpedoes hit. He, too, recalled the event:

Following the catastrophic explosions there was a split second's silence, the ship trembled like a wounded animal as the seas rushed into her gaping wounds, and then the all too familiar cries and screams of the wounded. Panic broke out in the sickbay as thick oily smoke reeking of cordite belched through the alleyways, filling our confined space. I felt sure I was about to die, but was terrified of dying like a rat caught in a metal box, sinking into the icy depths of the Arctic Ocean.

In a blind panic, I desperately struggled to pull myself over the cot side in order to fall to the deck and crawl out of this death trap. I had almost made it when a sailor rushed in and hoisted me onto his shoulder, "It's alight mate—I've got you."

With superhuman strength he battled his way over a tilting deck, through a milling crowd of seamen, up several iron ladders, and laid me on the open deck. He didn't wait to be thanked, even supposing I could have spoken any words through clattering teeth, but returned below to rescue others. A true, unsung hero.

Owing to the violent manner necessary to get me from below, my various wounds had all burst open, yet again I could feel the hot blood pumping from my stump. I might have bled to death, but for the fact I was laying on an open deck clad only in a hospital night-shirt, in a snowstorm, and minus 20 degrees F. the blood was literally freezing in my veins.

My body and mind were exhausted by the relentless punishment they had taken. The Arctic weather was rapidly freezing my thinly clad, tortured body, I felt no pain, even the spurting blood became bloody icicles. The vast ocean, the towering superstructure of the cruiser belching flames and smoke, the scream of escaping steam, the shouts and cries of crew about their various duties, all began to fade into a swirling, grey mist. I was dying and felt warm and contented.

The torpedoes' explosions were seen from the convoy, and the *Foresight* and *Forester* were detached to her assistance, followed shortly afterward by the Russian destroyers *Sokrushitelnyy* and *Gremyashchiy*. Escorted by them, she started the 250-mile return passage to Murmansk.

Although out of torpedoes, *U-456* continued to shadow and report the *Edinburgh*'s movements. Based on these reports, the Kriegsmarine Flag Officer, Northern Waters, ordered the destroyers *Hermann Schoemann*, *Z-24*, and *Z-25* put to sea and attack Convoy QP-11 with its depleted escort.

At 0540 hours on May 1, QP-11 was about 150 miles to the east-southeast of Bear Island when four Ju-88 torpedo planes attacked. John L. Haynes was part of the U.S. Naval Merchant Armed Guard detachment on board the cargo ship *Eldena*. As he remembered, it was his nineteenth birthday:

I wondered how we would celebrate the momentous occasion!! It didn't take long to find out. At 0445 six Junker Ju-88 torpedo planes attacked. Four of them came directly at us while two climbed into the clouds. Of the four on attack, two flew across our stern toward the ship aft of us, but turned off when both our ships opened fire. Both planes were observed to drop a torpedo but no tracks were seen. The other two bombers flew toward the ship ahead of us but veered off when we opened fire. Both, however, were seen to release their torpedoes. None of the torpedoes hit their intended targets. A plane flew around the convoy but was kept at a distance by gunfire from the escort ships. We had expended about 230 rounds of .50-caliber ammo.

At the same time, a U-boat was sighted and forced to dive by the *Amazon*. Frequent HF/DF bearings indicated that four U-boats were keeping pace with the convoy on different bearings, and at 0820 hours, course was altered to the southwest in an attempt to shake them off. Then ice was sighted in large quantities ahead, which extended some 20 miles to the south of the route, and course was again altered to the westward. The forenoon passed without incident. The weather was moderate, but frequent snow squalls caused the visibility to vary between ten and two miles.

At 1345 hours, the convoy was on course 275 degrees, skirting heavy drift ice to starboard, when the *Snowflake* reported three radar contacts bearing 185 degrees. At the same moment the *Beverley*, screening on the port bow, reported enemy in sight, bearing 210 degrees. The enemy proved to be the destroyers *Hermann Schoemann, Z-24*, and *Z-25*.

On receipt of the *Beverley's* sighting report, Commander Richmond, who was on the starboard bow of the convoy, moved across to the threatened flank and ordered the destroyers to concentrate on him. At once, the convoy (with the corvettes) carried out an emergency turn of 40° to starboard, the destroyers making smoke to cover it.

At 1400, the *Bulldog* turned toward the enemy on a southwesterly course with the destroyers in line ahead, with *Beagle, Amazon*, and *Beverley* following. The Germans at this time were about 10,000 yards distant, heading toward the convoy. At 1407, both sides fired torpedoes; none hit the destroyers, but a track was seen to pass close astern of the *Bulldog*.

After three minutes (1410), the Germans turned away and the British destroyers returned toward the convoy, making smoke. Repeatedly the two destroyer forces, in line ahead and on parallel courses, blazed away at one another with both sides loosing torpedoes. Each time the enemy turned to double back on their last course, *Bulldog* and her consorts turned also, always keeping themselves between the enemy and the convoy.

The British ships were frequently bracketed with heavy shells as the enemy tried to establish the range, but with each salvo falling to port or starboard the British force maneuvered into a new line of advance. The German ships, mounting between them ten 5.9-inch and five 5-inch guns, were far more heavily armed than the four remaining British destroyers, which between them mustered only six 4.7-inch and three 4-inch guns.

Amazon, second in line, was caught in a salvo that straddled her in a sudden sheet of flame and black smoke. Still in line and maintaining top speed, she sped on. As the smoke cleared, her captain, Lieutenant Commander Lord Teynham, stunned and bruised from the explosion, looked down from the bridge on a scene of destruction. The forward gun had been torn from its mounting; its crew, dead or wounded, lay prone on the fo'c'sle deck. The 4.7-inch gun aft, the 4-inch amidships, and the anti-aircraft guns had been smashed with their crews killed or wounded. The wheelhouse was shattered, and the main and auxiliary steering positions rendered untenable.

Careening along at 30 knots, *Amazon* was now out of control. As *Bulldog* made a tight turn to double back on the previous course, *Amazon* could only speed onward. It was only by cleverly executed maneuvers of the engines that her captain was able to bring her back into line at the rear of the column. She was immobilized as a fighting unit but it would not do to let the enemy be aware of this. Despite the fearful damage the ship had sustained, Lord Teynham somehow managed to maintain *Amazon* in line, so that to the enemy she still appeared a potential threat.

The German torpedoes running loose among the ice floes rose to the surface in a trail of bubbles and headed toward the merchant ships. A straggler, the Russian freighter *Tsiolkovsky*, was dead in line and a torpedo plunged into the engine room, rocking her to a standstill. Slowly she settled down by the bows, her screws high out of water. With the pungent smell of oil from her ruptured tanks came cries for help as the crew tried to launch rafts and boats.

The port lifeboat, although overcrowded, was successfully floated off, but on the starboard side panic prevailed. Twenty-five of the crew had managed to climb into the boat with the davits swung out, poised over the water some 30 feet below ready for lowering. Unfortunately the stern fall had jammed in the reel, slightly tilting it.

Despite all efforts to release the obstruction, matters worsened with the weight of those in the boat. In the confusion that followed, one of the two men operating the lowering mechanism took an axe in a moment of panic and severed the fall. The boat swung down hanging by the bow, throwing every man into the sea. In increasing terror, the second fall was now cut and the heavy boat plummeted on to the men below, killing many of those swimming around. Within minutes, the ship plunged slowly to her grave, with a small crowd of men packed high in the stern waving and screaming for help.

Moments later, *Lord Middleton* reached the sinking ship. Those who had survived the explosion and the numbing shock of immersion in the frigid waters were hauled aboard more dead than alive. Saturated in the black oil, it was difficult to grasp the men and lift them over the side. After thirty minutes of search, only a pathetic collection of bodies remained, washing about among the oil and mass of wreckage, and *Lord Middleton* made off at speed to join the distant convoy after rescuing only five people, leaving twenty-seven dead behind them.

During the course of the next four hours, the Germans made five separate attempts to reach the convoy, each of which was foiled by the aggressive tactics of the escorting destroyers despite their great inferiority in firepower to the Germans.

After a final exchange of gunfire at 1742, the Germans once more turned away. The British held on toward them for a few minutes until the rear destroyer disappeared into the smoke to the southeast. The *Hermann Schoemann*, *Z-24*, and *Z-25* had been ordered to attack the damaged *Edinburgh*, some 200 miles to the eastward, which is why they broke off their attacks.

Commander Richmond could not know this, and for the next three hours he kept his force cruising between the supposed direction of the enemy and the convoy. By 2155 hours on May 1, the convoy was in open water and the destroyers resumed their screening stations. The remainder of the passage was uneventful, and QP-11 arrived at Reykjavik at 0700, May 7.

Meanwhile, *Edinburgh*, unable to steer except with her engines, was making very slow progress eastward. On receiving information about the damage to the cruiser, Admiral A. G. Golovko, the Commander in Chief of the Soviet Northern Fleet, sent a message to the destroyers *Gremyashchiy* and *Sokrushitelnyy* that read: "If possible, render assistance to the British cruiser!" At the same time, the British minesweepers *Harrier*, *Niger*, and *Gossamer* were sent at 2150. At midnight on May 1, Soviet Tug No. 22 went out to the cruiser escorted by *Hussar*.

As the day wore on aboard *Edinburgh*, many acts of heroism and tragedy occurred in and around the explosion areas. Men trapped in small compartments were pulled to safety in the nick of time as oil threatened to engulf them. Men were caught in the blast of burst steam pipes in darkness until the flesh peeled from their bodies. Men were trapped alive in unreachable compartments, a voice tube the only link with the upper deck, as officers tried to reassure them they would soon be freed, knowing full well survival time was running out.

At 0630 hours on May 2, *Hermann Schoemann*, *Z-24*, and *Z-25* came upon the *Edinburgh* making about three knots under her own steam and steering with the aid of the tug on her port bow and the minesweeper *Gossamer* secured astern. First to sight the enemy was the minesweeper *Hussar*, which boldly opened fire with her single 4-inch gun. *Edinburgh*, although almost unmanageable, fought back and hit *Schoemann* with her second salvo, resulting in heavy damage to the German ship.

By now the destroyers *Forester* and *Foresight* had joined in the battle, which became one of hide and seek in and out of the snow squalls and the smoke screen laid by the destroyers to cover the *Edinburgh*. At 0650 hours, just as she had fired three torpedoes at the enemy, *Forester* received three hits, which killed her captain, Lieutenant Commander G. P. Huddart, R.N., and brought the destroyer to a stop.

The *Z-24* had also fired torpedoes, which passed under the *Forester* and sped on toward *Edinburgh*. One of these, almost at the end of its run, struck the cruiser on the side opposite to that against which the U-boat's torpedo had exploded, almost cutting the ship in half. Nevertheless, she continued to engage the enemy, but it was now plain to both the admiral and his flag captain that there was no longer any hope of saving her.

A moment later, Commander Jocelyn S. Salter in the *Foresight*, who had interposed his ship between the enemy and the damaged *Forester*, drew on himself the concentrated fire of the enemy ships at a range of about 4,000 yards. He went on to full speed and sought to retire under the cover of smoke, but four hits, one of them in a boiler room, brought his ship to a halt.

Foresight's casualties included Lieutenant R. A. Fawdrey, seven ratings killed or died of wounds, and eleven ratings wounded. The *Forester* lost her commanding officer, plus twelve ratings killed and nine ratings wounded. In addition, one officer and two ratings belonging to the *Lancaster Castle*, who were embarked in the *Foresight*, were wounded, and her master, Captain Sloan, was killed.

After a time, the badly damaged *Forester* and *Foresight*, taking turns to screen each other while repairs were effected, managed to get under way again, but to everyone's surprise and relief, the two remaining German destroyers retreated after rescuing some two hundred of the *Hermann Schoemann*'s crew and then scuttling her. Later, fifty-six more survivors were picked up from rafts by *U-88*.

However, for *Edinburgh* the end was obviously near, and the Admiral ordered the minesweepers to take off her crew. The injured merchant seamen in sickbay were carried to the upper deck and transferred to the minesweepers.

Once the minesweeper *Harrier* was secured along the port side and *Gossamer* starboard, the loading of the wounded and passengers began—a formidable undertaking up and down a sloping deck between the two vessels. But there was no time to complain. With the ship almost in two and likely to break up at any moment, time was of the essence.

Most of the wounded were on stretchers and had to be lifted over the side of the listing ship and lowered by whatever means available. The deck of *Harrier* was at least 12 feet below that of *Edinburgh*'s, and the transfer was made more difficult by the lifting and falling swell. One by one the stretcher cases were lowered as carefully as possible, but almost inevitably there were accidents. A few became dislodged from their stretchers and crashed to the decks below. Others, almost naked from their sickbay beds fell over the side and became entangled in the scrambling nets, nearly freezing to death in the Arctic wind.

Years later, Morris Mills wrote about the incident:

> *My stretcher had been placed some distance from the disembarking point, and watching the press of men trying to get off, I began to wonder if I would make it in time?*
>
> *At this stage a sailor settled down beside me and drawing a packet of cigarettes out lit two and gave me one. I thanked him through chattering teeth and inhaled deeply. We silently watched the desperate struggle to get the wounded onboard the* Harrier, *while several hundred seamen patiently waited their turn.*
>
> *Then, quietly, as though to himself he said, "Christ, mate, it's going to take a bloody miracle to get that lot off before she goes down!" Taking a deep drag on his cigarette, "How you feeling, mate?"*
>
> *"Bloody cold." I replied through chattering teeth. He nodded.*
>
> *"Do you feel up to taking a chance?"*
>
> *He pointed to a projection overhanging the* Edinburgh's *side — it was either a piece of wreckage, or a torpedo tube — he had noticed that every time the* Harrier *rose on a swell it was level with her deck. "If I give you a bunk-up you could crawl across." The will to live flared through my body, and I nodded eagerly. Without hesitation, he picked me up and placed me on the projection. "Good luck, mate." I had no time to thank him as I started to inch my way across. The surface was rough and jagged and several times I struck my raw stump causing it to hemorrhage a fine spray of blood.*
>
> *There was no time to worry about that as I clung to the metal and looked down on the freezing sea. Willing hands grabbed me and I was rushed down to a small cabin and placed in a bunk. The ship's surgeon was called and he applied a tourniquet and gave me a shot of morphine before dashing off on another mission of mercy.*

Once everyone on board had been taken off, the admiral ordered the *Foresight* to sink *Edinburgh* with a torpedo. A booming explosion rocked the vessel when it hit, sending a sheet of flame skyward that mushroomed into a pillar of black smoke. Slowly, *Edinburgh* rolled over on her side. The fore part broke away in a twisted mess of rending metal. The stern disappeared quickly, but the bow hovered for a moment before disappearing in a tumult of bubbling, gurgling water. Survivors were overwhelmed by the disgusting stench of oil fuel that coated the freezing water of the Barents Sea.

Edinburgh bore within her hull the bodies of fifty-seven men. Almost at the same moment, *Hermann Schoemann* was settling into her last resting place on the floor of the ocean with the bodies of those killed aboard her.

Aboard *Harrier*, the log recorded *Edinburgh* as sinking in position 71-51 degrees North, 35-10 degrees East. The time was 0900 hours May 2, 1942.

Minesweepers and destroyers moved away with one final look at the pool of oil and wreckage littering the surface over *Edinburgh*'s watery grave. The vessels geared up for their advance, moving forward again in the dark waters of the Arctic Ocean. They could linger no longer. It was time to make for the Kola Inlet.

As the battered British force moved toward safety, the crew of the Russian destroyer *Rubin*, which had joined them in the fight against the German force, found time to compose a wireless message. It was sent when the ships were off the coast and radio silence could be broken. It read:

SOVIETS SEAMEN HAS WITNESS OF HEROIC BATTLE
ENGLISH SEAMEN WITH PREDOMINANT POWERS
OF ENEMY. ENGLISH SEAMEN DID OBSERVE THEIR
SACRED DUTY BEFORE FATHERLAND. WE ARE
PROUD OF STAUNCHNESS AND COURSE ENGLISH
SEAMEN—OUR ALLIES.

When the badly battered force of warships returned to Murmansk, *Edinburgh*'s survivors had not had a hot meal for forty-eight hours, and the weather was bitterly cold. All the authorities were able to offer them was a bowl of thin, watery soup and a crust of hard rye bread. On this diet, supplemented by anything the visiting ships could spare, they would exist until repatriated. On arrival in camp, each man was issued one blanket and a piece of synthetic soap.

The Soviets had nothing better to offer. Food in the northern regions was short, and most of the population lived on a subsistence diet and were barely managing to survive themselves.

Merchant Navy survivors were taken up river to Murmansk, where a fleet of ambulances waited to take them back to the hospital they had so recently left. Morris Mills was one of those returning to the place he so desperately wanted to leave a few days earlier.

Quite a number of nurses who had waved us goodbye were there to greet us. Many cried and were quite desolate to find some of the original party had been lost. Those survivors who had thought themselves unlucky not to have been included in the Edinburgh party, anxiously questioned us as to what had happened.

We were too physically and mentally exhausted by our experience to go into detail, but what little we related caused great concern as they realised the insurmountable dangers of a return to the UK. Here and there, someone would ask after a shipmate only to learn he had not made it. An oppressive air of doom hung over the ward.

CHAPTER 5

WHITE NIGHTS
May 1942

A fter studying the reports from PQ-15, the British Admiralty recommended the Arctic convoys should be stopped, if not completely, at least until after the Arctic winter gave the protection of darkness to the ships. The First Sea Lord, Admiral Sir Dudley Pound, wrote to Admiral Ernest J. King, commander in chief of the U. S. Fleet, and informed him: "The whole thing is [a] most unsound operation with the dice loaded against us in every direction."

The problem facing British Prime Minister Winston Churchill and U.S. President Franklin D. Roosevelt was extremely serious. Shipments through the Arctic Circle to Murmansk and Arkhangelsk had reached only about half the amount that had been promised, and roughly 25 percent of every convoy was being sunk. For the USSR, the situation had become considerably worse since the beginning of the German spring offensive. The Caucasian oil fields were being deeply penetrated, and the Volga and the Don rivers were about to be reached by the invader. If supplies to the USSR were stopped, she very possibly would be unable to continue the fight against Germany, forcing her to sign a separate peace treaty.

Exacerbating the situation was the fact that the Allies were still losing the Battle of the Atlantic. U-boats ranged from the Arctic to the U.S. east coast to the Caribbean, South Atlantic, around South Africa, and into the Indian Ocean, sinking an average of thirty-three ships each week, and there was no end in sight. These losses far outstripped the combined British and U.S. shipbuilding capabilities.

Stalin learned early in May that ninety loaded ships were being kept at Tail o' the Bank and Loch Ewe in Scotland and at Hvalfjödur. They were bound for North Russia, but awaited convoy instructions. He sent a message to Churchill asking that "all possible measures be taken to ensure the arrival of the above-mentioned materials in the U.S.S.R. in the course of May as this is extremely important for our front."

Churchill understood the gravity of the Russian position and replied to Stalin: "Fight our way through to you with the maximum amount of war materials."

Churchill then addressed a meeting of the Chiefs of Staffs Committee:

Not only Premier Stalin but President Roosevelt will object very much to our desisting from running the convoys now. The Russians are in heavy action and will expect us to run the risk, and pay the price entailed by our contribution. The United States ships are queuing up. My own feeling, mingled with much anxiety, is that the convoy ought to sail on the 18th. The operation is justified if a half gets through. Failure on our part to make the attempt would weaken our influence with our major Allies. There are always uncertainties of weather and luck which may aid us. I share your misgivings, but I feel it is a matter of duty.

While these discussions were taking place, temporary repairs were completed to HMS *Trinidad*. The necessary repair plating was delivered by *Edinburgh* to the dry dock at Rosta. Russian women welders were brought in and, under the expert guidance of British construction engineers, the plates were jointed and fastened into positions with supporting girders of timber. But it was a temporary repair job, one that could not withstand an Arctic storm.

The *Trinidad*, escorted by the destroyers *Somali*, *Matchless*, *Foresight*, and *Forester*, left Murmansk in the evening of May 13. A force of four cruisers, *Nigeria*, *Kent*, *Norfolk*, and *Liverpool*, and four destroyers, *Inglefield*, *Escapade*, *Onslow*, and *Icarus*, under Rear Admiral Harold M. Burrough, was disposed west of Bear Island to cover her passage. In addition, a battle fleet, consisting of the *Duke of York* with Admiral Tovey on board as the senior flag officer, *Victorious, London,* USS *Washington, Tuscaloosa,* and eleven destroyers provided distant cover further to the south.

By May 12, about sixty *Edinburgh* survivors had arrived aboard the cruiser *Trinidad* as passengers, settling themselves in the canteen recreation space. This space had to be shared with an equal number of merchant seamen survivors of various nationalities from bombed and torpedoed ships of earlier convoys. Despite the cramped quarters, they were all happy enough to be returning home, particularly in a heavily armed cruiser which could well defend herself against attack. And those attacks would surely come in the sunlit nights that assisted the enemy but gave no cover to the British ships running the gauntlet between North Norway and the Ice Barrier. Just before midnight on May 13, *Trinidad* left the Kola Inlet in the gray aura of the Arctic night, with the sun low on the horizon peering through a thin veil of mist.

Throughout history, the sailing of a ship on the thirteenth of the month has been regarded by seamen as an omen of bad luck, and this was no exception. Many of the *Trinidad* and *Edinburgh* men openly expressed their apprehension. Two close friends of Jim Harper, a *Trinidad* seaman, confided in him that they did not expect to live much longer. They seemed aware of their fate, yet they behaved as though all was well. Strangely enough, the number thirteen had loomed significantly in recent months in respect of the Arctic convoys. The convoy in which *Trinidad* had torpedoed herself in March had been PQ-13. And QP-13, the convoy of thirteen ships *Edinburgh* had escorted out of the Kola Inlet on April 28, had resulted in her sinking. Now *Trinidad* was sailing on the dreaded date, the thirteenth.

At 0730 hours the next morning, *Trinidad* and her escorts were located 130 miles out by an FW-200 Condor. There were also several U-boat alarms, but no torpedo attacks or ice restricted the convoy's movement to the northward. By 1852 hours, two more BV-138 shadowing aircraft arrived. Their homing signals were intercepted by the British ships, but there was nothing they could do about it. Then at 2100 came the dreaded but expected news: In the radar compartment, bright against a black screen, the searching arm disclosed the approaching enemy with frightening clarity. Formation after formation of aircraft between the bearings 180 and 240 degrees were shown heading at speed in the direction of the cruiser. Reports to the bridge became almost continuous: "A wave of aircraft at 15 miles," "Another at 30 miles," "There are more coming in at 40 miles," "More at 60 miles." Then from the radar desk came a report that could not have been more complete in its bone-chilling finality: "The screen is full of aircraft, sir."

Air attacks developed shortly before 2200 that evening, when Ju-88s started dive bombing *Trinidad* and the destroyers. Frank Pearce was on *Trinidad*'s bridge that evening during the attacks:

> *Then came the first low whisper of the enemy. I was standing on the bridge beside Captain Saunders and Admiral Bonham-Carter heard the pulsating hum, growing louder with every passing second. There was no further need for radar reports for the first wave of bombers were already in sight. Small black dots against the ceiling of the Arctic world, they began a game of hide-and-seek, darting from the cover of one thin cloud to another. On the ship every eye peered anxiously into the scattered haze, while at the guns fingers closed more tightly around trigger keys. Darting out of the sky in concerted movement, the bombers peeled off and came screaming down at near vertical angles, their engines racing.*
>
> *But even as they began their dives the cruiser's guns blasted a defensive curtain of fire. A deafening roar that set the senses reeling as the barrage from the combined power of the 4-inch anti-aircraft guns, 2 pounders, pom-poms and Oerlikons went into action. With it, barely audible in the thunder of battle, came the voice of the first lieutenant, Lieutenant Commander Jack Herrapath, air defence officer, over the loud speaker system directing gun crews on to targets from his observation position half-way up the mast. With startling clarity, the first of the bombs were falling.*
>
> *Small and dark at first against the sky, they tumbled from the belly of the planes in a whining, wobbling descent of flight. Suddenly they were falling around the ship, missing by 40, 50 or 100 feet astern and abeam. Exploding on contact with the sea in ear-splitting eruptions, great waterspouts cascaded high above the ship's funnels, hanging momentarily before falling in an ice-cold deluge on the gunners in open cock-pits round the superstructure.*

After about twenty-five bombing attacks, in which no hits were obtained though all ships experienced near misses, about ten torpedo bombers came in at 2237. Eight minutes later (2245), a lone Ju-88 roaring out of the thin cloud immediately overhead released its stick of four bombs from a height of about 400 feet. Pearce, along with personnel on the bridge, watched with bated breath as the wobbling, screaming bombs fell directly toward the superstructure. With them came both the roar of the Junker's engines pulling out from its dive barely above mast height and the thunder of the ship's guns blasting a stream of shells into the attacking aircraft. Reduced to a fireball, the German plane plunged into the sea away on the port beam.

"The impact of four 500 pound bombs exploding almost simultaneously was terrifying," continued Pearce.

The little world around the bridge superstructure disintegrated into a pocket earthquake, blinding the senses, sending the bridge deck leaping. Officers and ratings were hurled in all directions. The damage to the ship was catastrophic. Each of the bombs had been on target. One had fallen outboard, gliding along the side of the ship aft of the forward "B" turret, in line with the bridge. Here it exploded under the waterline, blowing off the temporarily welded plates and sending a wall of water into the magazine and cordite compartments below the turret. All were instantly flooded, drowning every rating battened down in the area. If the explosion had occurred above the waterline flame and not water would have reached the cordite, in which case the ship and every man aboard would have disappeared in one great ball of fire.

The ship listed 14 degrees to starboard, but was still able to steam at about 20 knots. The carnage in the area of the recreation space where the *Edinburgh* and merchant marine survivors had taken refuge defied description. The explosion tore away steel bulkheads like cardboard. Decking between the recreation space and the messdecks around and below were ripped apart; stanchions, handrails, and piping were twisted like wire into grotesque shapes. Few men in the area survived

Torpedoes then just arriving from the torpedo bombers were avoided, as were other torpedoes a quarter of an hour later. By 2350, the attacks began to ease off. Captain Saunders was at last able to lessen the fanning of the flames by reducing speed to 12 knots, but by now this was too late to do much good. At midnight, with the sun shining above the horizon, the fires burned out of control. Below were those who remained alive, dazed and wounded, trying to grope their way to safety past flames and through choking smoke. Below them, in compartments that had become sealed off by fire, men were trapped at their duty stations.

Bert Soper and his friend "Blackie" Cass, passing through the fire area on their way to the upper deck, were mesmerized by the sight of a fellow seaman trapped in a light steel bulkhead that had been wound tightly round him by the force of the explosion. As the flames roared nearer, he was screaming his way to death. Every fire main in the area was out of action, and nothing could be done to extricate him.

By midnight it was clear that the fire was out of control, and in light of the distance from the nearest port, the presence of U-boats, and the certainty of further air attacks, the decision was made to abandon ship. The wounded and passengers had already been taken off by *Forester*, and the remainder were then embarked in the other three destroyers.

Engineer Lieutenant John Boddy attempted a gallant rescue. Some of his stokers were trapped below, shouting for help. The tall, young, faired-haired officer stepped through a hatchway to the decks below with the remark, "Can't leave my men below—must try to get them out."

A raging inferno had engulfed that part of the ship. Boddy could find no ladder or rope to lower himself below decks. Intense heat foiled any rescue efforts, and both Boddy and the men he had tried to rescue perished. Married just a week or two before the ship left Devonport, Boddy had sacrificed his life to reach his men. He was posthumously awarded the Albert Medal, subsequently renamed the George Cross.

High up on the 4-inch gun-deck, commissioned gunner Dicky Bunt and gunner Charles Norsworthy were manning the guns to the last to cover the remaining survivors while they climbed aboard the destroyer. Bunt, running between the port and starboard sides of the gun deck, was the first to spot the oncoming plane. With a shout of "Nosser, there's one bastard coming in over there," he and Norsworthy jumped on to the port gun mounting and watched the aircraft through binoculars and telescopic sights.

The He-111, approaching fast, was only about 20 feet above the sea and a mile away when first spotted. All the electrical circuits used to train and elevate the gun had been destroyed, so the two men were reduced to controlling the mounting by hand. With both barrels loaded, they waited. With *Trinidad* listing to starboard, they found even more trouble when they tried to depress the sights sufficiently to pick up the target. Norsworthy applied his eye to the telescope and directed the gun as best he could.

Changing to look through the open cartwheel sight, Norsworthy lowered the guns a little to get a target sighting between the bottom of the plane and the sea. He fired both barrels. The shells burst about three feet under the plane's port wing, lifting it with such a jerk that it almost capsized. The men who watched let out a great cheer. The enemy's torpedo dropped off at a crazy angle while smoke and flame poured out of the fuselage. Turning sharply away, the *Heinkel* slowly disappeared into the sea. These were the last shells to be fired from *Trinidad*.

The four destroyers and the minesweeper *Gossamer* stood off for some minutes to watch the last moments of the cruiser. The canting deck and settling bows revealed the distressed condition of the stricken ship. To hasten her end, Admiral Bonham-Carter on *Somali* gave the unpleasant but necessary order to *Matchless* to sink *Trinidad* with torpedoes. The crew and survivors watched the tubes being trained on the burning ship.

From *Trinidad*'s main and after masts, the large battle ensigns flaunted their emblems as if in defiance of the enemy and the leaping flames below. From a signal halyard on the main mast, a short line of flags, scorched by the heat, fluttered in the wind, broadcasting her last message to the world: "I am sailing to the westward."

On the destroyers' decks, the survivors watched as *Trinidad* sank into the frigid seas. Within the sinking hull, a great number of their messmates were being committed to the deep. So many of *Edinburgh*'s men had embarked with hopes of returning home to be reunited with their loved ones, but now they were dead, entombed within the disappearing ship. As the water reached the bridge, the stern lifted itself clear of the water. There she seemed to hang suspended for a few seconds as if reluctant to die. Then with a rush she plunged forward to disappear in a cloud of smoke and steam. It was 0120 hours on May 15: Ascension Day.

Now four of the five ships, crammed with survivors, put as much distance as possible between them and the German airfields, increasingly aware of the German reconnaissance planes, which never left but shadowed them continuously. But the boiler damage inflicted in their gallant defense of the *Trinidad* still limited the speed of both *Foresight* and *Forester*.

The destroyers rendezvoused with Rear Admiral Burrough's force and steered for Iceland. They were shadowed by enemy aircraft until 2000 hours on May 16, when about twenty-five Ju-88s attacked with bombs. Walls of water thrown up by near misses would at times completely hide one or another of the cruisers, which were bearing the brunt of the bombing. The Germans developed attack after attack, but after five hours, as the distance from the enemy airfields increased, they became less frequent. Despite the ferocity of their assault, every ship survived the blitzing and came through unscathed.

This attack took place more than 350 miles from the nearest airfield, which meant that in the future convoys had to expect to be attacked from the air during five days of their passage.

Rear Admiral Bonham-Carter's experiences in the *Edinburgh* and *Trinidad* left no doubt in his mind as to the hazards and dangers to which the convoys to North Russia were exposed. In his report to the British Admiralty, he wrote:

> *I am still convinced that until the aerodromes in North Norway are neutralised and there are some hours of darkness that the continuation of these convoys should be stopped. If they must continue for political reasons, very serious and heavy losses must be expected. The force of the German attacks will increase, not diminish. We in the Navy are paid to do this sort of job, but it is beginning to ask too much of the men of the Merchant Navy. We may be able to avoid bombs and torpedoes with our speed, a six or eight knot ship has not this advantage.*

These views were endorsed by Admiral Tovey, who repeatedly expressed his anxiety and more than once suggested that the convoys should at least be reduced in size. But political necessity overrode military considerations. The companion convoy QP-12 comprised of seventeen ships left Murmansk on May 21. PQ-16, with thirty-five ships—larger than any convoy to date—sailed from Iceland the same day.

QP-12 enjoyed a relatively uneventful passage. The convoy included the CAM ship *Empire Morn* and was escorted by the destroyers *Inglefield* (Captain P. Todd, Senior Officer), *Escapade*, *Venomous*, *St. Albans*, *Boadicea*, *Badsworth*, the anti-aircraft ship *Ulster Queen*, and four trawlers (*Cape Palliser*, *Northern Pride*, *Northern Wave*, and *Vizalma*). Though the visibility was generally good, the convoy was not sighted till the morning of May 25.

That morning, an FW-200 Condor, a BV-138 flying boat, and two Ju-88s appeared. In favorable conditions, the *Empire Morn* launched her Hurricane. The pilot, Flying Officer John Kendal of the Royal Air Force Volunteer Reserve, immediately found he had lost touch with his fighter direction officer, Sublieutenant P. G. Mallett in the CAM ship; his radio transmitter was faulty, though his receiver was functioning. Moreover, he also had lost sight of his primary target, the BV-138, in the cloud.

Undaunted, Kendal swooped down on a Ju-88 and began a long and dogged chase that culminated in both aircraft flying the length of the convoy. Kendal rocked his Hurricane from one quarter of the

The Arctic convoys were the most dangerous of all, under threat of attack by submarine, surface raider, and aircraft. Here PQ-18, en route to the Soviet Union in September 1942, is seen fighting a heavy attack by the Luftwaffe. (*IWM A12022*)

Icebound conditions on the deck of a British cruiser during escort duty on the Northern convoy route to Russia in February 1943. A return to the ice age can easily be imagined by the crews of these vessels, but the convoy got through all the same. (*Topham/AP*)

KMS *Admiral Scheer*, a Deutschland-class heavy cruiser (also referred to as a "pocket battleship"). Commissioned on November 12, 1934, and sunk by RAF bombers on April 9, 1945, while docked in Kiel.

KMS *Tirpitz*, a Bismarck-class battleship. Commissioned February 25, 1941, and sunk by RAF bombers November 12, 1944.

HMS *Bramble*, a Halcyon-class minesweeper commissioned in 1939. She served in the North Sea and as a Polar Convoy escort. She was sunk on December 31, 1942, by the battleship KMS *Hipper* and the destroyer *Z-16 Friedrich Eckoldt*.

Blenheims were used as both medium-range bombers and night fighters. They carried a crew of three and were armed with four .303 machine guns.

Known as the "Stringbag" by its crews, the Fairey Swordfish was obsolete when the war started in 1939. Regardless of that fact, the aircraft achieved an impressive record in combat over the next four years. (*IWM MH23*)

Martlets had considerable combat service, flying from both shore bases and aircraft carriers. The F4F was very maneuverable by European standards, and heavily armed with six .50-caliber machine guns, they were a serious threat to enemy aircraft.

Hawker Hurricanes were the first fighter aircraft delivered to the Soviet Union under Lend-Lease. Soviet pilots found it inferior to both Soviet and German aircraft in performance and armament.

The He-111 could carry 2,000 kg of bombs in its bomb bay or up to 3,600 kg of bombs externally. With a range of 2,300 km and a ceiling of 6,500 m, it was an ideal bomber for antiship operations. (*Bundesarchiv*)

One of the most versatile aircraft in the Luftwaffe's inventory, the Ju-88 served as a dive bomber, attack bomber, heavy fighter, night fighter, and torpedo plane. (*Bundesarchiv*)

The Condor was originally developed as a long-range passenger airliner. Equipped for antiship operations, the standard armament was one 20-mm cannon in the forward gondola and four 13-mm machine guns in the dorsal and beam positions. Later models carried radar mounted in the nose.

Jastrząb was the former US Navy S-Class *S-25* launched in 1922 and transferred to the British Royal Navy in November 1941 under Lend-Lease.

SS *Dekabrist* of Odessa, commanded by Captain Stephen Polukarpovic Belyev, was bombed and sunk on November 5, 1942 while sailing independently from Iceland to Russia. Although 87 crew members survived the attack, only ten eventually survived after being marooned for eleven months on Hope Island.

The *Zharky* was one of fifty-one flush-deck destroyers originally transferred from the United States to Britain. Several of these were then transferred to the Royal Canadian, Free Polish, and Soviet navies.

Sailors place a depth charge into position in a depth charge rack for dropping from the stern of the destroyer HMS *Eskimo* just out of harbor (possibly Hvalfjörður) after a U-boat hunt in the Atlantic. (*IWM A7414*)

Escorts and merchant ships at Hvalfjörður before the sailing of Convoy PQ-17. Behind the destroyer *Icarus* (1.03) is the Russian tanker *Azerbaijan*. The sea voyage to the north Russian ports of Murmansk and Arkhangelsk was the shortest route for sending Allied supplies to Russia. But it was also the most dangerous owing to the large concentration of German forces in northern Norway. The convoy PQ-17 was decimated by U-boats and the Luftwaffe after a communication from the Admiralty on July 4, 1942, ordered the escort to scatter. (*IWM A8953*)

Above • The 7,457-ton CAM ship *Empire Lawrence*, which was sunk during the PQ-16 convoy battle. Note the disruptive camouflage on her foredeck and the Sea Hurricane I sitting on the bow catapult. (*via Andy Thomas*)

Left • The escort carrier HMS *Avenger* with her full complement of six Sea Hurricanes from 883 Naval Air Squadron embarked. Note the special "Arctic" camouflage applied to her flightdeck for the PQ-18 operation. Avenger was sunk by U-boat *U-155* during the early hours of November 15, 1942, while escorting convoy MKF 1(Y) off the Portuguese coast. A single torpedo hit the ship's bomb room and ignited the munitions stored there, causing numerous secondary explosions. With her back broken, the carrier sunk in under five minutes, taking 68 officers and 446 ratings with it. (*R. Mackay via Andy Thomas*)

Below • An ammunition ship exploding during a Russian convoy, as seen from the deck of an aircraft carrier. (*IWM A12274*)

Above • Gun crews of HMS *Duke of York* under the ship's 14-inch guns at Scapa Flow after the sinking of the German warship, the *Scharnhorst* on December 26, 1943. (*IWM A21168*)

Below • An unidentified U-boat under attack by an 86 Sqn Liberator at 68,38N 08,59E, Germany, on July 18, 1944, in the Arctic Circle off Norway. (*ww2images.com*)

enemy plane to the other in a tenacious and perfectly judged attack, firing two long bursts of gunfire before overshooting his quarry. Black smoke began to pour from the engine nacelles of the Junkers. Her aircrew jettisoned their bombs in order to maintain height as the engine failed. Finally, the plane crashed into the sea. By now the Hurricane was short of fuel and the other German aircraft showed no signs of pressing an attack.

Kendal prepared to ditch near *Boadicea*, but the destroyer was approaching a patch of low, rain-bearing clouds, and Mallett advised Kendal to select a rear escort. Though he received no acknowledgement, Mallett was gratified to see the Hurricane break out of the cloud and double back to circle over *Badsworth,* while Mallett signaled the change of plan to the senior officer. Kendal now flew a tight, left-hand circuit and waggled his wings to indicate he intended to bail out rather than ditch. Flying east, he turned and, heading for *Badsworth*, climbed to gain height and vanished in the cloud.

The hundreds of men now watching from every ship in the convoy heard sound of the victorious Hurricane's engine cutting out. Then the fighter dropped out of the overcast and fell into the sea. A second later the figure of Kendal tumbled out of the sky, his parachute unopened. Just 50 feet above the sea, the canopy fluttered into life, but it was far too late. Kendal hit the water with the parachute imperfectly extended. A few moments later, *Badsworth* signaled *Empire Morn* that the young man had been picked up with grave injuries. Ten minutes later, Kendal died. He was buried at sea.

Luftwaffe aircraft continued shadowing through the afternoon. No air attacks were launched, and there were no submarine attacks even though U-boats were known to be in the area. Thick weather aided the convoy in avoiding trouble, and QP-12 duly arrived at Reykjavik intact and undamaged early on May 29.

After leaving from Iceland the same day, PQ-16 initially was escorted by the minesweeper HMS *Hazard* (Senior Escort ship) and four trawlers (*St. Elstan, Lady Madeleine, Retriever,* and *Northern Spray*). *Retriever* considered her speed insufficient to keep up with the convoy and returned to Iceland on May 24.

Graeme Ogden, captain of the trawler *Lady Madeleine*, was making his first Arctic Convoy run. Although he had experience with escorting convoys, Ogden expressed some trepidation at the new assignment:

At the Ardrossan Naval Base we had gone in for a new type of camouflage. The colour scheme was white, with light-blue and green triangles. By far the largest proportion was white, so we really looked very like a yacht, but, as we shall see, this nearly proved our undoing.

We left home behind us; we knew we should not be returning for many months—if at all—for we were going on "The Northern Crusade". I only hoped that ours would not be as disastrous as its medieval predecessors, which had left disease, death and ruin in their train.

One the four Russian merchant ships in PQ-16 was *Stari Bolshevik*, whose veteran crew was headed home on their fourth convoy. A DEMS gun crew provided by the Royal Navy was on board to assist in the ship's defense. The crew itself came from bombed, smashed, and burned cities and territories occupied by the Germans. A number of them had lost their entire families.

Also among the crew were four women. Of these, one was the second engineer's wife, a young, rather fragile-looking girl. Two others were pretty blonde stewardesses. The fourth woman was *Stari Bolshevik*'s Third Mate, whose husband was a tank commander on the Stalingrad front. She had not heard from him in months since she'd been at sea.

Two days after sailing, the escorts were joined by the anti-aircraft ship *Alynbank,* the submarines *Trident* and *Seawolf,* and four corvettes: *Honeysuckle, Starwort, Hyderabad,* and the Free French-manned *Roselys.*

The *City of Joliet* was one of the American vessels in convoy PQ-16, and this was her maiden voyage. Her crew consisted of thirty-nine seamen plus twelve naval armed guards commanded by an ensign. None of these ratings or the merchant seamen had ever been in a real air attack. One of them, Davis Doyle, had been twice shipwrecked, both times as the result of a torpedo attack. The sinkings had been almost instantaneous: violent shocks that made the ships shudder, bits of iron and wood flying through the air, a column of steam as the boiler groaned like a huge wounded beast. Both sinkings had been similar down to the smallest details. Davis remembered that he had hardly had time to be scared.

Rear Admiral Burrough, flying his flag on the *Nigeria,* sailed from Seydisfjord on May 23, with the *Onslow, Oribi,* and *Marne* as his destroyer escort. The cruisers *Norfolk, Kent,* and *Liverpool* later joined the force from Hvalfjödur. Together these ships were designated Force "Q."

Shortly afterward, a destroyer escort, consisting of the *Ashanti* (Commander R. G. Onslow, S.O.), *Martin, Achates, Volunteer,* and the

Free Polish destroyer ORP *Garland*, was detached to join PQ-16, the remainder of the force standing to the north-eastward for a position where it could also cover QP-12 approaching from the east. ORP *Garland* was the first warship flying Poland's red and white flag to visit a Soviet port since the beginning of the war.

At 0600 hours on May 25, the first FW-200 Condor arrived over the convoy, but the day passed fairly quietly, and Force Q was detached in the afternoon and returned to Scapa Flow. Convoy QP-12 was sighted at 1400 hours, and also reported having sighted a U-boat. An hour later, *Martin* sighted a U-boat 7 miles on the starboard beam of PQ-16 and carried out an unsuccessful attack. Although safe from U-boats for the time being, the arrival of a BV-138 flying boat meant that dive bombers and torpedo planes were on their way.

The first attack by six Ju-88 dive bombers and seven He-111 torpedo planes began at 1910 hours. Two Ju-88s fell to the convoy's gunners while out of the seven torpedo-planes, Pilot Officer Hay in the CAM ship *Empire Lawrence*'s Hurricane shot down one in flames and sent another staggering away heavily damaged and unlikely to reach its base. Overeager gunners on American ships fired at Hay's Hurricane as it flew low over the convoy after the dogfight. Although wounded, Hay successfully bailed out of his aircraft and was picked up by *Volunteer*.

Not a bomb or torpedo found its mark, though a near miss had immobilized one ship, the *Carlton*, which had to be sent back to Iceland in tow of the trawler *Northern Spray*. The day closed with an ineffectual attack by twelve Ju-88s between 2315 and 2330 hours.

One of the most hard-pressed vessels was *City of Joliet*, the target of eight torpedo planes and eighteen dive bombers during four attacks on just the first day of the battle. The Ju-88s and He-111s came in on the starboard beam at about 150 knots in line abreast, about 75 feet apart. Breaking formation, the bombers dove at a 50-degree angle and released three to five impact bombs, averaging 300 pounds each, from a height of 1,000 feet. The torpedo planes attacked in two groups, coming in 30 to 50 feet above the water and releasing torpedoes simultaneously at about 3,000 yards on the starboard side of the convoy. *City of Joliet* escaped with a severe shaking-up from near misses that twisted and buckled the hull plates.

In the early morning twilight on May 26, the American merchantman *Syros* straggled behind the convoy. As she labored to return, Kapitänleutnant Heinz Bielfeld on *U-703* found her and fired two torpedoes at the laboring ship. Raymond P. Holubowicz, serving as cadet-midshipman aboard *Syros*, sighted it as the track described a dim white furrow across the slate-colored sea. The torpedo had taken an abrupt right turn and was heading squarely for *Syros*. Holubowicz reported later what happened:

> Since I was the only one who had seen the torpedo up to this point and being the only cadet aboard, I shouted into the wheelhouse an order to put the wheel hard over. The third mate came running out to find what business I had giving the helmsman an order, and before he was able to say a word he saw the torpedo. He shouted an order to the helmsman. The captain, too, ran out to find why someone was giving the helmsman an order while he held the con. By the time the captain got out on the port wing, the torpedo struck. Just before the torpedo struck, I threw the General Alarm switch. But it was too late to do any good for the men on watch in the engine room, one of whom was my fellow cadet, John Brewster.

Syros carried TNT and ammunition. The torpedo struck her amidships. She exploded and sank within eighty seconds, wrapped in a vast white sheet of flame. She broke in half; the pieces reared as they buckled, then broke and plunged. Debris, lifejackets, shards of hatch board, and potatoes from the adrift and smashed locker lay on the dark wave crests where she had gone.

The crew of the *City of Joliet* saw a column of blinding flame rise to 9,000 feet, followed by a deafening roar, a suffocating displacement of air, and a searing wind on the face. The pillar of fire grew larger, became a gigantic egg, and changed color. From a blinding white it turned carmine, scarlet, and yellow. Then nothing. Not even a wisp of smoke against the pale blue sky.

Hazard and *Lady Madeleine* were detailed to look for survivors. Ogden on *Lady Madeleine* remembered the scene:

> I love ships of all kinds, and it hurts me to see them destroyed. They lie there in their death agony like some wounded animal. Some take longer than others to die—some sink gracefully and proudly and others break up in a frenzy of despair.
>
> When we got to her she was well down by the bows and her crew had abandoned ship. *Hazard* had arrived before us and was busy picking up survivors. We sent both sea-boats away and collected some more. She was an American ship, and I shall never forget one American seaman standing

up alone on a small raft making the hitch-hiking sign to us. The Americans were in very fine form and seemed to regard the whole thing as a joke. One Negro went straight from the life-boat to the wardroom, polished up all the glasses, borrowed a steward's white jacket and appeared on the bridge to ask if I cared for a "high-ball."

The "hitchhiker" story was told by the *Hazard* crew:

He was called Boston Blackie. It seems that he didn't even get his feet wet when Syros *sank. Blackie managed to step off the rail of the ship as she was sinking and onto a life-raft that was fortuitously floating by at that moment. He was alone on the raft and was next seen using his thumb to hitch a ride on an escort vessel that came alongside.*

Incredibly, twenty-eight men from *Syros's* crew of thirty-seven were rescued by trawlers.

There was only one air attack on this day: an ineffective effort by eight torpedo bombers and three Ju-88s at 1800. U-boats were sighted at frequent intervals, but were chased away or attacked with depth charges. The last encounter took place at 2300 hours, after which no more U-boats were encountered during the remainder of the passage.

But the departure of the four strongly armed cruisers (*Nigeria, Kent, Norfolk,* and *Liverpool*) meant a very serious reduction of firepower for the convoy. *Alynbank* was practically out of ammunition for her 5.25 pieces. Her decks were littered almost knee-high with empty shell cases. All the destroyers except the recently commissioned *Martin* were equipped with low-level guns. Their main batteries could not be elevated for high-angle anti-aircraft fire. A number of the merchant ships shared the same predicament as *Syros* before she was sunk; their ammunition was completely gone.

The Germans failed to take immediate advantage of that fact, though, and on May 26, delivered a lone, weak Luftwaffe attack, a combination of high-altitude bombing by Junkers 88s and a few runs by Heinkel 111s when torpedoes were released. *Martin* and *Alynbank*, supported by the escort's automatic weapons fire, drove it off without loss to the convoy.

Fatigue became a very serious factor for the merchant crews. Many of the men had no clear idea of their destination and had not been informed in any way at the outset of the voyage about the dangers they might encounter. Sleep had not been possible since the ships left Iceland. Clothing was not taken off, and most of the bunks were unoccupied. Instead, men sat briefly dozing in the mess rooms or the officers' saloons. They kept on their lifejackets, and some their rubber suits. Gunners who were off watch hung their steel helmets from their wrists by the chinstraps. The helmets were of the basin-shaped, World War I type, and the web linings served to hold cigarettes and identification papers.

Regular meals had been attempted for several days aboard a number of the ships. But it was impossible to keep the big galley ranges going while the vessels were under attack or while depth charges shook the frying pans spinning off onto the floor tiles. Sandwiches and coffee were the only rations.

Some men went mad. They sat babbling in the passageways, pitifully huddled, or screamed at each other when a near miss fell. One ran straight toward a descending bomb; another, bareheaded, stood for hours on deck, looking numbly aloft at the German planes. When he spoke, it was to ask why the Germans wanted to kill him.

The worst ordeal was for the men who served below in the engine rooms and fire rooms. They formed in little groups in the passageways a few minutes before they were to go on watch. It was useless for them to wear lifejackets, which were too bulky to move around in. They stood in their regular work clothes, dungarees, or khakis at the doorways, which led to the engine-room ladders.

They were pale with the terrible fear that gripped them. Sweat ran down their faces. Their eyes were deep-drawn, glaring. The fear was so great that some of them bent over, violently gripped with stomach pains from the stress. Many could not control the shaking of their hands. Men on deck duty who passed them looked aside from the group in a strange, irrational kind of shame.

Then one of the group moved. He stepped over the high, brass-bound sill and onto the grating at the head of the ladders. The others followed, closely crowding, eager now, wanting to return to the familiar warmth and noise, the white bulkheads, the shining steel, the gauges, the pumps, the massive turning of the main shaft, and the reddish orange throb of the furnace fires. They found reassurance below, although their fear could never be wholly checked.

The men on deck duty served emergency watches: four hours on, four hours off. The muster in some ships was reduced almost in half; too many men were no longer capable. Fatigue claimed them, and they sprawled, heads down on the mess-room tables, still wearing their mittens and helmets. There were others who were temporarily insane, or so shocked they moved as if in a trance.

For those who went in rotation from the guns to the wheel and then to lookout, time had begun to lose meaning. They walked the guns, around, around, once more around, gazing into the cloud-banked horizon from which the Heinkels veered low, black, fast. Their necks ached from staring at the planes in high-level flight. Cramps locked their arms and legs. They blinked the rheum from their eyes to regain full vision. Within the rubber suits, their bodies were clammy and had begun to stink.

Coffee mugs and bits of sandwiches were among the heaps of empties beside the guns. The men reeled, almost comatose, hanging to the gun grips to stay upright. When they were relieved by their watch partners or men of the next watch, they did not make the effort of speech. They nodded, and shuffled away along the catwalks over the deck cargo.

Bullet holes from German low-level strafing runs roughly barked the smooth khaki sides of the wooden cases that held trucks. The men noticed those and the scatter of shrapnel fragments without curiosity. When they came to the forward deckhouse and started to climb to the bridge, the effort was almost impossible.

Some men wept, not because of pain or fear, but from the weakness rent by exhaustion. They butted from side to side on the ladders, stumbled over the rungs, nearly tripped. Then, hauling themselves by the handrails, they went topside.

May 26 passed that way, and in the early hours of May 27, lookouts sighted pack ice close alongside. Some pieces were as high as the bridge wings. Men reported seeing polar bears that peered forth from caves in the ice. But the reports were disregarded.

On May 27, the air attacks reached a climax with attacks by Heinkels and Junkers lasting throughout most of the day. The German command was fully aware that the cruiser withdrawal meant a serious lessening of the convoy's defensive power. The weather was fair and the sea calm. The Luftwaffe pilots chose their targets at will. When their bomb or torpedo loads were expended, they returned to the six airfields they used in Norway and Finland, armed again, refueled, and flew back for another attack.

After an air attack that did no harm at 0320 hours, course was altered to the south-eastward for a couple of hours to avoid heavy pack ice. At 1115, there started a series of attacks by a large number of Ju-88s.

The dive-bombing attacks were pressed well home through the broken cloud cover at 3,000 feet, and the enemy was assisted by an intermittent filmy haze at about 1,500 feet, which made them very difficult to see.

Destruction reached across the length and width of the convoy. Immense hedges of explosive-surged water flung up between the ships. Dark and slick patches of oil from bombs and from ships whose hulls had been ruptured littered the seas. Dead men floated with their arms wide from the life jacket, heads lowered and faces beneath the surface. They were hurled waist-high from the sea with the impact of bombs, flopped back, and bobbed along the columns of ships. The wounded called out to the ships that passed, begging to be saved from the sea. But the ships could not stop. The order was to proceed at any cost.

At 1100 hours during the course of the attack, one of the bombers dropped a stick of bombs on *City of Joliet* from less than a thousand feet. The crew saw them falling obliquely and rather slowly. The pilot did not pull out as soon as he had dropped his load: he merely decreased his dive and continued toward the deck, machine-gunning as he came down. Green flames spurted from his wings. On the deck, one of the temporary wooden gangways built over the piled-up vehicles to allow the crew to circulate caught fire.

The bombs fell in the sea all around the ship. The Junkers streaked like a meteor over the deck at a hundred feet. Crewmen felt that they could almost have touched the huge black crosses bordered with white. They could see every detail of the aircraft, even the pilot sitting in his cockpit. The crew saw his broad shoulders, head, and goggles. It was strange to see an enemy airman at such close quarters. The Junkers did a thunderous zoom, still firing with its rear guns. Round, light-edged holes appeared on the new paint of the petrol trucks. The men put out the fire on the wooden gangway, which was blazing peacefully.

An hour later, another bomber dived on their ship. The pilot released his bomb, this time a large one, from less than five hundred feet. *City of Joliet*, whose helm was hard over to port at the beginning of the dive, was now swinging to starboard. The bomb fell in the sea 30 yards to port, making the ship shudder.

The first casualty occurred at 1310 hours, when the cargo ship *Alamar* was hit by two bombs and set on fire. She was abandoned at 1330, and Commander Onslow ordered the submarine *Trident* to finish her. The survivors were picked up by HMS *St. Elstan*, *Starwort*, and *Trident*. Charles J. Hayes, a U.S. Navy radioman on board *Alamar*, never forgot his Murmansk experiences:

I was a radioman third class at this time. However, there was nothing for me to do. The Alamar *already had a radio operator and there was just no sense to having both of us sitting in the radio shack monitoring the frequency for messages. (Transmissions were not allowed, as subs could zero in on the radio signals.) So, I became a volunteer loader on one of our .50 caliber machine guns. I teamed up with a young gunner's mate I'll call "Georgia" because that is where he hailed from. We had practiced in the quiet times before the planes came and we got to be a pretty good team.*

But on this particular day—May 27, 1942—they came in such numbers it was impossible to keep your eyes on them all. The Stuka dive bombers used the bright sun to their advantage. They came down from the sun and we usually couldn't see them, but fired at the sound they made in their dive. They made a piercing, screaming sound when they dived to drop their bombs and it could really unnerve you.

Our gun station was located amidships on the starboard side. There were ships on either side of us in the convoy and bombs were dropping between the ships. The noise was deafening between the planes, the bombs dropping and the antiaircraft guns firing from the ships.

While we were firing up at the Stuka coming in overhead, I bent down to get another load to keep feeding the gun. I looked back over my shoulder and saw a German Ju-88 bomber approaching us from starboard aft. I pounded on Georgia's shoulder and hollered at him. He swung the gun around to meet the plane, but it was too late.

We didn't hear the bombs coming down, but there was a tremendous explosion. The noise was unbelievable. The Alamar *leaned way over to starboard. The sea came up into the gun tub and both Georgia and I were picked up and carried over the side when the ship came back up and the wave of water went back down to the sea. I remember falling through what felt like a waterfall and then hitting solid water and going down like a rock below the surface.*

I came back up into the sunlight and there was Georgia a few feet away, hollering at the top of his voice. I looked back and saw the Alamar, *still afloat and listing to starboard. There was a lot of smoke coming from her deck and we could see the crew letting down the boats. Georgia was trying to let them know we were still around, but we were so far away I didn't think they could see or hear us.*

The next time I looked, Alamar *was gone. As far as we could see there was nothing but water. The ships and planes were all gone and just [us] two bobbing around in the ocean, we looked at each other and kind of nodded our heads. We were sure that this was as far as we would go.*

I don't know how long we were in the water. The cold Arctic water has the effect of putting you to sleep. I vaguely remember seeing a lifeboat and the face of Alamar's first mate as he pulled me into the boat.

When I came to, I was in a bunk on a British corvette. It was crowded with survivors. All of Alamar's crew, both merchant and Navy had survived. Georgia and I were the only ones who got wet.

Five minutes after *Alamar* was hit, the *Mormacsul* was sunk by a direct hit and three near misses; three of the ship's crew perished in the attack. *Starwort* and *St. Elstan* rescued the survivors (thirty-six merchant seamen and the nine-man Armed Guard) at 1330 hours.

Between 1405 and 1410 hours, five direct hits sank the *Empire Lawrence*, and another started a fire in the *Stari Bolshevik*, which was successfully fought by her crew for thirty-six hours; near misses damaged the *Empire Baffin* and *Garland*.

Garland seemed to be singled out for terrific attacks, but, for most of the day, neither bombs nor machine-gun fire hit her. Toward the close of that day, however, a Junkers 88, diving through a curtain of fire, dropped a stick of four bombs close alongside. *Garland* disappeared in a wall of water and of smoke.

The four bombs fell in a group abreast the bridge about 20 feet off. There was no underwater damage, but the *Garland* was riddled from stem to stern with splinter holes. It was thought that this unusual splinter damage was caused by the first bomb exploding upon striking the water and detonating the other three in the air. "A" and "B" guns, one Oerlikon, and No. 1 boiler room were put out of action. And, a fire was started in the fo'c'sle. *Garland* was not out of action, but she was badly damaged. Entire gun crews had been wiped out. Her decks were covered with dead and dying. Casualties amounted to twenty-five killed and forty-three wounded.

Yet *Garland* never ceased firing. Her gunnery officer, himself wounded, organized crews of artificers and cooks to keep the guns in action. At the stern sections, among the corpses of gunners, they continued to fire at the attackers. The paymaster, mortally wounded, handed over his store keys to a colleague before he died. One of the wounded, lying where he had been dragged to a precarious safety, wrote on the white paintwork above him, "Poland—how sweet it is to die for thee!"

The commanding officer of one of the British escort vessels said:

When I saw this happen, I said to my officers, "That's finished the Poles; what a tragedy; they fought so magnificently." But I didn't have time to finish what I was saying, as out from behind a wall of smoke and water emerged Garland, *still firing.*

Six Junkers sought the CAM ship *Empire Lawrence*, which they bombed and strafed. Bombs sent waves splashing over her decks, where the gunners fired as rapidly as they could load and serve. Great, frothy cascades tumbled down upon her wheelhouse and bridge. Cordite smoke from her guns drifted out to show that she still fought. A bomb hit her foredeck close alongside the catapult rig. The force of the explosion made the ship visible in almost her entire length for a second or so, and then she began to sink.

The crew of *City of Joliet* saw the ship bearing down on them like a hunted beast. The bombs from the first plane all fell in the sea. The second had no time to drop his. Hit by the ack-ack, he continued to plummet like a stone until he crashed with a terrible explosion on the bows of the cargo ship. An enormous column of seething black smoke billowed in the air. When it dispersed, they saw that the *Empire Lawrence* was listing badly by the bows.

Her stem post was only a few feet above the water. On deck a group of brand-new trucks were on fire, and the crew were running from this curtain of flame. The boats were lowered over the side, and the rafts were thrown overboard. The crew jumped into the water without waiting any longer. Unfortunately, in the rush several rafts had not been held alongside and floated away from the drifting ship. The men who had jumped into the icy sea had to swim a long way to reach them.

A number of her men got away in a lifeboat. They piled aboard her, released the davits falls, and paddled clear astern before she was caught by the suction of the sinking ship. Junkers pilots flew over the lifeboat, though, where the men lay two and three deep on top of each other. The Germans made strafing runs until all aboard the boat were killed.

Empire Lawrence passed quite close to *City of Joliet*, and they could see the unfortunate men swimming in the icy water. The lifeboats drew slowly away from the wreck. The exhausted swimmers seemed to find it terribly difficult to hoist themselves up on the rafts. Spent, they reached for their mates, who could see their white faces and even the fear in their eyes but could do nothing to help. Though screaming for help, their cries went unheard above the cacophony.

There was no question of stopping and picking them up. No merchant ship was allowed to do this, and the orders were categorical. They had to sail on, averting their eyes from these wretched men struggling in the water. Moreover, above the convoy other bombers had just broken formation and were selecting their targets.

Graeme Ogden in *Lady Madeleine*, assigned as one of the convoy's rescue trawlers, recalled the attack on *Empire Lawrence*:

> *At 1420 the* Empire Lawrence *was hit and pulled out of her place in the convoy. I could not see how badly damaged she was, so I took* Lady M *over to her to help take off her crew if necessary. When I was nearly alongside, I noticed that her port-side life-boats were hanging vertically down the side of the ship, so I yelled to her captain and asked if he wanted my boats in the water. He shouted back something which I shall never know, for at that moment Geoff (*Lady M's *Executive officer) and I heard the cruel whine of bombers, and, looking aft, saw three of them diving on us.*
>
> *I heard the swish of falling bombs, but couldn't move our ship. The next thing I remember is that Geoff and I were rolling about on our backs on the deck of the A/S bridge and the sky was full of strange shapes. We were covered with falling wreckage and enveloped in suffocating brown smoke. I thought we had been hit. When, minutes later, the smoke cleared away, there was no sign of the 12,000-ton* Empire Lawrence.
>
> *The first thing I did was to light my pipe—I wanted to know if I was still alive. An oily pool—fringed with wreckage and bodies—and the shattered remains of a life-boat were all that remained of the* Empire Lawrence. Lady M *was untouched, although we were lying with our engines stopped, the length of a cricket pitch away.*
>
> *We heard afterwards from* Hyderabad, *who was just astern of us, that when they saw* Lady M *emerge from the smoke cloud, her gay camouflage bright in the sunshine, they could hardly believe it.*
>
> *Onslow in* Ashanti *thought we were gone, for he signaled incredulously:* "Do you need assistance?"
>
> *I answered:* "Empire Lawrence *sunk, am picking up survivors."*
>
> *We had but a few yards to move to pick up the survivors. Some were terribly wounded, and our own lads jumped over the side to help get them inboard. Fortunately, trawlers have little freeboard, especially in the waist, and, the sea being like a millpond, I was able to manoeuvre* Lady M *alongside the badly wounded, who were unable to move, and get them aboard. Our sea-boats collected the others. Sixteen in all, including the radar officer, who was apparently unharmed.*

We agreed afterwards, when making out the report of the loss of the Empire Lawrence, *that of the six bombs aimed at her at least three must have been direct vertical hits and that they knocked the bottom out of her. She had sunk in a matter of seconds.*

Garland's casualties were twenty-five killed or subsequently died of wounds and forty-three wounded.

Meanwhile, *Stari Bolshevik* was hit by a bomb on her foredeck, starting a fire and forcing the crew to wage a double battle against the enemy planes and the conflagration. The gunners succeeded in bringing down one bomber and drove off the rest. The struggle to save the ship and its cargo continued, but the commander of the British escort instructed the crew of the *Stari Bolshevik* to abandon her and board one of the escorts. At the same time, he announced his intention of finishing off the damaged transport. In reply, the captain of the Soviet ship signaled, "We do not intend to inter our ship."

At 1415 hours, *Ashanti*, the escort leader, sent a signal to the corvette *Roselys*: "Go and help the *Stari Bolshevik*."

The *Roselys* drew in to within 10 yards of the burning ship and managed to convey hoses to the "old Bolshevik." While the two vessels sailed side by side, a new air attack developed. Luckily no aircraft dived in their direction.

Stari Bolshevik could not stay in column and dropped back astern, a vast black banner of flame-streaked smoke above her.

Lieutenant Ralph Wilson Gray Ransome-Wallis, RNVR, the doctor on board the destroyer HMS *Martin*, was sent to assist with *Stari Bolshevik*'s wounded. He later wrote about his most remarkable house call:

Stari Bolshevik *was starting to lag behind the convoy a bit, possibly having to reduce speed to keep the flames and smoke from sweeping back over the ship. A lull seemed to have arrived and* Martin *turned back towards the stricken Russian. We quickly loaded two Neil Robertson stretchers into the whaler which had been swung out and lowered in its davits until it was level with* Martin's *deck. As the boat's crew was scrambling into the whaler I realized that both my tin hat and an extra bag of dressings were still in the Sick Bay. I raced along the deck to the Sick Bay and grabbed them just as the alarm bell went for another air attack.*

I ran back towards the whaler but unfortunately just as I passed the 4-inch gun it fired over my head at some German aircraft coming in low on the beam. I did not realize it at the time, but it was probably the blast from this gun rather than bombs, which caused damage to my ears from which I did not fully recover until some years after the war had ended although it did not interfere with my service career.

I jumped into the boat as it was being lowered and in a trice we were on our own bobbing about in the Arctic Ocean with Martin *wheeling away at speed, firing furiously at attacking aircraft.*

Stari Bolshevik *had stopped about 300 yards away still burning fiercely with black smoke pouring out of her forehold and we started to row towards her. However the Germans were making a dead set at the ship and to our dismay she started to get under way again.*

The prospect of being left alone in a small boat in the Arctic and no doubt being machine-gunned by the Nazis, did not appeal and we started to row like blazes, the Sick Berth Attendant (SBA) and I double banking the oars. Several bombs fell between us and the Stari Bolshevik, *one near enough to soak us and make the boat rock violently. What with gunfire, bombs and the screaming engines of the dive bombers the row was terrific, but the effect on our rowing was electrical and the whaler surged along.*

A rope-ladder was hanging over the port side of the Russian ship and with a last despairing effort we got close enough for our bowman to grab it and hang on as the Stari Bolshevik *gathered speed. I scrambled up to the bow of the boat and jumped for the ladder which by now had been made fast to the bow of our boat.*

It was a horrible thing to climb as it was no longer vertical, as all good rope-ladders should be, but was being pulled out [at] an angle by towing our whaler. However I was spurred on to climb the high side of the Russian by seeing that our boat was being towed so fast that it was becoming unstable and was bumping alarmingly against the side of the ship. Eventually I arrived on deck to be met by three Russian women who were obviously and excusably very frightened but were making valiant efforts to be useful. They seemed to be acting as deck hands, but were probably cooks and stewards as well.

I tried to show the women the dangers that our boat was in but they failed to grasp this and led me to some bundles lying on the deck that I realized were badly wounded men. My SBA now appeared on deck with a line to which was attached the stretchers. Leaving him to haul these up with the help of the women, I ran towards the bridge and climbed a steel ladder but before I actually got on to the bridge I was met by an officer, possibly the Captain, who could not speak any English but quickly grasped my pantomime act demonstrating the necessity to slow down and after a minute or two speed was decreased.

Returning to the wounded, I found my SBA explaining to one of the women that it was not a good idea just to tie a rope round a badly wounded man and drop him into the boat. These women however were very helpful and one could not help admiring their astonishing courage in a situation in which no woman should be placed.

We lowered three men on stretchers and three other less severely wounded men were able to climb down the ladder with a rope attached to them.

I started then to look around me, noticing the ship had carried an anti-aircraft gun right up in her bow. The bomb which had done the damage had landed on this and had blown a hole deep into the ship into which most of the wrecked gun appeared to have fallen. Round the jagged edge of the hole were some bits of badly burnt bodies and a little further aft lay the twisted body of another seaman — very obviously dead.

I did not linger as there was nothing I could do, but I heard from some forgotten source later on, probably one of the wounded, that five men had been killed. We cast off our rope-ladder and the Stari Bolshevik, belching smoke like a volcano, clapped on speed and drew away.

I shall always remember her with admiration.

A near miss further opened *City of Joliet's* seams, and she could barely keep headway; her master was aware that she was fatally injured. The British ship *Empire Baffin* was in the same condition, held afloat by her pumps. A Heinkel torpedoed the British ship *Lowther Castle,* and she sank, losing only one man killed.

At 1945 hours, two bombs from a Junkers found the British merchantman *Empire Purcell,* which started a fire. The ship was abandoned; survivors were picked up by *Hyderabad* and *St. Elstan* under deliberate bombing attacks. Commander Onslow ordered *Trident* to sink any ships that were unable to proceed with the convoy. *Trident* went alongside *Empire Purcell,* some of her crew boarded the boat, an attempt was made to extinguish the fire, but it had gotten out of control. Much concern was felt for the safety of *Trident* and her crew because she carried several tons of TNT. Not long after the *Trident* parted, the *Empire Purcell* blew up. The blast, felt on the far side of the convoy, made men gasp. The scarlet pillar of her flame seared eyes and roiled the sea into a maelstrom.

At 1950 hours, the British Merchantman SS *Lowther Castle* was hit on the port side by a torpedo fired from an He-111, at 4,000 yards. The crew abandoned ship and she dropped astern. Commander Onslow ordered *Trident* to sink her, but observing that she was being subjected to repeated vicious dive-bombing attacks, Onslow then cancelled the order. It was obvious that the enemy would save *Trident* from wasting a torpedo.

On the other side of the convoy, Commodore N. H. Gale was knocked prone when his ship, *Ocean Voice*, was hit by a bomb that set her on fire and tore away twenty feet of her side plating abreast No. 1 hold within two feet of the water line and started a fire in her forward holds. The crew fought the fire for several hours until it was finally doused.

"I had little hopes of her survival," Commander Onslow later wrote, "but this gallant ship maintained her station, fought her fire, and with God's help arrived at her destination."

The day's last loss occurred later that evening. *City of Joliet* signaled that she was filling rapidly with water and sinking. *St. Elstan* took the crew off without injury or loss.

At 2130 hours, the enemy finally left PQ-16 in peace, except for the inevitable BV-138 shadower aircraft circling the horizon. Commander Onslow reported that the situation appeared far from rosy: in one day he lost five ships—20 percent of the convoy—and there were still three days to go before reaching Murmansk. Commander Onslow wrote in his daily report:

> *I felt far from optimistic. The question of ammunition began to worry me badly. I ordered all ships to exercise strict economy and restricted controlled fire in the* Ashanti *to one mounting at a time. We were all inspired however by the parade ground rigidity of the convoy's station keeping, including* Ocean Voice *and* Stari Bolshevik *who were both billowing smoke from their foreholds ...*

On the morning of May 28, the fog grew denser until visibility was reduced to a hundred yards. The ships lost sight of each other and began to sail whenever possible by the fog buoy towed by the vessel ahead. More often than not, they saw absolutely nothing. They had to sail a general course and maneuver to avoid the ice, listening for their neighbors' sirens, which were muffled by the fog.

PQ-16 sailed south through this ice on May 28 and 29 during hours of continual daylight. The ships had to maneuver the entire time. The escort vessels did their best to see that the slow procession was not broken up by ice flows or heavy fog.

On *Lady Madeleine*, Graeme Ogden was looking forward to finally getting to Murmansk:

At midnight the sun was still 5 degrees above the horizon, glowering at me like a sinister Polyphemus. To paraphrase Noel Coward's lyrics — "Mad dogs and Englishmen go out in the midnight sun." Well, there the wretched orb was, a beacon to incoming German torpedo-bombers and certainly devoid of any romance. I wondered how I was going to explain this to Sally [his fiancée]. I was beginning to hate the sight of the bloody thing: it was my enemy — Death in the Afternoon and Death in the Midnight Sun. I thought of it as an orange in a butcher's shop, surrounded by deep-blue tiles. We looked like being the meat on the slab if we weren't very lucky. To hell with the sun!

The Germans, however, had not forgotten that our most vulnerable position for a final attack would be as the convoy approached the Kola Inlet. The question was, would the Russian fighters turn up in time? We had one more day to go as we approached Kildin Island.

Early on Saturday, 30th May, we sighted a skein of high-flying single-engined planes, which we took to be the expected Russian fighters, but they turned out to be about forty Ju-87s from Petsamo, and a vicious dive-bombing attack developed. In the middle of this holocaust, as our gunners joined the A. A. barrage, I noticed a Heinkel-112 seaplane approaching us at sea-level. It just goes to show how wrong one can be, for I thought he was on fire, as there was a red glow under his wings. Seconds later, when his machine-gun bullets began to hit Lady M*'s smoke-stack, I came to in a hurry.*

At A. A. action stations in Lady M*, I was alone on the upper bridge, except for my signalman. We had to grin and bear being shot together. I had a pair of skeleton Lewis guns, which I used as shot guns (not by Holland and Holland, but lightened to be fired from the shoulder, with pans loaded one tracer to three). I seized my No. 1 gun and opened up. The Heinkel's tracers were now coming close enough for me to have lit a cigarette from them. There was nothing I could do but to keep on firing and reach for No. 2 gun.*

I yelled to Bunts (the signalman) to lie down. It was like being in a cowboy film. I must say I was more than relieved when the plane swerved off at about 100 yards range, and crashed into the sea with a splash like a leaping salmon. I then had some bomb-dodging to do from the Ju-87s, but nothing came uncomfortably near us.

The convoy along with *Lady M*'s crew was shaken up, but escaped unscathed.

At 1150 hours on May 29, three Russian destroyers, the *Grozny* (S.O.), *Sokrushitelnyy*, and *Kuibyshev*, in their palely mottled camouflage designs, joined the escort—a very welcome addition to its anti-aircraft firepower. Later that evening, six minesweepers, under the command of Captain Crombie in *Bramble*, also joined the convoy. Under their escort, with the *Alynbank* and *Martin*, six of the merchant ships were detached to Arkhangelsk. At 2330, while the two sections of the convoy were still in sight of each other, the Murmansk section was attacked by a combination of eighteen Ju-87 Stukas and Ju-88 bombers and the Arkhangelsk section by fifteen Ju-88s. According to the official report, no damage was suffered by the ships. But the men who weathered the attack tell of different results.

Sixteen-year-old Newfoundlander George H. Evans, a stoker on the explosives-laden Dutch ship SS *Pieter de Hoogh*, witnessed the Soviet destroyers' response to the attack:

> *The Russian form of defence was direct counterattack. The destroyers sailed out onto the exact courses held by the dive bombers and then opened with every gun aboard, they followed the low-sweeping German Heinkels along the columns, and pursued them across open sea.*
>
> *Russian gunners were deft in their use of the 37-millimeter Bofors cannon. They skipped shells from the surface of the sea; that of* Kuibyshev *struck the Heinkels in the belly, she went away damaged. Two more German planes were shot down; no more of the convoy ships were lost.*

The Luftwaffe attack was intercepted by Soviet Northern Fleet aircraft. Admiral Arseni Golovko recounted their actions in the fight:

> *Our airmen are giving direct cover to the convoys en route. This is what we were doing in the last allied convoy in May, when we lost the commander of the air regiment, Lieutenant-Colonel Boris Pheoktistovich Safonov, by now a Double Hero of the Soviet Union and the first man in the U.S.S.R. to achieve this in the war. The order announcing this was received today, a fortnight after Safonov's death. He died on 30 May in defense of PQ-16. The details of his end are meager, although there were many witnesses of it.*
>
> *The convoy was sixty miles from our shores when the Nazis hastened up to deliver a massive attack with bombs. Forty-five Junkers escorted by Messerschmitts took part in the raid. As soon as the alarm signal was transmitted by the escort ships, four of our fighters led by Safonov took off to intercept. The fourth machine (pilot Kukharenko) returned to base half-way out owing to engine trouble. The other three went on and gave battle. Three versus forty-five Junkers and an unassessed number of Messerschmitts!*
>
> *None the less every attempt of the Nazi pilots to break through to the transports in PQ 16 was defeated by our fighters — Safonov, Pokrovsky and*

Orlov, who excellently co-ordinated their actions with the barrage put up by the escorts. In full view of everybody Safonov shot down two bombers, and Pokrovsky and Orlov one each.

    Soon afterwards Vaenga [Air Base] headquarters heard the words "Cover my tail" … on the radio. These turned out to be Safonov's. Next the signalmen in the destroyer Kuibyshev, *escorting the convoy, saw Safonov rush in to attack a third Junkers, but at the same moment an enemy fighter dived out of the clouds and attacked him. After a short time headquarters picked up another message from Safonov: "Have damaged a third … engine …" The last word was a code word indicating the necessity of a forced landing.*

The rest, according to the ship's signalmen, happened as follows: Safonov's machine, losing height, glided toward the *Kuibyshev*, but fell into the sea about two miles short of the ship and sank immediately:

The air battle over the convoy had ended. Getting rid of their bombs anywhere and everywhere the Nazi planes made off in the direction of northern Norway, having failed to sink a single transport.

    Two hours after the battle Kuibyshev *searched the sea for Safonov, but failed to find him. The cause of his death thus remains unknown. Possibly the engine failed owing to machine gun fire. One thing was certain— Safonov had died on his 224th operational flight and in his 34th air battle, after his 25th individual victory over the enemy.*

    It is sad to have to admit this loss. It will remain forever linked in my memory with the code number of the last May convoy, PQ-16. The Northern Fleet lost an outstanding pilot and astonishingly talented officer. A courageous son of the Russian people, true to the Soviet Motherland and the Communist Party, Safonov was a model warrior of the air and commander-instructor.

Once more, Graeme Ogden on *Lady M* was in the thick of the fight:

The senior officer of the minesweeper flotilla, for some strange reason, took over command of P.Q.16 from Onslow *and attempted to split up the merchant ships into a Murmansk section and an Archangel section. The result was complete confusion, and the Ju-87s pounced on the convoy.*

    We were ordered to join the Archangel section, then the order was reversed. Whilst steaming between the two sections, a low-flying German plane came at us on our beam; I turned towards him and yelled to McTavish, but that wily Scot didn't need any advice from me. He waited until the Hun was about

400 yds. away (during which time I must say his bullets were whizzing past my head) and then let go. That was the end of that. "Well done, Mac," I yelled.

"The cheeky so and so," he replied.

The Ruski destroyers really saved this situation, as, having plenty of ammo, they put up a terrific barrage over the convoy. Now, to add to the confusion, the tardy Russian fighters turned up. I saw several planes crash into the sea, but as the Russians didn't take any notice of their own barrage, or anybody else's, I couldn't tell if they were German or Russian.

Before we had rejoined our section we were dive-bombed and, by the grace of God, I turned the ship the right way. The bombs exploded in the exact place where we should have been if I hadn't altered course. Poor Lady M got lifted out of the water and her engine stopped with a shudder. I thought we were hit, and, telling Geoff to take over on the bridge, I ran aft and down into the engine-room. Here I found Whitehead and the second engineer armed with a spanner about as big as themselves.

The chief did not speak, but gave me a look which I understood. All was not well in the engineroom, even the stokers' soot-covered faces looked pale. The engine's main piston had stuck and the chief was about to try and turn it over, in the same way as you crank a car with a starting handle.

The engine-room was full of steam and I had a nasty feeling Lady M had taken on a pronounced list to port. As I stood there watching, there was a thunderous explosion outside and Lady M again took a mighty heave. The chief and the second dropped the giant spanner, and we all panted for breath. The steam escape was worse and clouded the daylight out of the engine-room. Through a wet fog I saw the chief again wrestle with the huge spanner and, with the others, try to heave the engine over its dead centre. As these men, their half-naked bodies covered with sweat, strained away, I knew that if they didn't succeed Lady M was a dead duck.

The second explosion I had felt while in the engine-room could only have meant more bombs aimed at Lady M. Now I couldn't move the ship, she was at the dive-bombers' mercy. We were very obvious in our gay camouflage and, don't forget, we had just shot down a German plane. After what seemed an eternity the piston once again began its downward movement.

"She'll go now," Whitehead said thickly.

"Well done, boys," I answered and tore back to the bridge.

From then onward, Soviet Hurricanes gave air cover to the convoy as the crews began seeing signs that they were at last approaching land: floating tree trunks and land birds. At 1100 hours, they sighted the coast with its dark, rocky, pine-covered hills.

It was 1600 hours on May 30 when the Murmansk section formed single file to enter Kola Inlet. They steamed past Toros Island and through the minefield, took aboard their pilots. Commander Onslow held *Ashanti* on standby as they passed. He signaled them: "Reduced in numbers, battered and tired, but still keeping Perfect station."

Admiral Tovey, the commander-in-chief, Home Fleet, was agreeably surprised that, in the face of such a scale of attack, four-fifths of the ships of this large convoy ultimately reached their destination. He wrote:

The success was beyond expectation. It was due to the gallantry, efficiency and tireless zeal of the officers and men of the escorts and to the remarkable courage and determination of those of the merchant ships. No praise can be too high for either.

On the German side, Admiral Dönitz's, Commander-in-Chief, U-boats, wrote in his War Diary about the operation:

My opinion as to the small chances of success for U-boats against convoys during the northern summer ... has been confirmed by experience with PQ 16. Owing to the difficult conditions for attack (constant light, very variable weather and visibility, abnormally strong convoy escort, clever handling of the convoy, appearance of Russian aircraft forcing the U-boats to dive on sighting our own aircraft as well) the result, in spite of shadowing and a determined set-to by the boats, has been one steamer sunk and four probable hits. This must be accounted a failure when compared with the results of the anti-submarine activity for the boats operating ... U-436, U-703 have depth charge damage, unfit to dive to greater depths. Three more boats have slight depth charge damage, the effects of which ... will probably mean some considerable time in the dockyard.

Admiral Dönitz concluded, "The German Air Force would seem to be a better means of attacking convoys in the north in the summer" and suggested that these facts be taken into account rather more than they had been hitherto when U-boat operations in the north were planned.

The Luftwaffe greatly overestimated the effects of their attacks on PQ-16 and claimed to have destroyed the whole convoy. From the results of their reconnaissance flights, Luftwaffe officers were convinced that the convoy had dispersed as the result of the first attack in the evening of May 25. This was not the case.

The lesson the Germans drew from this attack was that the anti-aircraft defense could be dissipated and confused by high-level dive bombing closely integrated with the launching of torpedoes from a height of about three hundred feet. The method adopted for the torpedo attack, which was known as the "Golden Comb," was for the aircraft to approach in a wide line abreast and to drop their torpedoes simultaneously. It also was decided to attack at twilight with the ships silhouetted against the lighter sky. By June, forty-two torpedo aircraft had arrived in Northern Norway, and these tactics were assiduously practiced.

As a result, PQ-16 lost seven merchant ships: six to air attack and one to a U-boat. Seventy-four officers and 397 men were rescued from the seven ships. According to German sources, two U-boats were damaged during attacks by escorts and of the 101 Ju-88s and seven He-111s that attacked the convoy, three Ju-88s were lost with their two-man crews.

Even as both sides studied what happened to PQ-16 and QP-12, the next convoys, PQ-17 and QP-13, were being assembled.

CHAPTER 6

APOCALYPSE
June–July 1942

W hile the British and German commanders were planning their next moves, HMS *Gossamer* and her crew fought a desperate battle for survival far from the convoy routes. *Gossamer's* flotilla had been in Murmansk almost a year, escorting convoys as they approached the Murman coast as well as ensuring shipping channels were kept free of mines.

Leading Signalman John Maddern was on board *Gossamer* on June 24 as east and west the ship rode at anchor in the Kola Inlet north of Mishukov Point. The weather was fine and warm and the sky was clear but the water was cold. The crew were in jerseys, trousers, and shoes in the pleasant weather, so different from the freezing cold of the winter months.

Then at 0900 hours came the warning by the shore-based anti-aircraft guns and warning flags from ships in the anchorage of approaching enemy aircraft. *Gossamer's* gun crews were at their battle stations, and the crew waited for the impending attack. Eight minutes later, five Ju-88 bombers were seen flying from west to east through the slight haze. As they reached the sun, four turned toward the anchored merchant ships and began to dive. The fifth was lost sight of in the sun. Maddern was one of the first men on board to see the enemy, and he later wrote about the attack:

> Five aircraft came out of the sun and at least one attacked with bombs. The gunners opened fire but no hits were recorded. Two bombs hit us, and one near miss, virtually blowing our stern off at the break of the upper deck and quarter deck. The wardroom just disappeared with our Engineer Officer and two Deck Officers and several crew. There was a great deal of carnage but no panic. Some men below decks managed to get clear, but others were trapped as the ship was sinking fast.
>
> After the first explosion, I said to the captain there seemed nothing for me to do on the bridge—could I help below? I had just got to the ladder when a louder explosion threw me across the wheelhouse. This was the bomb that finished her, as she took a heavy list to starboard. On the upper deck—aft—two seamen were supporting an AB—one of the gunners. We lowered our port whaler to get the wounded away. I looked at some of my mates sliding over the port side whilst on the starboard side the guard rail was the only part above water.
>
> I saw a messmate sliding on his backside portside until reaching the bilge-keel and jumping into the water. At the height of our survival he, being a mess-deck wag, was heard to say even at a time of crisis—"Those bloody barnacles ripped the arse out of my pants."
>
> Soon there was only a P.O. and myself on that part of deck and he said the order had been given "Abandon ship: every man for himself." Two stokers appeared from the boiler room escape hatch and went over the side. One I never saw again—one survived. So I decided to jump.
>
> The whole business of the sinking took only ten minutes or so. Some small Russian boats headed towards us. We hastily climbed aboard, but our ship was now turning over, and the boat was being pushed under by the mast, so we had to abandon that one and board another in the vicinity.
>
> This then was the sad end to yet another gallant ship and crew with one exception. One of the enemy aircraft, still not satisfied, returned to survey the kill—flying low over the scene, machine-gunning the survivors in the water. It has since been related to me that three of the survivors in the confusion were hit by machine-gun bullets and died whilst swimming for their lives.

Gossamer turned over and sank at 0921 hours, eight minutes after being hit. Twenty-nine of her crew died in the attack. Three or four Russian powerboats and at least one rowing boat quickly reached the scene and pulled the survivors to safety. The loss seemed of little account to anyone—except the families of the men killed.

Even after the severe losses suffered by PQ-16, convoys PQ-17 and QP-13 initially were scheduled to depart on June 11 in order to keep with the three-week schedule as Churchill had promised Roosevelt. However, the British needed to mount a relief operation for the island of Malta in the Mediterranean. This operation required many of the British Home Fleet ships dedicated to supporting the Arctic convoys to serve as escort. Thus, the convoy sailing dates were moved forward to June 27.

This delay gave the Germans additional time to finalize their plans to ensure no ship made it through to Russia. Hitler had been informed on June 1 of the proposal to use Kriegsmarine surface ships against PQ-17; he was assured that the operation would take place only if it could be safely assumed that no superior enemy forces would be met with and that adequate air cover could be provided. Eventually he approved, but with the proviso that before the ships sailed, the Allied aircraft carriers' disposition must be ascertained so that they could be attacked by the Luftwaffe.

This proviso was tantamount to canceling the operation, as it would have delayed the sailing of the ships too long. Grand Admiral Erich Raeder therefore decided that the operation should be carried out in two phases. First, while waiting for the convoy to be located, the ships should transfer to sortie ports in the extreme north. Second, once in place, they should await Hitler's final sanction and orders to proceed.

On June 14, Admiral Otto Schniewind issued his orders for the operation, which was known as *Rösselsprung* (Knight's Move). The surface forces were organized in two groups: the Trondheim group, comprising the battleship *Tirpitz*, flying the flag of Admiral Schniewind, and the cruiser *Hipper*, together with six destroyers; and the Narvik group, comprising the pocket battleships *Lützow* and *Scheer*, with six destroyers.

On confirmation of PQ-17's approach, the Trondheim squadron was to move to Vestfjord and the Narvik squadron to Altenfjord. As soon as the convoy had reached the Barents Sea, the two German squadrons were to proceed to a rendezvous a hundred miles north of North Cape, and then attack the convoy west of Bear Island.

The Germans relied upon air reconnaissance and U-boats to provide early information about PQ-17's position. Of the ten operational U-boats available, three were sent to patrol the northeastern sector of Denmark Strait as early as June 5. By June 18, all had been disposed on the estimated convoy route.

As they prepared to assault PQ-17, the Luftwaffe applied lessons learned from PQ-16 a month earlier. The Luftwaffe had overestimated the effects of their attacks on PQ-16 and claimed to have destroyed the whole convoy. They were convinced that the convoy had dispersed as a result of the first attack in the evening of May 25. The lesson they drew from this attack was that the anti-aircraft defense could be dissipated and confused by high-level dive bombing coordinated with the launching of torpedoes from a height of about 300 feet. The method adopted for the torpedo attack, which was known as the "Golden Comb," was for the aircraft to approach in a wide line abreast and to drop their torpedoes simultaneously. It also was decided to attack at twilight with the ships silhouetted against the sky.

The British Admiralty was aware of the risks involved in sailing convoys in the face of growing German opposition. Ultra intercepts in June indicated that the Germans intended at last to bring out their main units to attack the next eastbound convoy to the east of Bear Island, and this threat formed the main preoccupation of the Admiralty. However, political considerations compelled them to continue with the sailings.

The Allies had suffered serious losses in the convoys, but they had been confined to what the British Admiralty considered acceptable limits. Nevertheless, those with personal experience viewed the prospect of continuing the traffic during the summer months with grave misgivings. It was difficult to see how the problem could be solved if the enemy chose to supplement his air and U-boat offensive by using his heavy ships for a surface attack in the Barents Sea. The strategic situation, wrote Admiral Tovey:

> ... was wholly favourable to the enemy. His heavy ships would be operating close to their own coast, with the support of powerful shore-based air reconnaissance and striking forces, and protected, if he so desired, by a screen of U-boats in the channels between Spitzbergen and Norway. Our covering forces, on the other hand, if they entered these waters, would be without shore-based air support, one thousand miles from their base, with their destroyers too short of fuel to escort a damaged ship to harbour.

Tovey proposed that the eastbound convoy, QP-13, upon reaching 10 degrees East longitude, should put back for twelve to eighteen hours, unless it was known that German ships were still in harbor or the weather prevented shadowing from the air. He hoped that this temporary course reversal would either tempt the German heavy ships to pursue, cause them to return to harbor, or compel them to cruise for an extended period among the eight British, one French, and two Russian submarines on patrol in areas off the North Cape, the Russians occupying the two inshore areas. These zones were to be moved east as the convoy passed north of them.

The Admiralty did not agree to this, though their instructions envisaged the possibility, under certain circumstances, of the convoy being temporarily turned back.

British Admiralty instructions also stipulated that the safety of the convoy against surface attack to the west of Bear Island must be met by British and American surface forces, and that to the east of that meridian, the convoy must be met by submarines. In addition, the cruiser covering force was not intended to go east of Bear Island, unless threatened by the presence of a German surface force which the cruisers could fight. In any case, they were not to go beyond 25 degrees East longitude.

This plan did not altogether meet Admiral Tovey's views, which from the first appearance of the German heavy ships in Norway had differed in several respects from those of the Admiralty as to the tactical dispositions best calculated to achieve the object. He was seriously disturbed to learn during the course of a telephone conversation with First Sea Lord Sir Dudley Pound under which certain circumstances the Admiralty contemplated ordering the convoy to scatter.

All the latest experience pointed to the vital necessity for ships to keep together for mutual support against the heavy air attack that was certain—weather permitting—to take place. Tovey strongly disapproved of an order to scatter, except as a last resort in the actual presence of attack by overwhelming surface forces.

PQ-17 sailed on June 27 with thirty-five merchant ships under Commodore J. C. K. Dowding on board the freighter *River Afton*, escorted by *Halcyon*, *Britomart*, *Salamander*, and four antisubmarine trawlers. One merchant ship grounded while leaving harbor, and another was damaged by drift ice in Denmark Strait and had to put back.

The Support Force under the orders of Rear Admiral L. H. K. Hamilton consisted of the British cruisers HMS *London* (flagship) and

Norfolk, the heavy American cruisers *Wichita* and *Tuscaloosa*, and three destroyers. The main task of this force was to intercept enemy aircraft and U-boats making their way toward the convoy.

The Covering Force, under the orders of Tovey on board the battleship HMS *Duke of York* (flagship), consisted of the American battleship *Washington* (in which Rear Admiral Robert Giffen flew his flag); the aircraft carrier HMS *Victorious*; the British cruisers HMS *Cumberland*, HMS *Nigeria*, and HMS *Manchester*; and a dozen destroyers and corvettes. This task force was to operate in the waters between Iceland and Spitzbergen, where it would shield PQ-17 from a possible thrust by German warships based at Altenfjord, Norway. It was also responsible for the safe return of a westbound convoy PQ-13. The close escort joined from Seydisfjord, Iceland, departed on June 30. It consisted of six destroyers: *Keppel* (Commander J. E. Broome, S.O.), *Leamington*, *Wilton*, *Ledbury*, *Fury*, and *Offa*; four corvettes: *Lotus*, *Poppy*, *Diayiella*, and the Free French *La Malouine*; and the submarines *P614* and *P615*, along with two anti-aircraft ships: *Palomares* and *Pozarica*. There were also three rescue ships: the *Zaafaran*, *Rathlin*, and *Zamalek*.

Westbound QP-13, also consisting of thirty-five ships, formed up off the Kola Inlet on June 27. This convoy was escorted by the minesweeper *Hussar*; corvettes *Honeysuckle*, *Hyderabad*, *Roselys*, and *Starwort*; the anti-aircraft ship *Alynbank*; destroyers *Achates*, *Volunteer*, and the Polish *Garland*; and trawlers *Lady Madeleine* and *St. Elstan*.

PQ-17's route skirted northern Iceland, took a north-by-east tack, went past the volcanic, glacier-covered Jan Mayen Island, continued northward toward Spitzbergen and Bear Island, and then swung southeast through the Barents Sea to skirt the Kola Peninsula and enter the White Sea.

The first few days passed quietly for the convoy, and all of the escorting forces proceeded on a northerly course through thick fog and heavy ice floes. The first sign of trouble came about 200 miles west of Bear Island on July 1 when a BV-138 reconnaissance plane sighted the convoy. The next day, six U-boats attacked but were driven off by the escorts.

Early on the morning of July 4, PQ-17 was about 60 miles north of Bear Island when twenty-six Heinkel He-111 torpedo bombers dove through the clouds and leveled off 50 feet above the water. The freighter *Christopher Newport* was hit by a torpedo from a Heinkel that dived in solo flight through a hole in the cloud cover. The crew immediately abandoned ship and was picked up by the rescue ship

Rathlin. One of the accompanying British submarines was detailed to finish the ship with a torpedo.

During the attack on *Christopher Newport*, one of her armed guard gunners rendered exceptionally gallant service. Seaman First Class Hugh Patrick Wright, USNR, manned a .30-caliber Browning machine gun in the starboard bridge wing of the ship and did his utmost to save her.

The torpedo released by the attacking Heinkel plane headed directly for *Newport*'s midships section. An order was passed to open fire on the German plane in an attempt to explode it before the ship was struck. Wright was squarely on target with his fire, but the small-caliber bullets bounced in futile ricochet from the torpedo. The merchant seamen who served as loaders for Wright's gun told him that the fire was wasted. They told him, too, that he should get out of the bridge wing before the torpedo hit.

But Wright kept on firing, bent down over the piece, cursing it for its lack of power. The merchant seamen ran for the port side of the ship. The torpedo struck the starboard side, almost directly below Wright's gun station.

Wright was still firing at the plane at the instant of explosion. He was flung off the flying bridge and down onto the main deck. That knocked him unconscious, and he also sprained an ankle. His shipmates hauled him into a lifeboat, and he was among the survivors brought aboard *Rathlin*.

At 1930 hours, there came a half-hearted attack by a few bombers whose nearest bombs fell through the cloud ahead of the convoy between the destroyers *Keppel* and USS *Wainwright*. It was meant to be a combined torpedo and bombing attack; half a dozen He-115 aircraft had been circling the horizon for some time, and a torpedo exploded harmlessly outside the convoy.

A more determined torpedo attack was made less than an hour later. The anti-aircraft ship *Palomares* detected twenty-five aircraft coming up from astern at 2020 hours. They attacked from the starboard quarter, flying fast and low. Their leader showed great determination, hitting the *Navarino* in the middle of the convoy with two torpedoes before he crashed in flames just ahead of the *Keppel*. The remaining pilots weren't as brave.

"Had they kept up with him, dividing and generally embarrassing the A.A. fire," wrote Commander Broome, "many ships would have been sunk."

As it was, the Heinkels did torpedo three other ships: the freighters *Navarino* and *William Hooper* and the Russian tanker *Azerbaijan*. The *Navarino* and *William Hooper* were so badly damaged they had to be sunk. At first *Azerbaijan's* bow was engulfed by flames, and lifeboats were seen leaving the ship, but she didn't sink. Led by women crewmembers, the fire was put out and the lifeboats hoisted back aboard. Fortunately, *Azerbaijan* was loaded with linseed oil for paint making, rather than fuel. She regained her station and continued with the convoy.

Commander Broome remarked on the good shooting of the escort and the convoy; four aircraft were thought to have been brought down, including one by the *Offa* and one by the *Wainwright*. The three rescue ships proved their value by picking up survivors quickly and efficiently. All told, the convoy lost three ships and ten men to the attack.

The convoy was 240 miles west of Norway's North Cape and still had more than 1,000 miles—five days' run—to sail before reaching Arkhangelsk. From the convoy's standpoint, everything was going well despite the day's air attacks.

The Germans, however, were still awaiting approval from Hitler for sailing the heavy ships to the attack. But the naval staff, fearing it might be delayed too long, had sanctioned the *Tirpitz* force joining the pocket battleships at Altenfjord (this had been done on the night of July 3/4). Admiral Tovey's covering force had been sighted some 300 miles southwest of the convoy early on July 3, and since then nothing had been seen of it. In view of Hitler's stringent orders that the carriers were to be located and put out of action before launching the operation, Grand Admiral Raeder decided that nothing further could be done for the present. They remained at Altenfjord until the afternoon of July 5.

At the British Admiralty, the situation was being watched with increasing anxiety. It had been known since July 3 that the German heavy ships had left Trondheim, and since the afternoon of July 4 that the northern squadron had left Narvik, but none of the ships had been located. That evening, Pound called a staff meeting to consider the situation. There was consensus that an attack might develop any time after 0200 hours next morning, July 5. If the attack was pressed home in full strength while Rear Admiral Hamilton's cruisers were still present, it seemed it could result only in their destruction, in addition to that of the entire convoy.

Against such an attack, the more widely the merchant ships were dispersed, the better their chances of escape seemed. Once the alarm had been given, the enemy raiders would not wish to spend more time than necessary in the neighborhood, rounding up odd groups and ships. But an 8-knot convoy takes some appreciable time to scatter effectively, and the matter was further complicated by uncertainty as to the extent to which the ice would permit maneuvering to the northward, away from the probable direction of the attack. On the other hand, the convoy was still some 800 miles from its final destination. Air and U-boat attacks had already started and were certain to continue on a heavy scale. Once scattered, the isolated groups and units of the convoy would present comparatively easy targets. Heavy casualties had to be expected.

Shortly after 2100 on July 4, the decision was made to withdraw the cruisers and scatter the convoy immediately.

The Admiralty's decision was conveyed to Rear Admiral Hamilton in the following three signals:

"Most immediate. Cruiser force withdraw to westward at high speed. (2111 B/4)"

"Immediate. Owing to threat from surface ships, convoy is to disperse and proceed to Russian ports. (2123 B/4)"

"Most immediate. My 2123/4 (message). Convoy is to scatter."

To Hamilton, these signals could only mean that the further information about the Kriegsmarine heavy ship movements the Admiralty had been hoping for at 1858 hours had indeed come in and was of such a nature as to render imperative the drastic measures now ordered. Actually, the emphasis on the use of high speed by the cruisers was due to reports of a massing of enemy submarines between 11 degrees and 20 degrees east, and the order to scatter was intended merely as a technical amendment of the term "disperse" (used in the previous signal).

The nuance in wording between "disperse" and "scatter" could not be known to the recipients, and the cumulative effect of the three signals—especially as the last had a more urgent priority marking than the middle one—implied that pressing danger was actually upon them. Ships in the convoy ordered to disperse would merely cease to keep formation, and each ship would proceed at her best speed to her destination. Because in the present instance all ships were bound for the same port, Arkhangelsk, they would obviously remain in fairly close company with each other for some hours. On the other hand, ships were ordered to scatter immediately; that is, they proceeded in accordance with a plan laid down on courses that would separate them from each other as quickly as possible.

Commander Broome expected at any moment to see the cruisers open fire and the enemy's masts appear on the horizon. In this belief, he decided to take the destroyers of the escort to reinforce the cruiser force and ordered the two submarines to stay near the convoy when it scattered and to try to attack the enemy, while the rest of the escorting ships were to proceed independently to Arkhangelsk.

The British Admiralty decision to withdraw the protective screen and scatter the convoy was based on false information: the German surface forces had not yet left their Norwegian bases, but simply moved to different anchorages. They did not leave them until the next day, July 5, when *Tirpitz*, *Scheer*, *Hipper*, seven destroyers, and three torpedo boats made a sortie off the North Cape. The Germans didn't find any Allied ships and returned to port without firing a shot.

Commander Broome relayed to Convoy Commodore Dowding the message to scatter. Dowding knew that such an order was used only in extraordinary emergencies. It had been issued only once before in the war, in November 1940 when *Scheer* attacked a British convoy in the North Atlantic. Thirty-seven merchant ships were guarded only by the British armed merchant cruiser *Jervis Bay*. After giving the order for the convoy to scatter, she was sunk by *Scheer*.

The *Jervis Bay* action was fought, though, in the middle of the Atlantic. Here, 240 miles east of the North Cape and within the confined waters of the Barents Sea, these merchant ships had a very slight chance of escape from the enemy. They were already at the edge of the pack ice and could go no further northward.

As the six escorting destroyers turned away, Broome signaled Dowding: "SORRY TO LEAVE YOU LIKE THIS. GOOD LUCK. LOOKS LIKE A BLOODY BUSINESS."

Within an hour, many of the ships had disappeared over the horizon, each sailing its own course to Arkhangelsk. Some ships stayed together in groups of three or four for mutual support.

Luftwaffe FW-200s and BV-138s combed the Barents Sea, searching for the convoy. What they found astonished them: merchant ships spread out all over the area without any escorts.

The planes' pilots sent radio messages that brought the Junkers 88s, the Heinkels, and the U-boats. The ships that had belonged to PQ-17 were sought singly and attacked until their ammunition was exhausted and they were defenseless. Then they were rapidly sunk unless in combat they had already received fatal damage.

Some ships' crews fought back after a bomb or a torpedo had hit. They believed it was better to keep on fighting than to freeze to death in the sea. Only three of the American merchant ships carried 3-inch cannon. The rest were armed with .50-caliber and .30-caliber machine guns. The ammunition used by the machine guns bounced off the armor plate of the German planes if not fired at almost point-blank range. Defense, the crews realized, did not mean much. But it was a relief for nervous tension and kept a man from going insane.

During that time, the Panamanian registry freighter *Troubadour* had engaged in some rather exceptional activity. She carried a U.S. Navy gun crew whose members shared action stations with the merchant seamen. *Troubadour* had been armed in the United States with a 4-inch cannon, four Browning .30-caliber machine guns, and a .30-caliber Lewis machine gun. But the supply of ammunition was inadequate.

Ensign Howard E. Carraway, USNR, the gunnery officer, emphasized the seriousness of this shortage to the master and chief officer. In his report made later in Arkhangelsk, the ensign wrote:

It was decided on 28 June to open the seals on one of the three M-3 U. S. Army tanks on the deck, part of the cargo, and to determine whether the 37 millimeter gun in it could be manned and used for the defense of the ship. This was thought advisable in view (1) of the small amount of mixed tracer and ball .30 ammunition in our lockers; and (2) of the short effective range of the .30 Lewis machine gun against aircraft. This done, the gun was found suitable for use. Ammunition (Armor Piercing with tracer) was broken out of the hold with the aid of the Chief Officer, the gun was test-fired and a two man crew trained and assigned General Quarters stations in the tank.

Next day a second tank was opened, the 37 mm. gun made ready and manned. One member of the Armed Guard and one of the ship's crew were used as crew for each of the tank guns.

The weather on July 5 was bright and sunny with some high, thin clouds. The sea was cobalt and retained the broad, white paths of the ships' wakes. Off on the starboard hand, to the northward, the ice wall lay lustrous and sheer. The Germans came quickly to the target and attacked in strength.

The British freighter, *Empire Byron*, was sunk by *U-703*. The combined attack of U-boats and Ju-88s destroyed four ships, which had bunched together farther north. These were *Earlston*, *Washington*, *Bolton Castle*, and *Paulus Potter*. Then the *Pan Kraft* was caught while she ran alone and sunk by aircraft. Commodore Dowding's ship, *River Afton*, was another victim of *U-703*. The fleet oiler *Aldersdale* was damaged and abandoned (she was finished off by a U-boat two days later). *Carlton* was destroyed, as were *Fairfield City* and *Daniel Morgan.*

Fairfield City was a sturdy American freighter with a good rate of speed. She used evasive tactics while her gunners fired furiously at the Heinkels. But her machine guns caused little if any damage. Three Junkers 88s stayed high out of range, and each dropped a stick of bombs. At 1645 hours, two to three bombs struck the ship on the port side at the edge of No. 2 hatch. The blast wrecked the wheelhouse, the Captain's house, and part of the Saloon house. All the ladders to the bridge were blown away, all the hatch boards were blown off No. 2 hatch, and the geyser of water from the explosion filled the lifeboats half full of water. The ship was stopped by the engineer on watch and reversed to get the headway off the ship. The ship sank by the head at 1740 hours with her American ensign still flying.

The thirty-four survivors abandoned ship in Nos. 1, 2, and 3 lifeboats. They were unable to lower No. 4. Two crewmembers jumped overboard and swam to a raft. They were taken aboard one of the lifeboats. Another man was picked up from the water. The master ordered the men in the boats to look for other survivors, but none were found. At 1850 hours, No. 2 and No. 3 boats were taken in tow by No. 1 lifeboat, which was the motorboat, and they headed for the island of Novaya Zemlya about 250 miles away.

Daniel Morgan, an American ship that mounted a 3-inch cannon, was not so easily destroyed. Her master maneuvered her away from nine sticks of bombs. The gunners drove off dive-bomber attacks, and shell bursts ripped the wings of two attacking Junkers. But then the breech action of the cannon jammed and could not be cleared. Two more attacks were made against her.

The German bombers pounded the *Morgan* from end to end. Though there were no direct hits, the enormous impact of the near misses in the water right around her sprung her plates wide at the waterline and below. Her pumps could not handle the rapid flow into her holds and engine room. She was abandoned, and her crew was picked up the next day by the Soviet tanker *Donbass*.

Washington's forty-six-man crew abandoned ship in two lifeboats. Despite the speed of her sinking, the wireless operators had had time to send out an SOS. But the men in the boats were convinced that the only effect of these messages was to let the Germans know the positive result of the attack.

The survivors in the lifeboats strove to avoid uninterrupted icepack. Then the ice seemed to be breaking up. Channels opened, and to the east beyond the fields of ice, the survivors could see expanses of sea dotted with ice blocks. In an easterly direction lay Novaya Zemlya, an archipelago 500 miles long situated between the Barents Sea and the Kara Sea and split in two by the Matochkin Strait. The lifeboats contained blankets, chocolates, pemmican (a mixture of fat and protein), powdered milk, sugar, biscuits, dried fruit, and watertight kegs of fresh water. The crew reckoned the archipelago to be a little less than 300 miles away, about five days' rowing. They were wrong.

The American freighter *Olopana* had heard their SOS and had gone off its course to pick up the shipwrecked men. Two crews from ships sunk at the same time as the *Washington* were rowing toward it.

The two lifeboats containing the *Washington*'s crew did not move. The sailors began to row toward *Olopana* and then stopped. The shipwrecked men from the *Washington* did not wish to be picked up. They thought that it would have been madness to reembark now in a ship, which, they figured, would suffer the same fate. In their lifeboats, they were comparatively secure. No planes would bother to drop bombs on them, and no U-boats would torpedo them. But to board another cargo vessel was to expose themselves for certain to bombs and torpedoes. It was far better to reach the shores of Novaya Zemlya.

Once they were there, the men thought, they could wait a few days until the Germans considered that their attacks on the PQ-17 were over. Then they would make their way close inshore to the south. It would be very odd if they did not meet some Russian boat, which, they figured, would pick up the shipwrecked men and take them to Arkhangelsk. The dangerous amount of open water to cross would then be shorter. The sailors of the *Washington* were fully aware that something unforeseen could happen in their plan, but anything appeared preferable to going aboard the *Olopana*. They discussed the matter while the ship was approaching, and all were in agreement.

The survivors of the other two ships climbed aboard *Olopana*, but the *Washington*'s crew refused to go aboard the *Olopana* and began to row eastward without waiting for *Olopana* to disappear to the east.

Meanwhile, after *River Afton* was bombed and sunk, Commodore Dowding managed to get aboard a raft with an able-bodied sailor and a messboy from her crew. They sat side by side on the flimsy plank-and-oil-drum craft, huddled close against the spray and the wind. Commodore Dowding was an Arctic veteran. He spoke to the others from time to time so that they would not lapse into the first phase of the drowsiness that led to immobility and then death from freezing.

There was no way to steer the raft. She drifted downwind, and across the men's backs spray became a crust of ice. Ice also formed on the planks of the raft. The freeboard was less than a foot. Within a few hours, as the ice load increased, the raft would sink.

Thrust by the wind, the raft slowly went past a lifeboat from a sunken British ship. A number of survivors were aboard her, and she was in a bad way. The boat was wooden. German machine-gun bullets had perforated the strakes, tearing jagged holes in the hull. She was taking on water, and most of the men she carried were soaked to the skin, cruelly chilled, and unable to use their hands in the simple motions of bailing.

But aboard the boat was a sailor who was determined to live and to keep his shipmates alive. He stuffed the bullet holes with pieces torn from his and other men's clothing. Cursing, prodding, shoving, he got men to bail, and small amounts of water were cast out of the boat. She began to show more broadside and became almost ready to be rowed. There was, though, one survivor who did not respond to any kind of incentive.

He sat stoop-shouldered on a thwart, a sodden and pitiful figure in the grayish haze, the boat herself spectral-seeming on the leaden sea. Dowding could barely distinguish the man, but he clearly heard the rasping, exasperated voice of the sailor who exhorted the boat survivors.

The sailor addressed the stoop-shouldered man. "Alfie," he asked, "why are you so bloody wet?"

Hours later, the Royal Navy corvette *Lotus* emerged from the haze and discovered Dowding's pitiful raft. Dowding and his two shipmates were taken off without having suffered serious injury. *Lotus*, at some risk, cruised slowly south and west, looking for other survivors. But the lifeboat Dowding had seen was never found.

Late in the day of July 5, the Germans found a group of four British vessels, and the rescue ship *Zaafaran* was sunk by aircraft. But HMS *Salamander*, a minesweeper, and the freighter *Ocean Freedom* saved themselves and escaped. *Salamander*'s crew took out of the sea the complement from *Ocean Freedom* and some of the people from *Zaafaran*. The men had not been in the sea too long and were saved before exposure became fatal.

But the day's destruction wasn't over yet. Aircraft destroyed the American freighter *Peter Kerr*. Torpedoes fired in unison by several U-boats sank another American freighter, the *Honomu*. Men were lost aboard each of these ships, and flotsam littered the sea where the survivors struggled. Lakes of oil stretched far and wide, glistening black and trapping bodies. The air smelled of cordite, scorched paint and steel, with, as a base, the bitter stench of the oil.

Ensign Carraway reported on *Troubadour*'s participation in the events after the July 4 order for the convoy to disperse had been obeyed:

> *We immediately swung out of column to port, took a Northwesterly course and headed for the East coast of Spitzbergen. At about 2200 a British armed trawler hailed us and directed us to follow her. Later we were joined by the SS* Ironclad *and the SS* Silver Sword. *On the morning of 5 July, we reached the southern edge of the ice fields and turned East, closely following the ice.*
>
> *During the afternoon the radio operator received several distress messages from other ships of the scattered convoy being attacked by planes of various types and submarines. Some of the ships attacked and abandoned gave positions as near as twenty miles from our D. R. [dead reckoned] position.*
>
> *The commanding officer of the trawler, the H.M.T. Ayrshire, signaled us to put as much white paint as was available on our starboard sides (to help camouflage the ships) and prepare to enter the ice. The Armed Guard was turned to and aided in this task. Within five hours the painting was completed and we were well into the ice.*

Before the ships were camouflaged, Lieutenant L. J. A. Gradwell, RNVR, in command of *Ayrshire*, had boarded each of the merchant vessels. He explained the need for banking ships' fires. A single wisp of smoke from a stack might betray their position here. He advised that the ships that carried tanks on deck follow the example set by *Troubadour*: open up the M-3s and use their 37-mm pieces to repel attack. Gradwell wrote in his report:

> *After going about twenty miles into the ice all ships stopped, turned their starboard sides to the sea and waited until late in the afternoon of 6 July, when they headed out of the ice, took an Easterly course along the edge of the ice fields, with the West coast of the island of Novaya Zemlya as the destination.*

The ships waited in the ice for three days. On July 9, Gradwell held a conference with all of the masters and commanding officers in the group while the ships were at anchor in an unidentified inlet on the coast of Novaya Zemlya. They agreed to proceed south to Matochkin Strait, where a radio station was thought to be located. Here a party would be sent ashore to attempt to get a message through to the British Naval Control in Arkhangelsk.

Ensign Carraway continued in his report:

> The C.O. of the *Ayrshire* requested that I prepare all available arms with adequate ammunition and select six men to accompany the landing party, prepared in case the station should not be in friendly hands.
>
> On 10 July at 1100 the Matochkin Strait was reached and a signal from the station assured us that it was friendly. The landing party went ashore, obtained the desired information and returned without incident. Early on the morning of 11 July we moved about two miles into the straits, where the SS *Benjamin Harrison* was at anchor. On 12 July all ships moved about ten miles further East into the straits for protection against air detection and attack.
>
> Earlier in the day a Russian tanker, a Russian armed trawler and an armed Russian icebreaker had joined the other ships.
>
> Three British escort vessels — corvettes — arrived in the straits on 20 July. A convoy was formed and at about 1400 we cleared the straits bound for the White Sea.

On July 6, *Olopana*, after answering the *Washington*'s SOS and picking up survivors, was torpedoed and sunk by *U-225*. All but six of her crew and the load of survivors she had picked up were able to escape into lifeboats or onto rafts as the ship sank.

HMS *Pozarica* and her sister anti-aircraft ship *Palomares* were kept busy guarding the small convoys as they made their way across the White Sea to Arkhangelsk, picking up men who for days had been stranded in lifeboats and on rafts. While off Kolguyev Island, 60 miles from the Russian mainland, the convoy the Royal Navy ships escorted came under very heavy German air attack when, at 2000 hours on July 9, forty high-level bombers emerged from the clouds.

The Germans bombed with precision. The American freighter *Hoosier* and the Panamanian *El Capitan* evaded direct hits. Near misses were so numerous, though, that both vessels were abandoned in sinking conditions. The American Liberty ship *Samuel Chase* veered between the bomb geysers, helm hard right, then hard left in evasive maneuvers, and avoided destruction. But many of her steam pipes were ruptured. When the ship bucked with the violence of a near miss right off the bridge wing, the compass was flung from the binnacle in the wheelhouse. The sailor at the wheel steered without one until a box compass was brought from a lifeboat and installed in the binnacle case.

The rescue ship *Zamalek* was almost as badly battered as the American vessel. Near misses shook her until waves clashed across her deck. Soot from her stack erupted in big, black flakes. The stubby 1,200-ton steamer carried survivors in all her quarters and on deck. Those who stood clung to each other or else were knocked from their feet. Her engines could not maintain the strain at full speed. Her master slowed her, and she fell astern with the bomb blasts very close.

Despite their losses, the Allies fought back. Gunners aboard *Pozarica* and *Palomares* were able to take four of the German planes out of the sky. The 5.9-inch shells went aloft with great accuracy whenever a bomber came within range. Showers of aluminum from torn wing tips stippled the sea, and then the smashed planes whirled down and disappeared, howling, in immense gouts of spray.

The enemy broke off the action at 0230 the next morning and flew southwest. Two Soviet Catalina flying boats arrived over the convoy half an hour later and protectively circled it. The ships slowed until *Zamalek* could get back on station. Commodore Dowding, who had assumed duties of command aboard *Ocean Freedom*, ordered a course steered for Arkhangelsk.

Three corvettes, *Poppy*, *Lotus*, and *La Malouine*, were on the coast to pick up survivors from the beaches and collect the merchant ships. Twelve men from *Olopana* were found in a poorly sheltered beach camp. Space to accommodate the 240 survivors picked up by *Empire Tide* was made aboard the naval vessels. They proceeded to Matochkin Strait, where Commodore Dowding picked up five more ships (*Silver Sword*, *Ironclad*, *Troubadour*, *Benjamin Harrison*, and *Azerbaijan*) as well as two other vessels, the Soviet ice-breaker *Murman* and a trawler.

The weather was bad. With a storm brewing, Commodore Dowding passed orders to get underway. Fog helped conceal the ships off Novaya Zemlya. Dowding brought the convoy through the White Sea and into Arkhangelsk on July 24, and the ships were berthed. It had been three weeks since PQ-17 had dispersed.

Meanwhile, as many as fifty boats with survivors were trying to reach Novaya Zemlya. The island was a prolongation of the Ural mountain chain, and extended to 77 degrees North latitude. Matochkin Strait was a transversal fjord, more than 60 miles in length and most of that a half-mile wide. The hills that rose 3,000 feet were shouldered by glaciers, and between them and the sea, in summer, were green fields.

A short and harsh grass spread across the fields. Willow trees and dwarf birches dotted the landscape. Further inland, pale in the distance, stood snow-capped mountains.

Sea birds in great, noisy crowds littered the shore-side cliffs. A few lemmings, wild reindeer, foxes, wolves, and bears existed on the plains of the southern part of the island. The local waters held cod, herring, and salmon. Seals crawled up over the pebbles among the masses of driftwood on the beaches. Whales cruised close offshore.

After being sunk on July 5, *Fairfield City*'s survivors hoisted sails on the boats and made landfall on Novaya Zemlya, 5 miles south of Matochkin Strait, on July 9. The men took the sails and boat covers ashore and made tents from them.

It was the birds that saved the survivors' lives. The men saw them first, dark, small specks high in the saffron-yellow sky above the land haze. Then they landed, and fumbling with weakness, the survivors killed enough to make a broth, providing each man with a meal, meager as it was. Time was not taken to catch fish; hunger was too insistent, and the birds were all around. Hunting of game for meat was not even considered.

A number of the survivors lacked sensation in their feet and lower legs. They hobbled ashore from the boats, helped along the strand by their shipmates. The prospect for them was gangrene and amputation. They sat rather still on the beach, seldom talking.

On July 10, the survivors were discovered by some Soviet Boy Scouts, who took a note to a nearby Soviet-manned radar station which sent word of the men to Northern Fleet headquarters Two days later, HMS *Ayrshire* picked them up and took them to Matochkin Strait. There they were placed on various ships. Eleven were put on the SS *Troubadour*, ten on the SS *Silver Sword*, and seven on the SS *Ironclad*; three remained on the *Ayrshire*.

Washington's crew reached Novaya Zemlya after spending six and a half days rowing through the icy seas in their lifeboats. By the time they landed, they were ravenous. They had finished the last of the boats' provisions the night before.

Hunger possessed the entire company of survivors. Geese cackled on the beach, but were too careless near the men. Eight goslings were captured, their necks quickly wrung. The armed guard officer from the ship, a young ensign, wore a .45-caliber issue Colt in a holster. He went hunting alone and shot a seagull. That sent the other gulls, hundreds of them, away in screaming flight. But the ensign's prize added materially to a soup cooked over a driftwood fire.

Alerted to the disastrous battle around PQ-17, the Soviet Ice Patrol vessel *Murmanez* was sent to search for survivors. Ice patrol vessels were charged with responsibility for both combat and transport operations in the Barents and Kara seas. The *Murmanez* crew included a five-man research and operations group. Among the crew was Valentin Valentinovich Dremlyug, the ship's twenty-four-year-old engineering officer. Later he wrote about what happened:

> *As she was heading out of the White Sea*, Murmanez *received a radiogram from the tanker* Donbass *informing us about the destruction of the ships of convoy PQ-17 by German submarines and torpedo-bombers. As it turned out*, Murmanez *proved to be the Russian vessel able to give the first and most important help to the survivors of PQ-17.*
>
> *As the* Donbass *departed, the* Murmanez *continued on her assigned mission. On 13 July, while off Gusinaya Island (south of the Novaya Zemlya Islands), we noticed a number of people on shore who were trying to get our attention with smoke and flag signals. Capt. Kotzov ordered a small boat put over. As the boat approached the shore, its crew—well armed with carbines—was prepared for anything. The two machine guns on the* Murmanez *also were aimed at the people on shore.*
>
> *Our hails to them in Russian brought no response, but when we tried English we were told that they were the surviving crewmembers of the SS* Olopana *(one of the PQ-17 ships), which had been torpedoed and sunk by a U-boat about 15 miles from Novaya Zemlya. After almost two weeks adrift in a lifeboat, the survivors—12 in all—had finally come ashore at Gusinaya Island.*
>
> *On 16 July we transferred the* Olopana *survivors to the settlement at Belushya Bay. An interesting footnote to the* Olopana *rescue is the gift to me, mentioned earlier, by the boatswain of the* Olopana. *As he was taken aboard the* Murmanez, *the boatswain still had with him the small tin cup with which each lifeboat was equipped for measuring out the daily rations of fresh water. He had carried it with him throughout his ordeal. He gave it to me as a token of gratitude. The cup, however, has been a treasured part of my household ever since.*
>
> *By 17 July we had seven lifeboats in tow, on which were about 100 American and British survivors from various ships. We towed the boats to the Gulf of Molier, where we transferred all of the survivors to the British transport* Empire Tide.
>
> *Between 13 and 17 July we were able to take aboard more than 100 seamen—survivors of the* Alcoa Ranger, Washington, Hartlebury,

and Paulus Potter—*in addition to the 12 crewmen from the* Olopana. *Our poor vessel was filled to overflowing.*

Later, we came upon the American transport Winston Salem, *which had been deliberately grounded in order to prevent her from sinking from the damage already inflicted by the U-boats. To prevent the* Winston Salem *from breaking up and going under, we took soundings to determine the depth of water in her vicinity, and prepared to tow her off at the next high tide.*

To tow the Winston Salem *we "married" our bow and stern anchors to her anchors to give us the leverage we needed to be able to tow her off at the next tide. We were assisted in this task by a Russian trawler and together were able not only to get her underway again but also, some time later, to witness the delivery of her full load of precious tanks and ammunition to the port of Arkhangelsk.*

Thirty-six ships left Hvalfjödur. Two had turned back to Iceland, air attack had destroyed thirteen (in addition to the *Zaafaran*) at a cost of six aircraft, and U-boats sank ten vessels without loss to themselves. The convoy started out carrying 156,492 tons of cargo. The ships that were lost took with them all but 57,176 tons of that—a loss of nearly two thirds of the precious cargo. The material sunk included enough to equip an army: 430 tanks, 210 planes, and 3,350 jeeps and trucks. The human cost was 153 dead men.

Winston Churchill said of PQ-17 in his history of World War II: "Unfortunately the destroyers of the convoy escort also withdrew (with the cruisers)."

Commander Broome, who had led the destroyer *Keppel*, wrote to the editor of the *Daily Telegraph* on October 30, 1950:

This [Churchill's] statement may reasonably create the impression that the destroyer force was free to remain with the convoy or withdraw.

It was from no misfortune that the destroyers under my command withdrew. It resulted from a direct order from the Admiralty to scatter the convoy. This order could only have been justified by the proximity of the enemy, and it demanded therefore that I should concentrate my destroyer force with the nearby cruisers.

The responsibility for the tragic events which followed must rest with those who, in contradiction to naval practice, elected to direct an Arctic convoy from London, instead of passing information and leaving the decisions to the commander on the spot.

QP-13, consisting of thirty-five ships (twelve from Arkhangelsk, twenty-three from Murmansk) under Commodore N. H. Gale in *Empire Selwyn*, left Murmansk on June 27. The convoy was heavily escorted by the minesweeper *Niger* (Commander A. J. Cubison, senior officer of escorts); *Hussar*; the corvettes *Honeysuckle*, *Hyderabad*, *Starwort*, and *Roselys*; anti-aircraft ship *Alynbank*; destroyers *Achates* and *Volunteer*; and trawlers *Lady Madeleine* and *St. Elstan*. Two days passed without alarm, but the ships were sighted by an FW-200, and everyone feared that Ju-88s, He-111s, and U-boats wouldn't be far behind. No attack came—partly because of heavy fog, but mainly because the Germans were concentrating on PQ-17.

Captain R. Kelsoe was the master of the big Panamanian registry freighter *Exterminator*. He was a tall Yugoslav with a shock of brown hair. A pair of Colt .45 automatic pistols were thrust inside the waistband of his trousers. A pair of ferocious German shepherd dogs followed him wherever he moved and stayed at his side in battle.

A. Andresen, a Norwegian national, was Captain Kelsoe's chief officer. Andresen was the best gunner aboard *Exterminator*. He was in command of the volunteer crew that worked the British 4-inch cannon mounted on the foredeck.

The chief officer went personally armed, a precaution taken by most of the other members of the crew. Everyone on board *Exterminator* was of several nationalities, and from countries under German occupation. Capture could mean instant execution by a German firing squad.

Captain Kelsoe and Andresen kept a terse logbook account of the PQ-13 voyage from Murmansk to Reykjavik, Iceland. The entry for June 29 read: "Day begins heavily overcast. At 10:15 a.m. altered course to 355°. At 2:45 p.m. altered to 297°. Day ends overcast with visibility good, speed 9 knots."

The entry for the next day marked the arrival of the first German patrol plane, the dreaded Focke-Wulf Condor, whose radio reports would bring the Junkers 88 bombers, the Heinkel torpedo planes, and the U-boats. It forecast very probable extinction. Captain Kelsoe's logbook read: "Tuesday, June 30th. Day begins overcast, visibility fair. Russian destroyers left the convoy. At 4:40 p.m. first air raid alert. At 5:30 p.m. all clear. At 10:20 p.m. altered course to 225°. At 11:00 p.m. altered course to 270°. Day ends cloudy and fine with speed 8.4 knots."

His entry for July 1 was: "Dense fog, heavily overcast. At 7:30 a.m. altered course to 254°. At 5:15 p.m. altered course to 263°. At 11:00 p.m. altered course to 228°."

Commodore Gale, within the fog cover, steered a series of evasive courses. He held on to the hope that he might lose the German reconnaissance planes that were sure to search the area as soon as the weather cleared. But they came the next day. Captain Kelsoe recorded the fact in *Exterminator's* log: "Thursday, July 2nd. Overcast, visibility good. At 9:00 a.m. two Blohm & Voss (BV-138) sea planes were circling the convoy. At 11:00 p.m. the planes left. At 11:25 p.m. altered course to 241°. Speed 8.5 knots. Day ends with scattered fog banks."

During the hours while the enemy aircraft were in sight, the escort made repeated attempts to shoot them down. The destroyers gave full throttle and whipped forward in a white, high-bow splatter, cannon firing as rapidly as they could be served. *Alynbank* joined with her heavier pieces.

The range was too great, and the German planes kept close to the haze-rimmed horizon in elusive flight patterns. There was nothing more to be done. The ships kept thumping and grinding on through the fog banks around them. The escort moved slowly once more in its usual screen formation. But aboard the escort vessels, men stood close alongside the depth charge racks and the gun mounts. They knew that U-boat attack might come at any minute.

The long minutes of waiting stretched into the next day. Captain Kelsoe wrote at the end of it: "Friday, July 3rd. Weather overcast with very thick fog and some ice. At 3:30 p.m. altered course to 196°. At 7:00 p.m. altered course to 210°. Ships passing through drift ice. Weather overcast with thick fog. Speed 8.3 knots."

Then, on July 4, during the hours of late afternoon, the men of the PQ-13 convoy fully understood what had saved them. Since July 1, they had heard intermittent rumbling from the southwestward. The loaded, eastbound convoy, PQ-17, was being attacked. The far-away noise was interrupted by long periods of silence. Fog lay thickly on the sea here; perhaps it spread, too, along the PQ-17 course track, protecting the ships.

Arriving off the northeast corner of Iceland on July 4, the convoy was ordered to split up. Sixteen ships, including that of the commodore, with part of the escort being routed to Loch Ewe and the remainder with the rest of the escort, went along the north coast of Iceland to Reykjavik. Captain J. Hiss of the *American Robin* was nominated as acting commodore of this section.

The weather during the previous two days had been cloudy, and it had not been possible to take sights during that time. As a result, the position of the convoy was uncertain. The radar carried by some of the ships of the escort was at that time not very reliable, and as the Iceland section approached the land, the weather deteriorated. It was blowing a gale from the northeast, raining, with the visibility down to about a mile. At 2000 hours, Commander Cubison decided to go ahead and try to make it to Iceland

Cubison realized that the ships must pass between the rugged coast of Iceland—now wholly unseen under a blanket of fog and rain—and a minefield, which extended for several miles to the westward out into the Denmark Strait. He decided to steer close enough to take a bearing of some sort. Weather conditions had made it impossible to take celestial sights for the past two days. Radar was unreliable. Visibility was down to one mile.

At 2200 hours on July 4, Cubison saw what he believed to be the North Cape. It was, however, an iceberg. He took a bearing on it and gave a radical course change of forty-eight degrees to due west. The convoy was ordered at the same time to form two columns so that it might sail safely between the outer minefield and the land.

A new minefield, closer to the coast, had been set since the PQ-13 formation had gone to North Russia. There were no charts available that gave the exact location of the field. The lack of charts would prove disastrous for the *Niger*.

Niger had been on duty in Russia for eight months, and her crew would be given leave as soon as she reached Britain after delivery of the convoy. A number of her men were discussing that when at 2240 she struck a mine. Before the ship went under him and he drowned, Commander Cubison was able to send a blinker message. *Niger*'s signal yeoman, swiftly pressing the trigger of the Aldis lamp, told Captain Hiss: "Suggest alter course to 222."

This was the course that had been previously steered, and Captain Hiss as acting commodore in *American Robin* was at once aware of it. He swung his own ship instantly and relayed the message to the rest of the convoy. But he lacked a chart that gave the minefield position, and suddenly *American Robin* was struck and seriously damaged by an explosion.

Due to faulty navigation, the convoy had sailed directly into the field. Within a brief space of time, four ships of the convoy had struck mines and foundered, and two more were seriously damaged.

Pale flames illuminated the scene as *Niger* sank, taking her commanding officer, eight other officers, and 140 crewmen with her.

The freighter *Hybert* hit a mine and sank, as did *Heffron* and *Massmar*. *Exterminator* and *John Randolph* were damaged. One of those lost was the Russian ship *Rodina*, which was carrying the wives and families of Soviet diplomats stationed in London.

Maria Amosovna Naumova Vyushina, who had four years of experience on steamships, was the baker on *Rodina*. Among the passengers were a young Russian woman and her young daughter, who shared Maria's cabin during the trip. The woman was going to meet her husband, who worked at the Soviet embassy in Reykjavik. Originally they were to have sailed on *Stari Bolshevik*, but at the last minute got passage on *Rodina*, which was departing sooner. Years later, in somewhat broken English, Vyushina recalled the voyage and its terrible end:

> The night we were to arrive in Iceland there was an explosion. I jumped up, flung the door open and found the corridor filled with water. The mother rushed out of a cabin with the girl on hands, without lifejackets.
>
> We ran to the boat deck where the boatswain supervised loading people into the life boats. The strong gale howled in tackles. As we got into the boat someone removed his own lifejacket and put on the girl. A strong wave picked up the boat and threw it against the sinking steamship. The boat turned over and plunged us into the icy water. It felt like I was burning and it was hard to breathe.
>
> Nearby appeared wide thick wooden hatch and I grabbed it, my hands where like iron crampons. Abruptly waves carried away me all further from a steamship. When a wave lifted me on an abrupt crest I saw Rodina strongly tilted as she sank.
>
> A man passenger floated not far away. He tried to come nearer to me and to grasp for same hatch, but couldn't reach it. In a wave there was a large timber which has knocked him on the head. On the water appeared a dark circle of blood began to creep away quickly, the man did not surface after being hit.
>
> My hands and body and I wanted to be let go of the hatch—I cannot unclench my fingers. Nearby the daughter of the passenger floated. The lifejacket's belt was weak and gradually slipped off the girl and I cannot help her. I looked back once again, but the girl already had drowned and was floating face down in the sea.
>
> It is better for me to sink, I thought, trying to be let go, but hatch and hands were as if one. Small ice floes, cross ties, bags with the wool, any wooden subjects around floated.

A big foreign boat passed near the sinking, I didn't think they saw me and again began to try to be let go of the hatch. I was exhausted and started to faint. Suddenly on hatch was a line with a big knot on the end. It was with the last bit of my strength I seized it with my teeth.

I regained consciousness as someone kneaded my body. It was the doctor. He saw I had regained my senses, and has started talking in language I didn't understand. I asked: "Where am I? How many of us survived?"

He didn't understand, but guessed and showed me ten fingers then four and three—17 persons escaped.

The doctor somewhere left. I lay there covered with a bed-sheet and reflected: "This is probably a fascist submarine and in an hour German officer which will torture and then shoot me."

Then door was quietly opened and I grew cold, but it was Katya Vushueva from Rodina. *She among the survivors was the mother of the little girl. Katya and I cried over the loss of our ship and comrades.*

SS *Massmar* carried a crew of thirty-eight merchant crew, sixteen Naval Armed Guard, and thirty-six survivors of the torpedoed SS *Alamar*, which had been sunk in PQ-13. Among these were the U.S. Naval Armed Guard detachment of the *Alamar*, all of whom survived the sinking and were assigned to *Massmar* for the return voyage to the States, via Iceland.

Charles J. Hayes, radioman second class, was one of *Alamar*'s Armed Guard detachment. Later he wrote about that terrible night:

The night of July 5, 1942 was very cold with dark clouds, strong winds and heavy seas. My assignment as lookout was on a hatch cover just forward of the bridge. I felt certain that with the size of the waves, no sub could possibly fire a torpedo with any chance of success, although we took nothing for granted and still kept a sharp watch.

When I was relieved of my watch, I went to my bunk which was just off the main deck. Of course, at this time and in these waters, we had learned never to be without our lifejacket—eating, sleeping or whatever.

I had just laid down when there was a horrendous explosion that shook the ship. The noise was louder even than that on the Alamar *when the bombs hit. I hit the deck and started for the hatch when another powerful explosion sounded. When I reached the main deck, it was already only three or four feet above the water.*

I looked down midships and saw a crew member trying to get a lifeboat free. The water was coming up so quickly the boat was already floating in the water before they had time to unhook the davits.

When I next looked over the side just in front of me, the deck was only a few inches above the surface. There was someone standing next to me—I don't remember who it was—and we both just stepped over the side into the water.

The sea was running high and those of us in the water would ride up to the top of a wave and then ride down into the trough, something like riding a small roller coaster. When you rose to the top of a wave you could see many people floating in the water and when you dropped down, you could see nothing but huge waves overhead. An overturned lifeboat floated by but I was unable to get to it.

Later, a lifeboat sailed by with a Navy Armed Guard sailor standing up in it! He had a big smile on his face as he sailed by. Some people called out to him from the water, but he didn't respond. He seemed to be in some state of shock and didn't seem aware of his situation.

All of a sudden, an overturned lifeboat came over the top of a wave, directly at me. There was a merchant seaman clinging to it and I noticed a line wrapped around the upturned bottom. The merchant sailor tried to reach me, but he was exhausted and wasn't able to pull me out of the water. I was able to grab the line that was wrapped around the boat and with some help from him I was finally able to climb onto the boat. We both were able to secure our arms under the taut line and this kept us from falling off. Then, as happened when the Alamar *went down, I fell asleep from the cold.*

Seventeen of *Massmar's* crewmembers, including the captain, plus twenty-three crewmembers from *Alamar,* including her captain too, were lost. Nine of the combined Naval Armed Guard detachments also perished.

At enormous risk to herself, the French corvette *Roselys,* under the command of Lieutenant de Vaisseau A. Bergeret, spent a hair-raising six and a half hours smelling her way around and into the minefield to pick up 134 survivors who otherwise certainly would have perished—a heroic action.

The trawlers *Lady Madeleine* and *St. Elstan,* with complete disregard for their own safety, also steamed about in the minefield for six and a half hours rescuing survivors, which included some from the cruiser *Edinburgh.* Between them they picked up 211 survivors, some of whom later died of exposure.

Graeme Ogden in *Lady Madeleine* wrote about his view of the disaster:

At 2040 I saw Niger *come steaming out of the gloom and take up a position about half a mile off our port bow. She made a visual signal to pass on to the Commodore to steer 270 degrees. While the signalman was busy calling up* the nearest ship, there was a heavy muffled explosion and, on looking round, I saw Niger had taken on a heavy list and was clearly in serious trouble. I made a hurried entry in the log:

HMS Niger torpedoed 2040.

Estimated position 66°3o′N 23°io/W.

I then took Lady M at full speed to Niger, broadcasting as I went that Niger was sinking. It was now a wild noisy evening but as Lady M plunged towards Niger I heard to starboard a quick series of heavy explosions. Through my glasses I could see merchant ships stopped and apparently sinking.

By the time we got to Niger, her bows were pointing skyward like a toy boat. The part of her bottom which was above water was unharmed. I thought at the time an acoustic torpedo must have blown her stern off. Some of her crew were clinging to the nearly perpendicular foredeck and others covered in black oil were hanging on to a Carley float some little way away. Within a minute, with a final hiss of escaping steam, she slid backwards into the hungry sea and disappeared before our astonished eyes.

The heavy sea running made it necessary to get to windward, thus making a lee and drifting on to the raft. Lady M's stern just missed the raft, but a heaving line was grabbed by the men hanging on to it and now began the struggle to get these men aboard. In those days we did not carry scrambling nets to help survivors climb inboard, and the task of rescuing those oil-covered sailors from the raft as it rose and fell in the heavy seas was heart-breaking.

I actually had my arm round Niger's oil-covered Australian first lieutenant when a wave swept him away never to be seen again. Apart from saving his life, if we had got this man aboard we might have solved the mystery of Niger's fate. As it was, the men we did get were engine-room ratings and very bemused as to what had hit their ship. As far as I know, all of her officers perished including Commander Cubison, her captain.

During this time the gunners on the merchant ships had opened fire indiscriminately, under the impression their ships had been attacked by U-boats on the surface or a German raider. Shells were whining in all directions and raising waterspouts as they pitched into the sea.

The convoy was now in a state of utter confusion. Nobody knew what was happening. Merchant ships were firing at one another, or anything they could see in the water, which was dotted with lifeboats from the sinking ships. Haiard and Hussar had disappeared into the fog with the leading ships and remained silent.

Graham Butcher, in St. Elstan, thought we had been attacked by U-boats on the surface using gun-fire and torpedoes. So did I, as apart from *having seen torpedoes I had seen a merchant ship which was stopped, hit fore and aft by shells. Conversation was difficult with* Roselys, *the French corvette. I believe Lieutenant Bergeret, her captain, thought we had run into a minefield, but I couldn't see how this could be possible.*

Firstly, because while on the same course the van of the convoy had steamed over the same ground unharmed, and, secondly, from the state of the sea, we were clearly within a few miles of the land. A quick look at the chart showed me that on my reckoning we were roughly on the reverse track PQ-16 had taken going north-east. Unless somebody had sown a new minefield while we had been away in Russia, the only one I knew of, and which was shown on our minefield chart, was miles away to the north-east in the Denmark Strait.

We began to pick up boat-loads of survivors from the American merchant ships. Unfortunately, they were mostly inexperienced seamen and terrified by the huge seas. They rowed for the sake of rowing, not looking where they were going or watching the treacherous waves. Some of them even pulled to my weather side and broke themselves to pieces against the ship.

I never expected to survive that night and the next morning. We spent hours and hours picking up and searching for survivors. Had we been in a minefield, we should have assuredly been blown up. If U-boats were about we were a sitting target, and if a raider was present we were helpless—our only chance was the fog.

Only HMS *Hussar* knew exactly where she was and where the minefield was; she led the remaining eleven ships out of danger and led the convoy to safety, arriving at Reykjavik on July 7. *Roselys* made port with U.S. Navy Catalina flying boats overhead that discouraged submarine attack. The remaining ships had arrived without further incident, and were already at anchor in Reykjavik harbor.

Although badly damaged by a mine, Captain Kelsoe believed that *Exterminator* was able to make port. He rejoined the convoy and entered in his logbook:

Monday, July 6th. First friendly plane appeared. Weather moderating and we are proceeding at 8 knots. The vessel was straining in No. 3 hold and was going down by the head. We requested a ship with pumps to be sent to our assistance. At 5:40 p.m. tug Empire Bascobel *was alongside and tried to pump out No. 2 hold. This proved unsuccessful and she cast off. Pilot on board at 11:35 p.m. At 11:45 p.m. tug* Empire Larch *made fast alongside, and we proceeded into inner harbor anchorage at Reykjavik.*

His entry for the next day read: "Tuesday, July 7th. At 12:45 p.m. ship anchored off Reykjavik. Salvage people came aboard and commenced work, taking on board pumps, etc."

Two members of *Exterminator*'s crew were convinced that celebration should not be delayed. The worst hazards of the voyage had been surmounted. A bottle they found in the engine room did not contain grain alcohol, though. It was a poisonous compound used in the cleaning of boiler tubes. The men died in intense agony after ingesting the poison.

After being rescued, Charles J. Hayes didn't wake up until arriving in Reykjavik.

I have no idea of the time that passed between the lifeboat and the hospital. I was told that we had been rescued by a Free French corvette. There were other survivors in the hospital, some in bed and some walking around.

I looked around for my Armed Guard shipmates from the Alamar. *There was just one other with me. He was the one who rode alone, standing in the lifeboat. He had no memory of that, although many others told of seeing him go by them while they were in the water.*

My partner, the gunner's mate, "Georgia" was gone, as were other mates, whose names and faces I still remember, but have not mentioned here.

Although it has been a lifetime since the Massmar *went down, I still remember those young men of the Navy Armed Guard—seventeen, eighteen, nineteen years old—who fought against an overwhelming enemy and survived only to lose their lives in an Allied minefield.*

However, in the poor conditions of storm and fog, we can understand the mistakes the Niger *made and sympathize with their loved ones over their loss. And we can never repay the courage of the French ship* Roselys, *who so bravely saved so many lives at great risk to their own.*

PQ-13's losses were four ships sunk, two badly damaged, and *Niger* gone from the escort.

Following PQ-17 and QP-13, the British Admiralty suspended convoys until September 1942. The growing demands on the Royal Navy in the Mediterranean and North Atlantic made it impossible it provide adequate protection for the Arctic convoys. Other measures would have to be put into place to keep some supplies moving to the USSR until September.

CHAPTER 7

TASK FORCES
July–September 1942

As the last survivors of PQ-17 limped into Murmansk, the British Admiralty was assessing the impact of the damage. News of the horrendous losses was first published in the United States, and the orders given by the British Admiralty were criticized by journalists and politicians in both the United States and the United Kingdom. Despite the public outcry, the Admiralty remained undaunted in its program to continue the convoys.

However, it was decided not to send more convoys across the Arctic Ocean until the days shortened. The uninterrupted daylight gave too great an advantage to the Luftwaffe, and no adequate anti-aircraft protection could be provided to defeat its attacks. Therefore the convoys were suspended until September.

This decision was reported to the Soviet High Command, which protested energetically. The USSR was hard pressed by the German offensive, and her troops had more need than ever of war materiel and munitions. In order not to leave the Soviets without at least some war-fighting materials, the Admiralty announced that it would send a special task force of transports consisting of warships. There was also the necessity of replenishing minesweepers, escort ships, and aircraft in Soviet ports with stores and ammunition that had been lost in PQ-17.

The question of providing better air reconnaissance and the possibility of bombing German surface ships also was raised. Air Marshal Sir Philip Joubert de la Ferté, commander-in-chief Coastal Command, pointed out that had torpedo aircraft been stationed in northern Russia, the Admiralty might not have considered it necessary to scatter convoy PQ-17. He obtained an agreement with the Soviet command to make arrangements for the temporary transfer of a balanced force of search and strike aircraft to Russian airfields during the period of the next convoy operation.

This force was comprised of four photographic reconnaissance Spitfires, No. 210 Squadron Catalina long-range seaplanes reconnaissance squadron, and Hampden torpedo-bomber squadrons No. 144 from the RAF and Royal Australian Air Force (RAAF) No. 455, all under the command of Group Captain F. L. Hopps, RAF.

The British destroyers *Marne*, *Martin*, *Middleton*, and *Blankney* were the first ships dispatched, sailing directly to Arkhangelsk, loaded with ammunition and new gun barrels, particularly for the anti-aircraft ships *Palomares* and *Pozarica*. They arrived on July 24.

A second task force, consisting of the U.S. cruiser *Tuscaloosa*, U.S. destroyers *Rodman* and *Emmons*, and HMS *Onslaught*, sailed from Glasgow on August 13. *Tuscaloosa* carried 300 tons of ammunition, explosives, radar parts, medical supplies, dehydrated foods, and thirty-six torpedoes. Each destroyer carried 20 tons of aircraft parts and 19 tons of mixed cargo. Seven British naval officers, three RAF officers, and 160 other passengers sailed with the three ships.

A German reconnaissance plane sighted the group on the evening of August 20 and apparently reported its position. The convoy's course was changed, and poor visibility helped concealment. *Tuscaloosa* broke radio silence to report the sighting to Commander in Chief Home Fleet, hoping that this would be interpreted by the enemy as routine patrol procedure.

And, as Captain Norman C. Gillette, commanding officer of *Tuscaloosa*, remarked, "God sent a fog," which concealed the ships for the rest of this anxious voyage. Two British and one Soviet destroyer met the group outside Kola Inlet and escorted them into Vaenga Bay on August 23. Their arrival had been timed to allow for unloading and fueling during a time of day when the Luftwaffe typically was grounded.

Arrangements had been made by local Soviet authorities and British liaison officers for discharging cargo, and all hands turned to with a will to get their lethal load on the beach. This was accomplished by 0700 hours the next day, August 24. *Tuscaloosa*, *Rodman*, and *Emmons*, plus the British destroyers *Marne*, *Martin*, and *Onslaught*, sailed that morning at 0749 with 240 PQ-17 survivors on board *Tuscaloosa* and an additional 300 men, including four Russian diplomats, in the five destroyers. Among the survivors on *Marne* were men from *Edinburgh* and *Gossamer*.

The Kriegsmarine command credited its successful operation against PQ-17 to the "exemplary cooperation between aircraft and U-boats," the results being in every way commensurate with those expected from the surface warships. It was decided in the future not to employ surface ships in attacks on the loaded PQ convoys, but rather to use them for attacking the returning QP convoys in the Barents Sea, which they could do with a minimum of risk. In addition to destroying the major Allied convoys, the Kriegsmarine command hoped to disrupt Soviet shipping in the Arctic that summer.

During August, two operations were set in motion to accomplish this. Operation *Unternehmen* (*Wunderland* [Land of Miracles]) was the most ambitious, employing the battlecruiser *Admiral Scheer* along with *U-209* and *U-601*. *Wunderland* was considered a preliminary stage for establishing control over the western Arctic. The second, Operation *Zar*, consisted of extensive mine-laying to be carried out by *Ulm*.

Preliminary moves of Operation *Wunderland* began three weeks before *Scheer* left Narvik. The moves were conducted by *U-601* and *U-209*, with primary attention focused on Belushya Guba, an administrative center located in southwest Novaya Zemlya, a move designed to distract the Soviets from *Admiral Scheer*'s raid in the Kara Sea.

The first action occurred on July 27, when *U-601*, under Kapitänleutnant Peter-Ottmar Grau, attacked the town of Malye Karmakuly near Belushya Bay and shelled two anchored seaplanes and three living and two storage huts.

I. P. Mazuruk piloted one of the Soviet seaplanes. He and his crew had spent a long day searching for survivors of PQ-17. They'd spent twenty-four hours flying, but failed to find anything. Utterly exhausted, they planned to rest and refuel overnight before setting out again. There wasn't enough room for everyone to sleep ashore, so the aircraft commander, Kozlov, and mechanic, Serov Kosuhin, stayed overnight in the plane while Mazuruk, the navigator Zhukov, and copilot and radio operator Syrokvasha Cholyshev made themselves comfortable in one of the huts. Later, Mazuruk recalled that evening in an interview:

> We'd started to settle in when Zhukov said: "Maybe everyone's found already and we'll find nobody" as he pulled off his boots.
>
> "Anyway, we will seek, as long as possible," I replied. "Tomorrow we'll go once more over the coast. Maybe someone landed ashore."

While the men bantered back and forth, Grau readied U-601's gun crew for the attack. For half an hour, Grau carefully observed the structures on the shore and the seaplane through the U-boat's periscope. Moving to within 2,000 yards of the shore, Grau took another look to ensure there were no threats to the U-boat. Seeing none, he surfaced and prepared to attack.

Mazuruk had just fallen asleep when a shell hit the window under which he was sleeping, splashing the airman with small fragments of glass. The embossed frame flew over his head and hit the opposite wall of the house. Stunned, Mazuruk jumped up and looked out the broken window. Mazuruk continued his story:

> The first thing I saw was a flaming torch, an aircraft and a submarine, sitting on the mirror surface of the bay. At the submarine's bow, gunners were busy reloading and an officer on the bridge in a fur jacket showing his gunners where to fire.
>
> Kozlov jumped from the burning plane and furiously swam to shore.
>
> Not paying more attention to the aircraft, the submarine officer waved his hand toward the shore, and immediately following a projectile hit the roof of a family hut. The roof of the hut, as if projected from below by an unknown force, jumped up and collapsed on the walls of the building. Immediately it caught fire from the barrack's oven. From the ruins half-dressed men jumped out and, bending down, and fled into the interior of the island under cover of the rocky spurs.
>
> I and my comrades ran out of the hut, and as soon as we got clear, it was smashed into splinters by a projectile.
>
> After firing more shots the gunners one by one dropped in the conning-tower hatch and the boat slowly sank into the water.
>
> Shivering from the cold and the shock of the shelling, people were returning to the village. Several people were injured, the plane burned with mechanic Serov trapped inside. The Ice Station was half destroyed.

Grau was satisfied and thought that the work was well started. Without expending a single torpedo, he destroyed most of the Soviet polar station and burned a seaplane.

On the night of August 1, Grau received orders to move north toward Cape Desire and be prepared to raid the Kara Sea. This order was the beginning of Operation *Wunderland*. But before heading north, Grau decided to inspect the area one more time. Through the periscope, he saw the white, rocky, snow-capped mountains of Novaya Zemlya, beaches, rugged coves, and numerous bays. All previous attempts to get there had been thwarted by Soviet patrols, a minefield, and an antisubmarine net.

Grau turned the periscope without regret from the shoreline toward the sea and sighted an unescorted Soviet ship approaching the island. At 0023 hours, Grau fired a single torpedo, which hit and the vessel started to sink.

His target was *Krestyanin* (Master A. G. Nikolaev). Loaded with coal, she was approaching Belushya Guba Bay (Beluga Whale Island) when the torpedo hit. She sunk in three minutes; five sailors and two passengers died in the attack. The survivors abandoned ship in two lifeboats and were questioned by the Germans, who gave them the direction to the shore.

F. Stepanov, First Lieutenant of *Krestyanin* (Farmer), wrote about the sinking in his memoirs:

Krestyanin *was without escort. The short distance from Naryan-Mar to Belushya gave rise to the illusion that the area was safe since there hadn't been any attacks against our ships.*

My first thought after the explosion was of our ship's carpenter Gennady Lebedev and his wife Tase. The torpedo struck their cabin.

The Boatswain's Mate Lebedev, rushed to a lifeboat and with the help of three sailors, quickly lowered it overboard. I was in the second boat that got away before the ship sank.

Sadly Engineering Officer Pavel Barabkin didn't have time to get out of the engine room. Sending up a young fireman, Lenya Baukova, Barabkin apparently tried to run pumps to bail out the engine room, but there wasn't enough time, and he went down with the ship.

The two boats filled with survivors remained near where our ship went down, searching for other survivors, but in vain. Tase was not among them. Neither was the Orderly Nikitichna Mezdrikovoy Olga, an elderly woman of fifty-three years nor was twenty-year old Ghali Kambuznitsy Bestuzhev.

Suddenly the surface began to seethe and the submarine conning tower with the number of U-601 soon appeared.

When the water subsided on the bridge officer appeared in a fur jacket. For several minutes he looked at the people in the boat, and then in pretty clear Russian said:

"What is the name of the ship? What cargo?"

"Farmer. Arkhangelsk. Went in ballast," I yelled, although I was aware that the Germans could see perfectly that the ship was loaded.

The German still for a moment looked at the sailors and, choosing his words carefully, said: "Sorry. It's a pity we spent torpedoes."

Then, not paying more attention to the remaining people in the stormy sea, the U-boat captain descended into the bowels of the boat, closed the hatch, and submerged.

The wind grew stronger and, worst of all it was blowing from the shore, taking the crippled boat out to sea. Sailors piled on top of the oars, but rowing only warmed the people and the boats drifted westward. Yet the sailors did not give up. Stronger men replaced the feeble. The storm didn't grow stronger; nor did it subside, although the wind direction changed a bit.

On the second day, the fireman Lenya Baucom died, although there were older and weaker survivors than him. For some reason he lost his strength. Perhaps he had a cold after having jumped out of the boiler room to chill stuffy air. Who knows why, since we didn't have a doctor among us.

For over two days we fought wind and waves, fighting to stay near the shore. Finally the day came when we were able to reach Novaya Zemlya. The boats, grinding their bottoms along the rocky shingle, got close enough for the people to jump overboard and make onto the beach. However, final salvation was far away.

We landed on the desert shore and for many miles around there was no shelter. For no particular reason we decided to move along the coast to the south.

Walking was a little easier than rowing. The road was blocked by piles of rocks, sometimes descending to the water's edge, narrow winding bays, far from crashing into the shore. We were forced to deviate from the straight path. Sharp rocks tore our shoes, and bruised our bodies.

The Novaya Zemlya bird rookeries were far apart, and the food from them now was not enough—there were no eggs in the nests, and we couldn't catch the larger chicks with our bare hands.

The starving, ragged, hard frozen survivors marched to the south. They were brave in a battle; they did not give up now. Courage and perseverance won.

I went ahead, and climbing up to the next rock, saw in the distance, at the foot of the mountains two fishermen huts. Above one of them rose smoke. Happily smiling, I whispered "We live" then sat down on cold stone, waiting for my friends.

After sinking *Krestyanin*, *U-601* continued its patrol and on August 8 entered Kara Sea to gather information about Soviet shipping as well as ice and weather conditions. She took up a key position off the north point of Novaya Zemlya island.

After unsuccessful hunting in Kara Gate and Ugorski Shar Straits, *U-209* (Kapitänleutnant Heinrich Brodda) at last got her chance to leave a mark on the Arctic Naval War. This mark was destined to be exceptionally gruesome. On August 16, an NKVD (Soviet Secret Police) representative in Chabarovo, a small port on the south shore of Ugorsky Shar Strait, authorized the departure of two ocean tugs, *Komsomolets* and *Nord*, which were to tow barge *P 4*, lighter *Sh-500*, and the tug *Komiles*, which had a malfunctioning engine, to Naryan-Mar.

The *Sh-500* carried construction materials, but the *P 4* had 328 construction crewmen and workers of the Pechora port, Narjan-Mar, some of whom were probably political prisoners from Norilskstroi Gulag concentration camps. According to long-standing practice, the NKVD considered itself a separate and independent power inside the state. As such, the Soviet Secret Police never bothered to inform White Sea Naval Command about their departure, and as a result, the convoy left harbor unescorted, even though minesweepers *T-54* and *T-62* were available in Chabarovo.

As noted in *All World Wars: Operation Wunderland*, at 0700 hours the next day, two miles from the north shore of Matveev Island, near the western entrance to Ugorski Shar Strait, Brodda spotted *Komsomolets* with *P 4* in tow, behind her was *Nord* with *Komiles* and *Sh-500*.

Brodda ordered *U-209* to surface and shell P 4. The shells ignited fires that engulfed the barge, sparking chaos. Inmates were released from the hold by the guards, and everyone began jumping overboard to escape the flames. While *U-209* shelled P 4, *Komsomolets* cast off the towline and attempted to leave the area while her radioman, Kozhevina, reported the attack to Chabarovo.

Brodda saw *Komsomolets*'s attempted escape and ordered his gun crew to fire on the tug. After several direct hits, this tug, too, caught fire and began to sink. Brodda was certain that *Komsomolets* was doomed and returned to finish off *P 4*.

At 0720, after two failed attempts to torpedo the burning *P 4*, *U-209* turned to pursue *Nord*. In the meantime, *Nord* was able to bring *Komiles* and *Sh-500* closer to the shore of Matveyev Island, where she cast off the towline and left in the direction of Ugorski Shar. At 0800 hours, *U-209* shelled *Komiles*, whose crew abandoned ship and were able to reach the safety of the shore.

Ten minutes later came *Sh-500*'s turn. At 0810 hours, Brodda shelled *Sh-500*. After several hits, the cargo lighter slowly went down.

P 4 was still burning when *U-209* moved in to finish the job. Almost out of ammunition, Brodda launched a torpedo which smashed into the barge's exposed side, sinking it quickly. Brodda noticed that one ship escaped. Concerned that it had sent out an alarm, he headed north to the shores on the Novaya Zemlya.

As soon as the men stationed at Chabarovo learned about the massacre on Matveyev Island, minesweepers were dispatched to pick up survivors. At 1140 hours, *T-54* and *T-62* met *Nord*, which turned back and joined the rescue force. Four hours later, the ships picked up *Komiles*'s survivors and also found *Komsomolets*, which eventually reached the island with only five of the original nineteen crewmembers on board still alive. From the total amount of 328 men on board *P 4*, only twenty-three were rescued. Not one of the construction workers, inmates, or guards from *P 4* survived the ordeal, and 305 people remain forever at the bottom of the Pechora Sea.

On August 19, *U-209* attempted to enter Belushya Guba, but was spotted by the motorboat *Poliarny* and two Soviet minesweepers, *T-39* and *T-58*. A firefight promptly erupted. Neither side sustained any damage, but with so much opposition in the area, *U-209* headed for quieter waters.

As U-boats wreaked havoc in the Kara Sea, Luftwaffe reconnaissance planes detected two convoys on August 15. Consisting of more than fifty ships in total, the convoys had left Arkhangelsk a week before and turned to the east to Belushya Guba, heading toward the Vilkitsky Strait. Both convoys were accompanied by almost all the icebreakers the Soviet Chief Administrator of the Northern Sea Route had at his disposal.

Admiral Scheer, commanded by Wilhelm Meendsen-Bohlken, set out from Narvik to the Barents Sea on August 16. Because so much depended on the accurate decoding of Soviet radio traffic, *Admiral Scheer*'s crew was joined by a Kriegsmarine *Funkaufklärung* (radio intelligence) team, most of whom spoke fluent Russian.

Weather conditions remained a major concern, and German planners were careful to take this into consideration. In addition to submarines and a network of stations stretching from Spitzbergen to Novaya Zemlya and even to the mouth of Lena River, five BV-138s were to patrol along the most important shipping routes.

An ice conditions report, transmitted by *U-601* to Kriegsmarine headquarters in Narvik on August 15, looked promising. The Germans decided to proceed with Operation *Wunderland*. At 1500 hours on August 16, *Admiral Scheer*, accompanied by destroyers *Z-16 Friedrich Eckoldt, Z-15 Erich Steinbrinck*, and *Z-4 Richard Beitzen*, left anchorage in Ofotfjord, Norway. Reaching Bear Island, approximately 400 nautical miles northwest of Murmansk and on the main Arctic convoy route in complete radio silence, Meendsen-Bohlken parted with his escort and proceeded eastward at full speed.

Foggy, cloudy weather and poor visibility favored *Scheer*'s run across the Barents Sea. On the evening of August 18, *Scheer* entered the Kara Sea and lowered her Arado seaplane on the water for a reconnaissance flight. After nine days of searching fruitlessly for Soviet convoys, *Scheer*'s lookouts sighted an enemy ship at 1100 hours on August 25. It turned out to be the old Soviet icebreaker *Alexander Sibiryakov*

An Arctic workhorse, *Alexander Sibiryakov* was one of the most well-known ships to sail along the Northern Sea Route. After the start of the war, *Sibiryakov* was armed with two 76-mm naval guns, two 45-mm guns, and two 20-mm anti-aircraft Oerlikons, and her crew was joined by thirty-two gunners. During the first year of the war, *Sibiryakov* was employed mostly in the White Sea carrying troops, artillery shells, and food rations and evacuating the wounded.

On August 23, *Sibiryakov*'s captain Anatoly Kacharava was ordered to deliver supplies for the weather stations on Severnaya Zemlia near the Taymyr Peninsula across the Vilkitsky Strait between the Kara and Laptev Seas. The crew and construction materials also were to be delivered for the new planned station on Cape Molotov. *Sibiryakov* was loaded with 350 tons of supplies for the weather station and a large cargo boat known locally as a *kungas* used for delivering supplies to shore. In addition, three hundred barrels of gasoline fuel were stored on deck. *Sibiryakov* had a crew of 47 sailors, 32 gunners, and 23 civilians (mostly personnel for the weather stations), along with two officers of the White Sea Naval Command in charge, for 104 in total.

By midday on August 25, *Sibiryakov*, on course to Cape Olovianny on Severnaya Zemlia, approached three islands, Belukha, Centralny, and Dolgy, which already had become visible on the horizon in the clear and cold Arctic air. At 1317 hours, as the crew was going to have lunch, Senior Signalman Alexeyev reported that he observed smoke from an unknown ship. Kacharava ordered his radioman Sharshavin to request identification.

Three messages were sent, but *Scheer* didn't reply. "Large capital ship," reported Alexeyev. "Yes, battleship or cruiser," replied Kacharava, observing the ship with his binoculars. "Here goes the bridge, massive gun turrets ... Emergency message to Dikson in clear: 'Battleship near Belukha Island, country of origin is unknown.'" Kacharava was puzzled: there was no reason to sail in friendly waters without a flag.

On board *Admiral Scheer*, Meendsen-Bohlken faced a difficult dilemma. He could open fire immediately and quickly sink the old icebreaker, but with *Arado* grounded due to a lack of fuel, he also desperately needed information from the Soviets about ice conditions and the convoys' movements.

Scheer turned in the direction of the icebreaker, hoisted an American flag, and identified herself as *Tuscaloosa*. But the trick didn't work. Due to a German signal mistake, *Sibiryakov* signalmen read the name of the ship not as *Tuscaloosa*, but as the Japanese-sounding *Siyasima*.

Even if Alexeyev had got the name right, Kacharava knew that the American cruiser *Tuscaloosa* occasionally visited the Barents Sea and that, in fact, it entered Kola Bight in the evening hours of August 23 and left Murmansk on the following day. It was physically impossible for the American cruiser to be near Belushya Island on August 25, 1,300 miles from Murmansk.

Kacharava realized the approaching ship could only be German and ordered course to be set for Belushya Island. He then ordered a general alarm. Guns were quickly prepared for action as the firefighting crew connected water hoses and ship medics deployed a makeshift hospital to treat wounded.

At 1338 hours, Kacharava ordered his radioman to send a message in clear to Northern Sea Route Command in Port Dikson that an unknown battlecruiser had hoisted an American flag and was approaching fast. Dikson replied immediately that there were no American or Japanese ships in the area and that the ship in question could only be an enemy's raider, confirming Kacharava's suspicions. *Sibiryakov* was instructed to act according to standing battle orders.

The radio team on board *Scheer* was carefully monitoring radio messages from *Sibiryakov* and understood at once that their disguise hadn't worked. They demanded the Soviet ship stop radio transmission immediately. Receiving no reply, *Scheer* hoisted the Kriegsmarine battle flag and ordered *Sibiryakov* to stop her engine.

Sibiryakov was in a desperate situation. Belushya Island was still 10 miles away, and it would take the icebreaker more than an hour to reach it. At the same time, the distance between the ships was too large for *Sibiryakov*'s 76-mm guns to be effective.

Kacharava and his crew decided to fight. He sent a message to Port Dikson: "Enemy ship is closing on us, we will fight," followed shortly by one more message: "Shooting has started," and a last message, several minutes later: "… continue to fight …"

The last two messages were not received by Dikson because *Scheer*'s powerful radio transmitter jammed all frequencies.

"Open fire," Kacharava ordered his gunnery officer Nikiforenko. *Sibiryakov*'s guns fired, but the distance was too great and the shots fell short of the German battlecruiser.

Nikiforenko saw through his rangefinder that the cruiser's dreaded 280-mm guns began to move. Kacharava ordered: "Smoke screen, helm to port, set course for Belushya Island, full ahead!"

The first German salvo slightly overshot the target, the close explosions shaking the ship. The phone line between the bridge and the guns was broken. Splinters cut down the fore-top-mast and destroyed the radio antenna.

At 1353 hours, *Scheer*'s next salvo landed right on target: a 305-kilogram shell struck the gun platform on the stern. The explosion was enormous. Kacharava saw pieces of boxes, trunks, boats, and spent shell cartridges flying high through the air. The stern gun was destroyed, its crew killed in the blast.

A third salvo straddled the icebreaker, this time hitting the bow. Hot splinters pierced gasoline barrels and many exploded, quickly spreading fire. Kacharava was heavily wounded and fell unconscious, his arm heavily damaged and bleeding.

The fourth salvo sealed *Sibiryakov*'s fate. Shells tore through the deck and exploded below, damaging the boiler and ripping gaping holes in the hulk. *Sibiryakov*'s engine went silent. At 1405, second in command Lieutenant Elimelach ordered everyone to abandon ship and launched the only undamaged lifeboat. But not everyone heard or followed this order. Some were left on board or were unwilling or unable to leave the ship, wounded or cut off by the wall of fire from the burning barrels of fuel.

An enormous column of smoke completely obscured the ship. Closing in on her victim, *Scheer* waited more than twenty minutes for the flames to begin to subside. *Sibiryakov* was visibly low in the water, but was refusing to sink. Miraculously, her last gun continued firing. Meendsen-Bohlken decided to deliver a *coup de grâce* and at 1428 ordered a final salvo from point-blank range, which at last silenced *Sibiryakov*. The valiant ship finally sank at 1500 hours.

Before the battle began, Kacharava ordered his chief engineer, Bochurko, to scuttle the ship in order to prevent the Germans from searching and seizing the icebreaker. Receiving word that Kacharava had died (a false rumor) and that a German launch was approaching, Bochurko decided to act and descended into the bowels of the ship, never to be seen again.

Meanwhile, still hoping to get information they needed, the Germans decided to capture survivors and lowered the launch, which quickly approached *Sibiryakov*'s lifeboat as it carried Soviet survivors. Stoker Matveyev, who was in the boat, threw an axe at a German officer and was shot on the spot.

German sources reported that some sailors refused to be rescued, instead jumping overboard. They were left behind in the ice-cold water, doomed for death. Several Germans jumped into the captured lifeboat and beat up survivors with gun butts, forcing them to board the German launch. Of the compliment of 104, the Germans picked up twenty-two survivors, including the wounded and unconscious Kacharava, radioman Sharshavin, and Zolotov, the head of the planned weather station on Severnaya Zemlia.

Meendsen-Bohlken was disappointed. *Sibiryakov* made *Scheer*'s presence in the Arctic known. The ensuing skirmish had warned the Soviets in the most deadly manner about the presence of the Germans, and the convoys certainly would react to the danger. Captured crewmembers could tell their captors only the name and destination of the ship. Because *Sibiryakov* was not part of any convoy, the Germans were unable to obtain any new information about other ships.

Meanwhile, the wounded Kacharava remained unconscious. The Germans assumed he was a regular crewmember; his true identity was only revealed much later. Also, as it turned out, Zolotov, the unlucky head of the polar station, was a geologist, not a meteorologist, and he knew little about the general conditions of the weather or the ice in the area. Nor was he aware of the current forecast, information that would be of the most value to the Germans.

At 1545 hours, August 25, the Germans intercepted a radio signal from the Soviets' Western Sector Command Headquarters of the Northern Sea Route Main Directorate, warning that an enemy auxiliary cruiser was operating in the Kara Sea. Soon *Scheer*'s lookouts spotted a Soviet boat, apparently looking for *Sibiryakov*, which at that time didn't notice the Germans. But with increasing Soviet naval activity, it was time for *Scheer* to leave the area.

Even after being discovered, Meendsen-Bohlken still stubbornly hoped to meet Soviet convoys near Cape Zhelaniya. But he received orders to turn northwest, into the empty Kara Sea. During the night, *Scheer*'s lookouts saw only the occasional ice field, and by the morning hours of August 26, Meendsen-Bohlken decided that because the element of surprise had been lost, he would be unable to intercept any Soviet ships in the open sea.

A more promising idea was to attack a port. There Meendsen-Bohlken not only could find merchant ships at anchor, but he also could capture senior commanders, enemy headquarters with documentation about convoy movements, detailed maps of the area, weather forecasts, naval codes, and other troves of information.

Meendsen-Bohlken could choose between two ports, both of which were among the most important centers of the Northern Sea Route in the Kara Sea: Amderma and Dikson Island. The Germans erroneously believed that Amderma was the key center for unloading Allied convoys because of the constant Luftwaffe bombing sorties against Murmansk. Meendsen-Bohlken knew, though, that if that were true, Amderma, located on the southwest coast, most likely would be well protected by shore batteries. In addition, the port was situated uncomfortably close to Soviet naval and air bases.

The remote Port Dikson looked like a much more promising target. Careful analysis of Soviet radio traffic during *Sibiryakov*'s ordeal indicated that Dikson functioned as a hub in the Arctic support network, transmitting orders to other ports and ships, and, because of the amount and type of radio communications it was most likely Western Sector Command Headquarters. If Port Dikson could be damaged or destroyed by heavy bombardment and searched by a landing party for intelligence information, the main aim of the Operation *Wunderland*—suppressing navigation along the Northern Sea route—could still be attained.

Unknown to the Germans was that in July 1941, the head of the Soviet shipping company Glavnoe Upravlenie Severnogo Morskogo Puti (GUSMP), Ivan Papanin, contacted Admiral Nikolai G. Kuznetsov and asked to reinforce Dikson defenses with "some guns." Papanin, an NKVD associate, had developed personal connections with Stalin and military brass and was able to submit his requests directly to Soviet leaders. Thus, Port Dikson's defenses were enforced with two batteries: #226 Naval with two 130-mm guns, and #246 anti-aircraft with two 45-mm guns. Later, another heavy battery, #569 equipped with two heavy 152-mm siege guns forged in 1910.

Dikson's senior officers met on board the *Dezhnev* during the evening hours of August 26 to discuss the port's defense. They decided to form two groups of local militia under the leadership of the Dikson polar station chiefs, Sidorin and Statov. Women and children were to be transported to a small hunters' settlement on River Lembrovka. GUSMP secret documents were to be stored there as well and prepared for burning on short notice.

Meanwhile, Lieutenant Kornyakov, commander of the battery #569 at Port Dikson, acting on his own initiative, ordered the 152-mm shells for his guns unloaded from the barge and selected volunteers for the gun crews from local longshoremen. Key commanding figures of the defense, Commissar Babintsev from the White Sea Naval Group and Senior Lieutenant Gidulianov, captain of SKR-*19*, decided to strengthen port defenses. Just before midnight, these two men left port on a motorboat to check the shoreline of Cape Kretchatik on Dikson Island to determine the best place to install 130-mm batteries. Their boat was accompanied by the port tug *Molokov* towing a barge carrying both the 130-mm guns and ammunition.

Dezhnev had the same light armament as *Sibiryakov* of four 76-mm guns, four 45-mm guns, and four 20-mm Oerlikons aircraft guns, none of which was remotely effective enough to fight a battlecruiser. Naval forces were not markedly enhanced when, later that evening, Port Dikson defenses were joined by the merchant ship *Revolutionary*, under the command of Captain Panfilov, of North Sea Route command. *Revolutionary* was armed with one 76-mm gun, one 45-mm gun, and two anti-aircraft Oerlikons, and she was carrying a cargo of timber. To make matters even worse, the third and the last vessel in Port Dikson was the unarmed cargo ship *Kara*, loaded with several hundred tons of ammonal, a powerful explosive used for mining and creating canals of clear water in the ice fields.

At 0105 hours on August 27, militia lookouts near the former position of gun battery #226 in the northwestern corner of Port Dikson caught a glimpse of the dark silhouette of *Admiral Scheer* moving to the south along the western shore of the island. The lookouts immediately contacted Dikson. An alarm was sounded, and the Port Dikson radio station began transmitting in clear the frightening news of the impending attack.

After the enemy's approach was reported, two lookouts picked up the only available rifle with a single 5-cartridge clip. They ran along the shore, keeping *Scheer* in sight and prepared to open fire on a possible German landing party. Indeed, if Meendsen-Bohlken had known that Dikson Island, GUSMP headquarters, and its radio station were not protected by any naval guns from the west, his landing party could easily have captured the island. Instead he chose to attack Dikson Island, Port Dikson on the mainland, and ships in the inner harbor simultaneously.

Dezhnev, standing near Conus Island coal terminal in the middle of the inner harbor, under command of Gidulianov's second in command, Lieutenant Krotov, began to move away from the terminal. But there wasn't enough time to take up a safer position under the protection of the shore. In twenty-five minutes, *Scheer* passed Skuratov navigation station at the entrance to the south harbor, 4.5 miles from the port.

Meendsen-Bohlken decided to take Dikson Island with a well-armed, 180-man landing party, supported by 280-mm and 150-mm naval guns. In order to minimize the landing party boats' exposure to the Soviet fire, *Scheer* had to launch landing operations as close to the GUSMP center as possible and needed to suppress any Soviet artillery. He foresaw no serious opposition, at most anticipating some disorganized and inaccurate fire from one or two merchant ships, several light guns of shore defenses, and counterattacks from the Port Dikson garrison, which, according to their estimates, consisted of the half-company (fifty to sixty soldiers) of NKVD border guards troops armed with rifles and, perhaps, a few machine guns.

In fact, the garrison also had two 37-mm antitank guns, one 76-mm anti-aircraft gun, and a 75-mm field howitzer. Border guards and approximately three hundred local militia armed with rifles, carbines, and hunting guns patrolled the port. But light artillery and hunting guns would not be enough to survive for long under the 280-mm guns firing at point-blank range.

Since Port Dikson already started hectic radio transmissions, the Germans knew they had lost the element of surprise and the shock effect of the heavy naval bombardment.

Meanwhile *Dezhnev* at last left the coal terminal, and Krotov changed speed from slow to full ahead, turning his ship toward the enemy. He decided to attack *Scheer*'s portside. If *Dezhnev* was damaged, he figured, the ship could be sunk between Pirozhok Island and the Vega shallows, blocking the entrance to the inner harbor. As *Dezhnev* passed the pier, her crewmen saw artillery crews and volunteer longshoremen trying to manually maneuver the heavy, unwieldy artillery pieces into firing position on the dock.

As *Scheer* closed to within 4 miles, Krotov, who wanted to buy as much time as possible, ordered his signalmen to send a message to *Scheer* asking her to identify herself. This time the Germans didn't try the "Tuscaloosa routine" again. As soon as *Scheer*'s fire control got visuals on the ships in the port, the German battlecruiser opened fire.

Dezhnev's bow guns fired back and then Krotov turned slightly to port to open *Scheer* for the guns on the stern. Gunners targeted not the impenetrable steel hulk, but her bridge, fo'c'sle, and rangefinders. It was their only chance to inflict at least some damage. They claimed later that they observed several bright flashes from hits on the battlecruiser's superstructure, but German sources don't mention any.

Soon *Dezhnev* was buffeted by two salvos. She then was hit by a third, between the third and fourth cargo holds. At first the Germans used armor-piercing shells, which passed almost harmlessly through *Dezhnev*'s hull, but the German gunners soon understood their mistake and switched to the high-explosive shells. Heavy shells damaged *Dezhnev*'s rangefinder, both 76-mm guns, and a heavy machine gun. Splinters ripped open a number of underwater holes; the biggest, found later in the hulk, was two square feet. Splinters also produced some leaks in the coal storage compartment, which were inaccessible for quick repairs. Six members of the crew were killed instantly from the blasts. One more died later the same day, and twenty sailors were wounded.

Dezhnev put up a smoke screen and started to move slowly to the entrance of Samoletnaya Bay, which provided better protection from the murderous fire of the heavy naval guns. At 0146 hours, *Dezhnev* discontinued the battle. She already had taken on tons of water, and her captain, Gidulianov, was determined to prevent capsizing. But he soon faced another problem. Eight minutes later, the ship ran aground and became a stationary target with almost all her armament out of action. The damage control party later reported that it would take at least three hours to cover all holes and pump the water out.

With *Dezhnev* out of the picture, *Scheer* concentrated her fire on *Revolutionary*, which was barely visible through the smoke screen. In just five minutes, *Revolutionary* took three hits which started fires on the deck and wooden bridge, damaged several compartments inside the ship, and destroyed the steam line and anchor winch, preventing the ship from weighing the anchor and making her an easy target.

Luckily for the defenders, *Scheer* had yet to observe the third ship, *Kara*, heavily laden with explosives and invisible behind the protection of the rocky shore and *Dezhnev*'s smoke screen. Even one well-placed shell would spark a huge explosion and completely obliterate the port and defense forces. That hadn't happened yet, but *Kara*'s discovery was only a matter of time.

In mere minutes, the Soviets had found themselves on the verge of complete annihilation. All their naval forces were out of action, and it seemed nothing stood between the German landing party and the command center of the Northern Sea Route.

In this crucial moment of Operation *Wunderland*, Kornyakov's 152-mm guns opened fire. No hits were registered, but high columns of sea water rose in the air close to *Scheer*.

According to *All World Wars*, Kornyakov had positioned his guns not on the pier itself, where they would be visible against the water, but near where the pier connected to the shore, making the guns much less visible. Because of this position, with its dark, rocky background, along with the murky haze of the late summer Arctic night, fog, and *Dezhnev*'s smoke screen, no one on board *Scheer* knew how many guns the Soviets had or where they were located.

Nor did Meendsen-Bohlken know that he was dealing with vintage siege guns of pre-World War I design or that they were standing in the open without any camouflage, firing blindly through the smoke and fog without any rangefinders or any observation posts. He didn't know that the guns were serviced by poorly trained crews and untrained, though enthusiastic, volunteers under the command of an inexperienced lieutenant from backwater Arctic shore defenses.

But Meendsen-Bohlken had been well aware of the fate of the heavy cruiser *Blucher*, which was sunk by the antiquated Norwegian gun battery in Oslo-Fjord on April 9, 1940. He also knew about the disastrous end of the battleship *Bismarck*, which, in May 1941, received a hit in the fuel tank and later another hit in the steering compartment, enough for the British to close in for the kill. He thought that if *Scheer* attempted to move closer, sooner or later she could be hit and that any damage, even minor, in the middle of the inhospitable Arctic might prove fatal.

The main problem for Kornyakov, in the meantime, was not *Scheer*'s return fire, but how to handle the enormous recoil at unprepared artillery positions. The guns' spades were sliding on a slippery surface, and, weighing in at almost 8 metric tons, the artillery pieces were being thrown by recoil so far back that crews had to use a small port truck on the pier to return the guns into position. Later, the men used logs to block the spades and the rate of firing increased.

At 0146 hours, after battery #569 fired forty shells, Meendsen-Bohlken decided to disengage. After laying a smoke screen, *Scheer* disappeared behind Cape Anvil four minutes later. But Meendsen-Bohlken was still certain that even now, when the enemy's heavy artillery remained unsuppressed and the landing part of the operation had to be aborted, his trump card—accurate fire—could still overcome the Soviet defenses, or at least inflict irreparable damage on the port.

Moving north along the shoreline of Dikson Island, from 0214 to 0219 hours, *Scheer* shelled the Great Bear Island weather station. Kornyakov's battery again opened fire, aiming at the sounds of *Scheer*'s guns and the reddish glare of distant salvos, but didn't hit anything.

Scheer stopped firing to assess inflicted damage to the port infrastructure. Meendsen-Bohlken apparently was satisfied with the report: the oil depot and coal storage on Conus Island were burning fiercely, several radio masts were cut by splinters or toppled over, and the radio center and its power station were ablaze, as were several buildings in the settlement.

During the bombardment, Meendsen-Bohlken received reports that 20 percent of the ammunition on board the *Scheer* had been expended. Fire from the Soviet 152-mm battery continued, and he at last decided to lay a smoke screen once again and disengage rather than risk wasting precious ammunition. *Scheer* turned sharply starboard and disappeared in the vastness of Kara Sea. The battle for Port Dikson was over.

The Germans considered the battle a success. Two ships were heavily hit, one of which ran aground; port installations were destroyed; oil storage was burning; and the radio center and weather station on the Great Bear Island had been shelled into oblivion. It looked like the hub of the Northern Sea Route was put out of action for a long time. In addition to optimistic observation reports, the Germans soon intercepted a Soviet message that the Soviet ship *Valerian Kuibyshev* was lost. Meendsen-Bohlken assumed that she was on the Port Dikson anchorage as well, though in reality *Kuibyshev* was sunk on August 24 by *U-601* to the northwest of Dikson. The ship's crew perished and it was two weeks before the wreck was found.

In fact, the permanent damage inflicted by the bombardment was negligible. The port was not taken, and no vital information about the Northern Sea Route was captured. Steel radio masts were promptly fixed and erected, the power station remained intact since shells hit only barrels with spent oil stored nearby, and the fires on Conus Island were soon extinguished. Port Dikson resumed regular transmissions in just two days, even before *Scheer* reached Narvik.

Revolutionary was repaired in three days, *Dezhnev* in six. Miraculously, except for seven sailors aboard *Dezhnev*, nobody else was killed by *Scheer*'s shells. The icebreakers *Litke* and *Taimyr* were sent to Port Dudinka on the Enisei River and in three days returned with enough fuel to supply Port Dikson for the next Arctic convoy.

Scheer's retreat was uneventful. At 2000 hours on August 28, the battlecruiser met with her escort destroyers near Bear Island. Two days later *Scheer* entered anchorage at Tielzund in Schemenfjord. Soon after returning to her base, British reconnaissance planes discovered *Scheer* at anchor. The British Admiralty informed the Soviets that because all German capital ships were found at their Norway bases, the Kara and Barents seas were at last free from German surface raiders.

While the battle for Port Dikson was raging, the Kriegsmarine minelayer *Ulm* left Narvik at 0400 hours on August 24. Mine-laying was to have started on the night of August 27. But before reaching her destination, *Ulm* ran afoul of the British destroyers *Marne*, *Martin*, and *Onslaught* on their way back from Arkhangelsk. In addition to their normal crews, the three destroyers were carrying *Edinburgh* and *Gossamer* survivors.

The morning after leaving Arkhangelsk in company with USS *Tuscaloosa* on August 24, as a consequence of an Ultra intercept, the Admiralty ordered Joe Selby, commanding officer of *Onslaught*, to leave the escort of *Tuscaloosa* and take *Marne* and *Martin* with him.

Selby had been given a position to steer southeast of Bear Island, then a second position due south to North Cape. Naval intelligence informed him that he likely would encounter light surface warships that were suspected to be in the area.

At 2155 hours, British lookouts reported a well-camouflaged enemy merchant ship in the area. A minute later, the three destroyers increased speed to 25 knots, while the enemy turned to port until she was steering directly away. Six minutes later, *Onslaught* opened fire at a range of 9,000 yards, followed immediately by *Marne*.

According to a November 1942 British report, upon first sighting the group of destroyers, Kapitänleutnant der Reserve Ernst Biet, *Ulm*'s commanding officer, at once realized the hopelessness of his position and gave the order to haul down the German flag and hoist the U.S. flag, hoping to deceive the approaching enemy ships. Many in *Ulm* thought the destroyers were Russian, which made them even more anxious owing to the Russians' reputation for taking no prisoners.

Ulm altered course to the westward and then back to southwest and started zigzagging. Her executive officer, Leutnant zur See der Reserve Heinrich Birckenstadt, was on the signal deck. He pointed out to the captain that the U.S. flag was still flying. Biet replied, "Yes, yes, I know" and appeared very agitated. He ordered it to be hauled down and the German flag to be hoisted instead. He then ordered the 10.5-cm gun to open fire.

Ulm was no match for the three British destroyers. While *Marne* and *Martin* straddled *Ulm* with their 4.7-inch armament and the minelayer replied with her only two guns capable of returning fire, *Ulm* scored two hits on *Marne*, knocking out "Y" gun and killing an ordnance artificer. In addition, three men among the *Edinburgh* and *Gossamer* survivors were killed and another five were wounded.

By 2216 hours, the range had closed to 2,500 yards, and the British opened their anti-aircraft guns onto *Ulm*'s bridge to destroy any radio or fire control gear. According to Biet, this burst of fire was responsible for most of the casualties among his ship's company, nearly all of whom had mustered by the bridge preparing to abandon ship.

Marne's salvoes began to fall close to *Onslaught*, so the latter increased speed to 30 knots past the enemy to clear the line of fire. When clear of the smoke, *Marne* was ordered to cease fire and *Onslaught* turned to fire another torpedo. The enemy was swinging slowly to port at the time and eventually stopped, heading approximately 030 degrees.

After firing two torpedoes that missed, *Onslaught* fired her third torpedo at 2231 hours, hitting *Ulm* abreast the foremast and causing a huge explosion and detonating onboard ammunition. An officer who survived the blast reported that it hit *Ulm*'s magazine. The ship broke up completely, sinking in just two and a half minutes at 2235.

Marne closed the sight and rescued fifty-four survivors, but some thirty to forty survivors were left swimming in the water, the British ships considering it imprudent to remain any longer in the vicinity due to the presence of enemy aircraft. Of *Ulm*'s complement of 186 souls, 132 died. Those left behind in the water were among the dead.

After the ground support crews transported to Russia on board USS *Tuscaloosa* were in place, Royal Australian Air Force (RAAF) 455 Squadron and RAF 144 Squadron readied their thirty-two Hampden bombers for the long flight from England. The flight was about thirty minutes beyond the normal endurance of a Hampden. There was some apprehension among the aircrews; it was a long flight toward an unknown destination over inhospitable country and enemy territory, with little hope of a safe forced landing.

On Wednesday, September 2, the aircrews packed small kits of personal belongings into cardboard containers to be carried in the empty bomb bays. It was a beautiful day, and the airmen were in high spirits for an easy flight to the departure point at Sumburgh in the Shetland Islands (the closest airfield to Norway). First into the air was 144 Squadron. They wheeled around and beat-up their home base of Leuchars airfield, some aircraft actually hopping over parked aircraft as they flew around showing off. Wing Commander Grant Lindeman, 455 Squadron's commander, came onto the radio and sternly announced "455 will take off like gentlemen." The ensuing flight was routine as they crossed over the North Sea, which sparkled as they headed north.

The group commander toyed with the idea of sending the aircraft off on the night they arrived to get ahead of bad weather. Fortunately the idea fell through on account of the refueling necessary to make the long trip to Soviet bases. The squadrons were told too late that they would be expected to operate within a day or two of their arrival at the Soviet airbase. Naturally, the squadron commanders objected to this short notice, pointing out that they might easily be held up by bad weather. The arrangements were fixed to a rigid timetable that did not take the weather into account.

Weather was the greatest concern, and it was not looking good. The Group Command was worried that if the squadrons could not fly and be in place at the Soviet airbases in time, questions would be asked in high places. On September 3, Group Command got overexcited and tried to dispatch the squadrons despite a shocking weather report, believing the next day might be even worse. Wing Commanders James McLaughlin and Lindeman refused to take their squadrons into certain disaster, unwilling to lose half their aircraft and men simply to save

Group's face; it would be no use if only a handful of survivors made it to Russia. Their only chance against capital ships was to attack in large formations; anything less would be an ineffectual sacrifice.

So the squadrons waited for the weather to clear. A reasonably clear forecast came in the afternoon of September 4. The decision to go was made. The thirty-two aircraft dispersed around the crowded taxiways of Sumburgh and had their fuel topped off. At the final briefing for pilots and navigators, they were warned of a "nomad," or breakaway barrage balloon, drifting across their track and were warned to steer clear of Rovanimi fighter airfield in Finland.

The support party and reserve crews stood watching as the small airfield resounded to the throb of so many engines starting. Engines were run up to full power against brakes before the aircraft began to slide down the downhill runway. There was no room for error: the airfield runway ended with a 200-foot drop to the sea.

On the ground, Squadron Leader Jimmy Catanach, RAAF, couldn't restrain himself to wait his turn; he taxied into the first gap in the line and was away. Catanach was full of unbridled energy. He didn't drink or smoke and talked at an incredible speed. He couldn't stand still, hopping about all the time. For all that, he was an excellent flight commander and one of the most liked men in the squadron.

Once airborne the aircraft turned north, heading for Burra Firth at the top of the Shetlands. From there they were to set a course to cross the Norwegian coast at 66 degrees North (the Arctic Circle is 66.6 degrees North). The last light faded from the sky as they flew up the Shetlands, and the islands below looked grim and black.

Occasionally they saw a glimmer of light from the window of a cottage below. Lindeman mused about the scene and their situation:

> *How cosy the occupants must be by their fire in the lamplight, whilst we airmen roar through the night high above with a long stormy passage ahead. In an hour or two they'd yawn and go off to bed and we'll be miles away over the North Sea, bucketing about in rain and cloud, not knowing what evil ones might be lurking in the murk.*

These thoughts made him so miserable that he gave up and brooded over the engine gauges instead. Everything was normal. "George," the automatic pilot, was behaving. After take-off, the autopilot often seemed to want to fly at a fixed altitude, and Lindeman had worried he would have to fly manually all the way.

They departed from Muckle Flugga lighthouse, far north in the British Isles, flying over the sea under some unpleasant low cloud. A positive sign was the sight of flickering flame floats, which had been dropped by leading aircraft to calculate drift. They felt less lonely up there in the great empty blackness as they followed the friendly trail— each of those fairy lights bobbing on the water was being watched by someone else who had passed a few minutes earlier. Navigator Les Oliver observed, "Gosh look at 'em all. It's like Bondi Esplanade [in Sydney] on a Sunday night."

The cloud base thickened as they went north, and to stay below it they were forced down to 500 feet, a mucky altitude where great white-capped waves lashed underneath. One aircraft actually bent the tips of one propeller after clipping a wave-top.

Lindeman decided to try to climb above the thick cloud and heavy rain. At 7,000 feet, he broke into clear sky with stars overhead. After some time, he and his fellow flyers noticed the cloud below breaking up, and they soon were able to see the sea and make out the horizon.

Ahead of them was a faint glimmer on the horizon. As they approached, it grew bigger and looked like an orange flame flickering on the sea. Lindeman estimated it to be at about the point where they would turn east to the Norwegian coast. He called up his navigator, Les Oliver. "Yes," replied Oliver. "I've been watching it for some time. Looks like an aircraft burning on the water, doesn't it?" That agreed with Lindeman's assessment, and he instructed his crew to look out for German night fighters in their path. Colin Bastian, the upper gunner, searched the sky ceaselessly.

Lindeman was puzzled: the flame was growing larger, but they didn't appear to be getting any closer. At last the penny dropped. It was the horn of the moon rising out of the sea, partially masked by some low black cloud, which gave it an odd shape and a flickering effect.

Turning toward the Norwegian coast, they could see the thick cloud ahead, which rose to 6,000 feet. To clear the Swedish mountains, they needed 8,000 feet, so they began a steady climb to get above the cloud.

Breaks in the cloud as they crossed the coast and the rising moon made flying easier. Ahead were the great black mountains; below fjords and lakes. But they could not see enough detail to fix their position. Oliver advised everyone that they were on track. Lindeman hoped he was right. Flying under radio silence so as not to give their position away to the Germans, they could not use radio navigation to fix their position. They had kept to their compass course faithfully but had no idea what navigational errors had been introduced by wind drift, compass variation over Sweden, or even the angle of dip caused by using unsuitable compasses in high latitudes.

The weather forecast was for fine weather at dawn over Finland and Russia. The plan, if their track was approximately correct, was that they should be able to spot the Gulf of Kandalaksha on the western end of the White Sea. This and a single railway line were the only landmarks in the surrounding wasteland. Crossing Sweden, the cumulus clouds gave way to a great flat expanse of low-level cloud blotting out the ground. They droned on at 7,000 feet.

Aircraftman Murray Cryer was an engine fitter in August 1942 when he found his name on the noticeboard as nominated to fly overseas on aircraft "A" (for "Apple"). It was replaced by "K" (for "King") just before they left. Cryer noted during the flight that the autopilot required constant course adjustment to maintain track, and over Sweden the crew were surprised to fly over towns with lights on. The rest of Europe was blacked-out each night.

As UB-K (King) ("UB" was the squadron designator for 455 Squadron) climbed to 10,000 feet over the Swedish mountains, Colonel C. Storry and his crew, including Snowy Lovell, Bluey Collins, Sargent R. Sheedy, and Murray Cryer, found the cold unbearable, even with the hot-air pipe jammed up the trouser leg of the heavy Arctic Tropex kit they wore. The ventral gunner at the end of the pipe was the worst off. Over Finland, gun flashes split the darkness as forty anti-aircraft guns opened up. Storry dived to 3,000 feet as a cannon shell passed through the tail and two more hit the wings.

On board UB-H P 5304, after crossing the Norwegian coast, the aircraft was tracked by a German fighter from Bodø across the Swedish border before being shot down. The entire crew was killed in the subsequent crash, though it was many years before facts became known.

As dawn broke over Finland and Russia, the airmen's worst fears were realized—they didn't know where they were and their fuel was running low. Below was a cold, barren wasteland, sparsely wooded with light trees and dotted with myriad lakes. The land was without a significant landmark. A forced landing looked possible for a pilot mindful of his fuel position, but for how many days would they have to walk to find help? Who would help them: Russians or Germans?

Jack Davenport piloting UB-B had only one thought as he looked down: Finding a tree, lining up, and having a pee. After eight hours flying in the cold, he was busting. The crew was jumpy. Now it was dawn, and the scene they saw below was different from any they'd seen in Scotland, England, France, or Germany. Harry Harrison, the upper gunner, sent a chill through the crew when he shouted "Fighters!"

"It's okay! They're Hurricanes!" Davenport fired the recognition flare colors of day.

"They're attacking!" screamed Harrison. The Hurricanes wheeled around, guns blazing. The fighter-like qualities of the Hampden were handy as Davenport avoided first one attack and then a second. Between jinxing, Davenport lowered the wheels and waggled his wings. Harrison waved both arms to the Russians.

The Hurricanes then came alongside and forced the Hampden down. Only late in his approach did Davenport realize he was landing on an airfield. Earth-covered shelters for the Hurricanes camouflaged it so well he wasn't able to make out the field. Later, Squadron Leader Dennis Foster of 144 Squadron also was escorted into what he later learned was Monchegorsk aerodrome.

UB-R, flown by Robert Holmes, was also well north of the track and weren't sure of their position. Earlier he and his crew had been fired on by light, accurate flak while over Finland. Navigator Frank Dick was lost because their compasses were so affected by the iron in the mountains and the angle of dip (i.e., where the compass needle points downward to the North Pole) in the high latitudes.

With "R" for Robert flying at about 8,000 feet in the brightening sky over Finland, Dick spotted light flak coming up. To relieve the boredom, he called up the supernumerary, Bob Raebel, who had probably not seen flak from the receiving end. "Bob," he said, "if you look out to port you'll see some light flak coming up."

Silence.

"Bob? Bob, you there?"

"Yeah."

"Did you want to see the flak out to port?"

"No," came the sullen reply. "I don't want to see any bloody flak!"

At last the crew sighted the coast bordering the Barents Sea. Below was an airfield. They set down cautiously. There appeared to be Hampdens in the dispersal area. As they circled, a green light winked, inviting them to land.

The Hampden was often visually confused with the German Dornier Do-17 bomber. On the final approach, Frank Dick in the nose suddenly called to his pilot Robert Holmes: "Bob, those planes have got crosses on them!"

Holmes pushed the throttles open and got the undercart up. As they went over the end of the airfield, anti-aircraft mortar bombs called "Flying Onions" whistled past them trailing cables.

Now they knew they were at Petsamo in Finland. Following the coast, they located the Kola Inlet. Again they were met by a barrage of anti-aircraft fire, this time from the Soviet Naval Base at Polyarnoe. Turning south, they flew past Vaenga and picked up the Murmansk–Kandalaksha railway, which would lead them to the Soviet Afrikander air base.

To Dick, Afrikander appeared busy with Hampdens dispersed around the field. Fuel was getting critical, and there was a light mist at ground level. Holmes made a normal approach down to 20 feet when suddenly the mist thickened and the ground disappeared. Below, airmen ducked as wheels came through the mist and Holmes went around again. The mist held off on the second approach, and they were able to land.

In PL-K, Sergeant John Bray, also lost in the Petsamo area, was shot down by a Messerschmitt. Bray parachuted clear, but his crew was killed in the ensuing crash.

"Jeep" Patrick in UB-L came a little later into Afrikander. After several attempts at landing in the mist, his fuel position also was critical. He flew toward Kandalaksha, searching for an emergency landing ground. All he could find was an area where the silver birch trees had been cut down, leaving tall thin stumps. Jeep elected to make a wheels-up landing. Turning to approach, both motors stopped. He was gliding. With the supernumerary aboard, it was cramped as the crew braced themselves against the wing spars. In the cockpit the navigator, Leo Clohessy, braced himself for the crash.

The Hampden hit and slithered on her belly, tree stumps tearing at her until she came to rest. Miraculously, she was largely intact and on an even keel, and no one was hurt. Ronny Bryans, the supernumerary, rushed back to collect the cardboard container holding his kit. These containers were strewn along the crash path when the bomb bay had been torn open.

As Bryans reached for the container, a bullet smacked into the ground at his feet. He dropped to his knees, thinking of the revolver stashed in the container. Looking around, he could see no one. For the second time that morning, an Australian acknowledged the Russian mastery of camouflage.

Heeding the warning shot, Bryans ambled nervously back to the others at the aircraft, forgetting the revolver. As they waited, knowing that they had an unseen guard, Bryans removed the clock from "L" for London's instrument panel as a souvenir.

Further north Sergeant W. Hood, piloting a 144 Squadron machine AE356, broke through cloud over the Kola Inlet. Suddenly the crew found themselves in the middle of a fighter dogfight. It was unclear whether Soviet or German bullets brought them down. Hood brought the aircraft down to a forced landing in a lake.

Everyone except the lower gunner, Sergeant W. Tabor, was more or less unhurt and tried to get out of the aircraft. They came under Soviet rifle fire from the shore. The Soviets knew it wasn't one of their aircraft. Meanwhile, a desperate struggle developed to get Tabor from his compartment in the sinking aircraft. But they failed, and Tabor was trapped. Later, he was buried at Vaenga.

In UB-K, Murray Cryer, the engine fitter, sat nervously on the D spar behind the pilot.

"Fighters! Coming in from port!" yelled Sheedy, the upper gunner.

Cryer grabbed a spare Vickers machine gun from its rack and attempted to push it out through the beam-gun port. He had to fight the slipstream to get the gun mounted, and then he found the port wingtip occupied most of his field of fire. The moment passed as the gunner called, "Hurricanes! They must be Russian Hurricanes!"

Jimmy Catanach's aircraft UB-C had crossed the mountains, but compass error had pulled him well north of the track. Catanach crossed the coast over the Barents Sea near Kirkennes on the Finnish–Norwegian border when he was forced down by flak from the German armed trawler, *Ubootjager 1105*.

With his fuel tanks punctured and leaking, Catanach knew he could neither return nor go on, so he elected to make a wheels-down landing on a beach. Fate stepped in as the aircraft stopped exactly where a German patrol was waiting. The crew was captured before they had time to destroy their aircraft. Catanach himself, Australia's youngest squadron leader at the time, was shot by the Germans two years later in reprisal for his part in the "Great Escape" (a mass escape attempt of Allied prisoners in 1944; fifty men were summarily shot as a warning to others). The Germans found papers on the aircraft referring to the radio organization for PQ-18 and QP-14, which when put together with a deciphered signal to the Soviet 95th Naval Flight Regiment, gave them a good picture of the convoys' routes and timetables.

Mystery surrounded Sargent Sandy Smart and his crew in UB-H. Some airmen were positive that he was seen over Afrikander, while others stated that fighters over Finland were seen chasing him. Another firmly held theory was that he had been brought down by Swedish flak;

this is unlikely given the desolate area they crashed in. It was learned later that the entire crew was killed when their aircraft crashed at Aravst Uttar, Sweden.

144 Squadron was less fortunate, losing six aircraft, the most spectacular of which was PL-J serial AE436, piloted by Pilot Officer I. Evans. With one motor overheating, the pilot could not maintain altitude as he crossed the Swedish mountains. He flew into rising ground on a scree-covered slope of Tsatsa Mountain, about 15 miles north of their track. The aircraft broke up badly, wrapping around on itself, nose against tail, but staying right-side up. Only the pilot and supernumerary survived. Relatively unscathed, they walked for three days before happening on the village of Kvikkvok, 20 miles southeast of the crash site.

It quickly became apparent that very few Russians had been told the Hampdens were expected. Even the Soviet pilots covering the narrow air corridor assigned to the flight seemed largely unaware. The whole area north of Kandalaksha was a war zone, and isolated crews were thought to be Germans by the simple soldiers and peasants—and they were treated accordingly.

Davenport, after landing at Mongiegorsk, found his aircraft surrounded by peasants with pitchforks. "Harry," he called to the upper gunner, "the natives don't look friendly, better stay by your guns." Still harboring a strong desire to empty his bladder before negotiating, Davenport climbed down. Relief was almost his when suddenly the embarrassed young Australian noticed there were many women among the peasants. "Angliyskiy," he called pointing to himself. "Churchill, Stalin, RAF."

His words were met with blank stares. The English gunner called down insubordinately, "Tell 'em the truth you mug. You're a bloody Australian."

At last the Russian-speaking Commissar, Kapitan Nikolaev, arrived. Recognizing they probably weren't German, he had Davenport and his crew escorted to an underground bunker. What the British believed to be glasses of water were offered around in an amusing ceremony, and the young fliers followed the Commissar's example, knocking them back in one gulp. They had never drunk vodka before. Breathless and reeling from the fiery spirit, they fought to speak.

Milling around near the wreck of their aircraft UB-L, Jeep Patrick and his crew fidgeted, knowing they were being observed and guarded by an unseen sniper just 15 miles inside the Eastern Front.

Eventually a troop of soldiers arrived and, thinking the Australians were the hated Nazis, treated them quite roughly. One story has it that Jeep Patrick was bayoneted in the backside, though Ron Bryans had no memory of the incident.

Things got better when they were taken to an underground interview room. An English-speaking commissar was able to understand their wondrous tale and verify it through Afrikander. Later they were reunited with the squadron at Afrikander.

The next day, a Russian SB3 bomber escorted the Hampdens, three at a time, to Vaenga. As Cryer's aircraft made a port turn onto its final approach to land, the port motor quit, probably due to a mix-up changing fuel tanks. The loss of an inboard motor was normally fatal turning at low altitude and low speed. The inner wing of the turn would stall; the faster outer wing still giving lift would flip the aircraft over into an incipient spin. Typically, the aircraft would crash into the ground before the pilot could recover control. On this occasion, however, Cryer managed to keep control and land normally. Even the Russians came forward to congratulate him on saving the aircraft.

Overall the losses were a disaster, losing nine of thirty-two aircraft, precisely the loss rate anticipated for an attack on a major warship. 455 Squadron lost three aircraft; 144 Squadron was less fortunate, losing six aircraft.

Challenges continued throughout the month of September for the Allies working in and around the Arctic Circle. On September 26, 1942, sailors of the Soviet timber ship *Sacco*, passing near Belushya Island, saw a strange bearded man on the beach wearing rags, desperately waving a large white flag and obviously trying to attract their attention. *Sacco* stopped the engine, but was unable to launch a rescue boat because of high waves.

The ship's radioman reported the sighting to Port Dikson and got everybody at GUSMP HQ highly agitated. The stranded man could only be a sailor from the icebreaker *Sibiryakov*, sunk by *Admiral Scheer* in August. Fortunately, a Soviet seaplane piloted by Kaminski was in the air at the time, not far from Belushya and Dikson, and was ordered to pick up the survivor or to at least drop some food and a note for the man, asking him to hold on until he could be rescued.

Due to stormy conditions, the seaplane wasn't able to land, so the pilot dropped a bag with cacao powder, condensed milk, bread, medications, and warm winter clothes, along with a note promising rescue as soon as the storm subsided. Three days later, Cherevichny, one of the most experienced polar pilots, approached the shore to rescue the man. Excited, the man couldn't wait, jumped into the icy water, and started swimming to the seaplane. After being rescued, he was treated for malnutrition in the hospital. Later, he told his incredible story.

Nikolai Vavilov had been a stoker aboard *Sibiryakov*. He had been on board the burning icebreaker with two other men, sailor Safronov and gunner Dunayev, but couldn't escape in time, cut off by the flames and almost suffocated by smoke. When *Sibiryakov* went down, sailors were sucked under by the huge water maelstrom. Safronov and Dunayev drowned, but Vavilov managed to clasp a piece of wood and surface, alone in the middle of the Arctic. He was about to give up when he saw an empty lifeboat floating on the icy sea, survivors from which had only recently been transferred to the *Scheer*. Vavilov managed to reach the boat and pull himself out of the water. In the boat he found the corpse of fellow stoker Matveyev, who died of a gunshot wound.

When *Scheer* disappeared on the horizon, Vavilov decided to set out for Belushya Island, still 5 miles away but likely his only chance for survival. On his way to the island, he found and rescued a blind dog, heavily burned, and collected some floating debris, including a bag with wheat middling (fine particles of wheat bran and fine particles of wheat shorts, wheat germ, wheat flour, and offal from the "tail of the mill"). He also located an emergency supplies box under the bench and secured an invaluable emergency kit with three cans of food, two axes, a loaded handgun, a compass, a sleeping bag, some clothes, matches, a bucket, a flask with water, and a couple of signal flares.

When Vavilov reached Belushya, he unloaded all his treasures on the shore and started his polar odyssey, which would last thirty-four days. Belushya was completely deserted. Vavilov found only the ruins of an old lighthouse. His situation soon became desperate after his boat was crushed by waves during a stormy night and his food and matches were depleted. Vavilov was preparing to give up and die when he saw *Sacco*'s silhouette on the horizon.

Officials visited Vavilov in the Port Dikson hospital, but all he really knew was that the ship went down and that he was the only survivor.

Hopes of the relatives of *Sibiryakov*'s crew, who thought that, after Vavilov's miraculous rescue, other survivors would be found, quickly vanished.

While these battles were being waged, planning went ahead for PQ-18 and QP-14. Both German and British commanders alike believed they had the situation under control and would come out of the next confrontation victorious. No one asked the men at the sharp end of the spear what they thought about the situation.

CHAPTER 8

AN AUTUMN IN HELL
September–December 1942

By the end of August, the British Admiralty was ready to sail convoys PQ-18 and QP-14. Because German reconnaissance aircraft were patrolling over Iceland, where most of the previous convoys had sailed from, it was decided to sail PQ-18 from Loch Ewe on the northwest coast of Scotland.

On September 2, the forty-four ships in PQ-18 under Rear Admiral E. K. Boddam-Whetham serving as a commodore set out for Arkhangelsk. In company were the two tankers *Gray Ranger* and *Black Ranger* for refueling the escorts and the rescue ship *Copeland*. As soon as the long line of ships cleared the Outer Hebrides, they encountered the full force of an Atlantic gale, which delayed their progress. They were thirty-six hours late at the rendezvous with the ocean escort.

The ocean escort comprised the two anti-aircraft ships (*Ulster Queen* and *Alynbank*), three destroyers, four corvettes, and four trawlers, all of which joined the merchant ships on September 7. The escort was augmented on September 9 when Rear Admiral Robert L. Burnett in command of the fighting destroyer escort, flying his flag in the anti-aircraft cruiser *Scylla* (commanded by Captain Ian Macintyre), joined the convoy.

For the first time the escort aircraft carrier *Avenger* sailed with the convoy, carrying twelve Sea Hurricane fighters and three Swordfish antisubmarine aircraft. However, the Hurricanes were of the oldest type, and as Admiral Tovey remarked to Churchill, it was ironic that transports crammed with the latest type of Hurricanes for Russia had to be protected by their outworn predecessors.

Additional cover was provided for Convoy QP-14 by a cruiser force under Vice Admiral Stuart Bonham-Carter, consisting of his flagship *Norfolk*, *Suffolk*, and *London* with two destroyers, which operated to the westward of Spitsbergen between September 17–20, in support of *Cumberland*, *Sheffield*, and *Eclipse*, which were landing reinforcements and stores for the Norwegian post at Barentsburg.

Four submarines were stationed close off the coast of Norway to intercept enemy ships going north from Narvik. These were soon joined by three more submarines, forming a shifting patrol line to cover the passage of the convoys east of Bear Island.

In addition to the *Avenger's* aircraft, improved antisubmarine protection, and reconnaissance by Coastal Command aircraft from Iceland and Russia, the convoys had the support of the two squadrons of torpedo-carrying Hampden bombers based in Russia against possible attack by surface ships in the Barents Sea.

The number of warships assigned to cover PQ-18 and QP-14 totaled seventy-six, a massive accumulation of firepower, but the Germans were ready for them. As mentioned in Chapter 7, Jimmy Catanach's Hampden of RAAF 455 Squadron crashed in Norway, and the Germans found papers referring to the radio organization for PQ-18 and QP-14. This information, when combined with an intercepted signal from the Soviet 95th Naval Flight Regiment, gave the Germans a good picture of the convoys' routes and timetables. The Luftwaffe, whose torpedo bomber strength had increased to ninety-two, was ready and anxious to try to repeat its success against PQ-17. Also, between eight and ten U-boats formed a scouting line across the convoys' projected paths.

German reconnaissance aircraft located PQ-18 late on September 8, but the Germans soon lost sight of it. Thanks to low-lying cloud and occasional fog banks, reconnaissance planes did not find it again until 1320 hours on September 12. However, U-boats had managed to gain and maintain contact during this period, although they were kept at a respectful distance by the *Avenger's* antisubmarine aircraft, which made several attacks on them and assisted the escort ships in their attacks. It was estimated that there were now no fewer than eight U-boats around the convoy, and the destroyers had a busy time fending them off. In one of these attacks, the destroyer *Faulknor* sank *U-88* at 2100 hours on September 12.

The following day at 0855, *U-408* and *U-589* avenged the loss of their comrade by sinking the freighter *Stalingrad* and tanker *Oliver Ellsworth*, in the outside starboard column. *U-408* fired three torpedoes, one of which hit *Stalingrad* on the starboard side at the coal bunker. She sank in less than four minutes. The starboard lifeboats were destroyed by the explosion, leaving only the portside boats for crewmembers and passengers to use. Adding to the loss, one of the portside boats capsized when reaching the water. Sixteen crewmembers and five passengers were lost. Master A. Sakharov was the last to leave the *Stalingrad*. He spent forty minutes in the freezing water before being rescued.

One of the torpedoes hit *Oliver Ellsworth* (Master Otto Ernest Buford), igniting her cargo of oil. Her crew immediately abandoned ship. But the vessel still had headway, which caused both starboard boats to swamp. One of the portside boats struck a raft and sank. Due to the quick reaction of the British rescue ship *Copeland* and HMS *St. Kenan*, forty-three crewmembers and eighteen gunners were picked up; one armed guard drowned.

The U-boats had scored; now it was the Luftwaffe's turn. The first attack came at 1500 hours when half a dozen Ju-88s dropped their bombs through gaps in the clouds from a height of about 4,000 feet, with no loss to either the convoy or themselves. This was only a taste of what was to come.

Half an hour later, thirty Ju-88s and fifty-five He-111 torpedo bombers carried out a mass attack, the latter employing the Golden Comb technique, approaching in line abreast, 100 to 150 yards apart at a height of about 35 feet above the sea in perfect formation. Each aircraft carried two torpedoes, and all were dropped simultaneously, threatening the convoy with 170 torpedoes.

The pilots launched their torpedoes only at the precise moment when they had just enough space to pull out before crashing into the ships' masts. Riddled by anti-aircraft fire, some of them caught fire and crashed into the sea, but none failed to press home the attack. Ships fired on the planes, the trajectories of their shells crossing the fire of the targeted ships and forming a net of fire over the sea.

Above the deafening din of the ack-ack could be heard the explosions of ships hit by torpedoes. In every ship, the crew was certain that it was quite impossible that their vessel could come unscathed through this inferno.

For Boddam-Whetham, convoy commodore, the contingency plan for massed torpedo attack was a simple 45-degree alteration of course, either to port or starboard using the appropriate international sound signal backed up by a single flag hoist. Its efficacy relied upon good lookouts, prompt response, and coordinated repetition of the signal down the columns. The commodore made his port-turn signal, but the ninth and tenth columns failed to respond due to the sheer size of PQ-18. The outer starboard ships failed to execute the turn and caught the worst of the attack.

One plane flew so close to *Wacosta* that the torpedo failed to hit the water and instead dropped through her No. 2 hatch, exploding inside her hull. The ship had been slowing down, her engines disabled by the terrible explosion of the ship immediately ahead. Leading the ninth column, the *Empire Stevenson* was suddenly enveloped in a tower of flame and smoke, which, when it cleared, left only an oily slick on the water. This was the dreadful penalty of carrying explosives. Although no one from the *Empire Stevenson* survived, all the crew of the *Wacosta* were rescued.

Similarly loaded with tanks and war materials, the *Macbeth*, second ship in the tenth column, succumbed to two torpedoes, while the *Oregonian* ahead of her capsized rapidly after three torpedoes stove in her whole starboard side. Only twenty-seven of her fifty-five-man crew were rescued by the *St. Kenan*, many of them in a fearful condition having swallowed oil and been immersed in the freezing sea.

Macbeth's crew was rescued by *Offa*, whose commanding officer, Lieutenant Commander R. A. Ewing, ran her alongside the Panamanian freighter, so close that several of the destroyer's guardrails and stanchions were crushed. Torpedoes also hit the Russian ship *Sukhona*, as well as *Afrikander*, a Panamanian ship chartered to the U.S. Maritime Commission. Both were abandoned as they sank, their crews efficiently picked up by the close escort ships. Although the rescues were a bit of good news, the day was going poorly for the convoy. With the exception of the *Mary Luckenbach*, the outer two columns of PQ-18 had been annihilated.

The loss of the two outer columns was by no means the end of it all. More losses would come. Leading an inner port column, *Empire Beaumont* was set on fire after a torpedo struck in the only hold not containing explosives. The ship was successfully abandoned. Less fortunate, however, were the crew of the *John Penn*. The three men on duty in her engine room were killed when two torpedoes exploded in their midst.

Amid the confusion, *Copeland,* the trawlers, and the motor minesweepers picked up the merchant sailors from their rafts, lifeboats, and the freezing sea. *Daneman,* one of the four trawlers, was steaming at the rear of the convoy. Seaman Gunner G. R. Lunn, one of the survivors from *Empire Stevenson,* wrote later:

> *One of these four seamen couldn't swim and we put it down to his threshing madly about in the sea which kept him afloat and warm enough to survive. Another older man was about to be rescued when the planes attacked again and we had to get under way and leave him to drown. I can still see him, cold in the water, trying to reach one of our sailor's hands to get a grip so that he could be pulled aboard to safety, but we were being attacked by a torpedo-bomber and the skipper rang full-ahead.*
>
> *We had to leave him and watch his bald head and red football jersey, vanish behind us; as we were the last ship in the convoy he would never be picked up.*

St. Kenan rescued sixty-four survivors during and after the mass torpedo-bomber attack. These included survivors from the American SS *Oregonian.* Ten of her survivors were snatched from the sea, all in horrible condition after swallowing oil and water and being plunged into the icy seas.

Among *Sukhona's* survivors were a man and his wife who had suffered several broken ribs. Their two children were not among the survivors.

Eight ships had been lost in less than fifteen minutes. Luftwaffe losses amounted to only five aircraft.

The following day, September 14, began with another loss for the convoy. Returning to station from an ASDIC contact, HMS *Impulsive* obtained a second echo and had begun a run in to depth-charge it, but before she could, *U-457* (Korvettenkapitän Karl Brandenburg) torpedoed the tanker *Athel Templar. Impulsive* then lost contact as *U-457* dove under the convoy amid the noise of the propeller races and escaped.

Although she was hit in the engine room, the tanker's volatile cargo did not explode. But fire soon made it impossible for her crew to do anything more than abandon ship. The master, forty-two crewmembers, and eighteen gunners were picked up by *Copeland* and *Offa,* one of whose crewmen, James Green, jumped into the icy sea in an abortive attempt to rescue a drowning boy. Green was recovered and revived with difficulty after his exertions. Another sixteen *Athel Templar* crewmembers later died from their injuries.

HMS *Onslow*, following a sighting by one of *Avenger*'s Swordfish, bagged *U-589*, which was stalking the convoy. At 1235 hours, the Luftwaffe again joined the battle with about twenty torpedo aircraft targeting *Avenger* and *Scylla*. The attack cost the Germans another eleven planes, but the losses didn't deter them from further attacks.

As the initial wave of torpedo bombers in this attack disappeared over the horizon, a dozen Ju-88s appeared overhead and started dive-bombing. Several ships, including the *Avenger*, made narrow escapes while the Germans lost another aircraft. Almost immediately, twenty-five torpedo aircraft came in from ahead, dividing as before into two groups, one of which made a dead set for the *Avenger*. *Avenger* had ten fighters in the air, and these, together with the ship's guns, shot down nine more enemy aircraft, but one ship, *Mary Luckenbach* in the starboard wing column, was torpedoed. She blew up with such force that *Nathaniel Greene* right behind her in the column was covered with debris and several of her deck cargo crates burst. Sublieutenant Robert Hughes witnessed the explosion from his gun director on *Scylla*.

> *Tracers began to fly upward from all over the ship as a plane skimmed the masts. Oerlikon gunners lay backward, strapped to their guns, the muzzles pointing skyward and slewing as the gunners scrabbled the deck for purchase to move sideways. The plane kept on steadily though shells kept hitting her, and headed for the* Mary Luckenbach *on our starboard side. She headed on pursued by a few shells, and other targets presented themselves. Suddenly there was a dull roar from starboard, and Freeman shouted and pointed. "Look !"*
>
> *The* Mary Luckenbach *had gone. In her place a stupendous column of smoke was rocketing to heaven, and as we looked an immense glow lit the column, and great cerise, orange-and-yellow fragments arched outwards towards us.*
>
> *"Oh, Good God Almighty," prayed someone.*
>
> *I shuddered in fear. "Oh, God," I prayed. "Oh, God, why have you sent us here? What have we done, what have we done?"*
>
> *"Duck!" came my voice from somewhere deep down, and five heads bent as in prayer, and perhaps we did pray.*
>
> *Still we waited and the seconds flitted past, but there was no crash of metal on top of us. We raised our heads. Fluttering down into the director came large pieces of ash.*
>
> *Mead caught a piece on his hand and smeared it into his palm. "Just like burnt paper," he said quietly and wonderingly.*

The great smoke column was still thousands of feet high and mushrooming out where it met the clouds. At its base flames still flickered, and the following ship was altering course to avoid them. The Mary Luckenbach *had gone, and forty men had died. This was their memorial and the smear on Mead's palm.*

The death toll from *Mary Luckenbach* was forty crewmen and twenty-four armed guards. Incredibly, one man did survive. He was walking along the deck carrying a cup of coffee for the captain when the ship exploded. Next thing he knew, he was in the water a half mile away. Unfortunately, Hughes wasn't able to record his name, just his story.

During this action, three Hurricanes were shot down by the convoy's guns, but the pilots were saved. The final attack of the day began at 1430 hours when about twenty aircraft approached from astern and bombed intermittently through gaps in the cloud for about an hour. Despite the difficult conditions that provided only fleeting glimpses of the attackers, another aircraft was shot down.

The next morning, two large Russian destroyers, *Gremyashchiy* and *Sokrushitelnyy*, and two smaller ones, *Uritski* and *Kuibyshev*, joined the convoy escort screen. When rounding Cape Kanin at 0820 hours on September 18, twelve He-111 torpedo aircraft delivered an attack from the starboard quarter of the convoy dropping their torpedoes at between 3,000 and 4,000 yards range. Although in the commodore's opinion the ships had a good opportunity to avoid them, one ship, *Kentucky*, was hit. Fortunately no one was killed.

A similar attack an hour later was synchronized with a bombing attack by Ju-88s. *Kentucky* was hit again and sunk. All her crew got away safely. The Hurricane aircraft in the CAM ship *Empire Morn* shot down three aircraft and damaged another. The pilot then flew on and successfully landed at a Russian airfield with only four gallons of fuel left in his tank.

At last, on the evening of September 19, the convoy reached the Dvina River leading to Arkhangelsk. PQ-18 lost fourteen ships, more than a third of the total convoy, during the voyage.

Meanwhile, westbound QP-14 with twenty ships sailed from Arkhangelsk for Loch Ewe on September 13. With the convoy of fifteen ships were the rescue ships *Zamalek* and *Rathlin*. The commodore was J. C. K. Dowding, on board the *Ocean Voice*, which also was his ship in PQ-16. The close escort of the two anti-aircraft ships *Palomares* and *Pozarica*, two destroyers, four corvettes, three minesweepers, and three trawlers was under the command of Captain J. F. Crombie, R.N.

After the air battle around PQ-18 on the afternoon of September 16, Admiral Robert L. Burnett began transferring forces from PQ-18 to QP-14. He did this gradually in three groups so as to make it less obvious to the enemy. In addition to *Scylla* and her destroyer escort force, he took the aircraft carrier *Avenger*, the anti-aircraft ship *Alynbank*, the tankers *Gray Ranger* and *Black Ranger*, and the submarines *P 615* and *P 614*.

The weather during the convoy's passage through the Barents Sea was thick with patches of fog and intermittent snow squalls, which favored the defenders and hampered the work of the enemy shadowing aircraft. It was bitterly cold, too, and severe icing conditions impeded the work of the *Avenger*'s antisubmarine aircraft in maintaining constant air patrols around the convoy. Catalina aircraft working from the Kola Inlet assisted in the patrols.

As for the Kriegsmarine, instructions had been given to eight U-boats to patrol along a line 200 miles to the east of the passage between Bear Island and the South Cape of Spitzbergen, but by the time this line was established, the convoy was well to the west of it. When this was discovered from a report of a shadowing aircraft that caught sight of the convoy at 1100 hours on September 18, the U-boats took up the chase at full speed. Escorts sighted three of them astern and northeast of the convoy that afternoon.

The thick weather seemed to offer an excellent opportunity to throw the U-boats and Luftwaffe off the scent, and Burnett decided that when the convoy passed the South Cape of Spitzbergen on the morning of September 19, he would alter its course to take it up the west coast of Spitzbergen, which would increase its distance from the enemy airfields in north Norway.

The deception worked for twelve hours before the U-boats again found the convoy. Their first victim was the minesweeper *Leda*, stationed astern of the convoy. She was torpedoed and sunk by *U-435* (Korvettenkapitän Siegfried Strelow) at 0520 hours on September 20, resulting in the loss of forty-six lives, including two merchant seamen survivors. Six others were among the eighty-six of the ship's company who were rescued.

It was estimated that five submarines were in contact with the convoy. Counterattacks by destroyers and aircraft continued throughout the day, but without success. Then at 1720 hours, *U-255* (Kapitänleutnant

Reinhart Reche) laced two torpedoes into the American freighter *Silver Sword* (Master Clyde Wellington Colbeth). The first struck in the bow, and the explosion destroyed the forward part of the bridge. The second hit the stern, blowing off the stern post, the propeller, and the rudder and causing the after magazine to explode. The seven officers, twenty-nine crewmen, twelve armed guards, and sixteen passengers abandoned ship in two lifeboats and one raft. Of the sixty-four survivors, fifty-five were picked up by the British rescue ship *Rathlin* and nine by the *Zamalek*, but one oiler later died aboard of wounds. The sixteen passengers aboard *Silver Sword* also had survived ships lost in PQ-17: fifteen from *Honomu* and one survivor from *Peter Kerr*, which had been sunk by German aircraft on July 5.

Silver Sword was one of the ships of Convoy PQ-17 that Lieutenant L. J. A. Gradwell of the trawler *Ayrshire* had preserved from destruction. It was tragic that a ship that had survived such great dangers should have been stricken when she was two thirds of the way back on the return trip.

In the afternoon of September 20, Admiral Burnett decided to detach the carrier *Avenger* and his flagship, the cruiser *Scylla*, to return to base independently because the convoy was now beyond the range of heavy air attack. He had requested aircraft from Coastal Command to take over the antisubmarine air patrols and so relieve the *Avenger*'s pilots, who were exhausted after ten days of continuous operations under extremely severe conditions. Burnett also considered that the U-boat threat was so great that it was inadvisable to retain these two valuable ships close by any longer.

After transferring his flag to the destroyer *Milne* (Captain I. M. R. Campbell, R.N.), the two ships parted company, but hardly had they disappeared over the horizon before *U-703* (Kapitänleutnant Heinz Bielfeld) fired a spread of three torpedoes at the destroyer *Somali*, commanded by Lieutenant Commander C. D. Maud, R.N., at 1955 hours. One torpedo struck home. The explosion blew the torpedo tubes over the side and cut all of the port side main stringers so that the ship was held together only by the upper deck and starboard side as far as the keel. The port engine fell through the bottom of the ship, and the engine and gear rooms filled with water. The leaking bulkheads on either side were promptly shored up and seemed to be holding, but there was no light or power except from an unreliable auxiliary diesel generator that powered the bilge pumps.

The British rescue ship *Zamalek* was alongside within minutes after the hit, but she was sent back to the convoy. The trawler HMS *Lord Middleton* took off most of the 190-man crew and transferred them to other ships. Only a skeleton crew of eighty men were left aboard *Somali*, and all of them were forbidden to go below except for any critical work. HMS *Ashanti* then took her crippled sister ship in tow, cruising at a slow 7 knots in a flat and calm sea, to crawl to Akureyri, Iceland.

Three more destroyers and *Lord Middleton* were detailed to escort her. This left the convoy with twelve destroyers and the close escort of nine ships. The presence of twenty-one escorts didn't trouble the U-boat captains and their veteran crews, which *U-435*, commanded by Korvettenkapitän Siegfried Strelow, proved in dramatic fashion.

At 0630 hours on September 22, *U-435* penetrated the screen and torpedoed three ships within five minutes of each other. They were the tanker *Gray Ranger* (Master Howard Douglas Gausden, DSO), the *Bellingham* (Master Soren Mortensen), both of which were survivors from PQ-17, and the Commodore's ship *Ocean Voice* (Master Harold James Kay). Once again Commodore Dowding found himself waiting to be picked up out of an icy sea. *Gray Ranger* suffered the loss of six of her crew of thirty-three. Surprisingly, no one on board either *Bellingham* or *Ocean Voice* was lost.

This was the last attack, as soon afterward the U-boats were ordered to withdraw. But now another hazard beset the convoy in the shape of a northerly gale, which swept down upon the ships riding high in ballast and tossed them about, making steering and station-keeping a torment. Thankfully the storm didn't claim any ships, so the battered sixteen made it safely into Loch Ewe on September 26.

Meanwhile, *Somali* was slowly making her way south under tow. All but two officers, one of whom was the commanding officer, Lieutenant Commander Maud, and eighty ratings had been taken off the *Somali*. By that time, everything possible had been done to make her seaworthy, but as the wind increased and the rising sea caused the water-logged ship to labor more and more, the towing hawser sprang taut out of the sea one moment, only to fall back slack the next. It soon became obvious that disaster was in the offing.

The captains of the two ships conferred over a telephone line that had been run between them. It was a battle against lengthening odds. Maud ordered all hands on deck as a precaution. It was well that he did so, for the end came with dramatic suddenness. Early on the morning of September 24, with the wind howling through the darkness and the angry hiss of the waves rolling up from astern, there was heard the ugly, frightening sound of rending metal as the ship broke in half. This was followed by the shattering thud of bursting bulkheads as the two sections drifted apart, slowly turned over, and sank. Only thirty-five of the eighty men on board were plucked out of the icy water, including Maud, who was unconscious when rescued.

Captain Richard Onslow (later Admiral Sir Richard Onslow), commanding HMS *Ashanti*, wrote about rescuing *Somali*'s survivors:

> We had come up on the weather side, beam to sea, drifting fast down over the position where she had sunk. The rescue nets were over the side and some of our better swimmers ready with lines round their bodies. I signalled to the other two ships to get to windward of me. In that weather it was hopeless to try to hold the ship head to sea. The only possible manoeuvre was to stay beam on and, by backing and filling, pick up as many as we could to leeward.
>
> It was heartbreaking work. The ship was rolling drunkenly and we were drifting so fast that inevitably a few of those in the water were trapped under our bilge keel before we could grab them. And a few swept past our bow or stern, when to have moved the ship would have meant losing those we nearly had.
>
> We could only pray that the ships to windward would see them in the blinding snow and spindrift. I was proud of our men that night. Many of them showed great courage and endurance, particularly those who went over the side, at the risk of themselves being caught under the bilge keel. But their courage was of little avail. Of those they brought on board none was still breathing, and only one responded to artificial respiration. He was the captain, Lieutenant Commander Colin Mead.
>
> When we could see no more men to leeward we worked round to windward again. Between us we covered the area until all hope was gone. The three of us could count the living on one hand, and it took some time to find out from the Lord Middleton how many she had.
>
> We had lost sight of her in the storm and could get no answer on the wireless, so we spent a very anxious time while we spread on a line of search to find her. When she got her radio working again we learnt that she had rescued over thirty (men). Thank God for the Lord Middleton was our thought. But we had lost some forty gallant officers and men. I am haunted still by the thought that perhaps I should have foreseen and avoided it.

In the two convoys, sixteen merchant ships had been lost (a loss rate of 29 percent), together with the large destroyer *Somali*, minesweeper *Leda*, fleet tanker *Gray Ranger*, and four fighter aircraft (three of whose pilots were rescued).

The commander in chief, Admiral John C. Tovey, did not consider the losses excessive in view of the scale of air and submarine attacks to which they had been subjected. The Germans lost thirty-three torpedo planes, six Ju-88 dive bombers, and two long-range reconnaissance aircraft—a total of forty-one; three U-boats had been lost and five damaged, and another had been sunk by a Catalina aircraft off Iceland while lying in wait for QP-14. Approximately 250 aircraft torpedoes had been fired in order to sink ten ships. No one tallied the human losses to death or injury or to the incredible amount of stress each person suffered.

Convoy PQ-19 was cancelled because Operation *Torch*, the invasion of North Africa, required the support of a large number of British Home Fleet units. In order to keep supplies following to the Soviets, the British Admiralty started a series of independent single-ship sailings, both east- and westbound, codenamed Operation *FB*.

It is not clear whether the British or Americans originated the idea for Operation *FB*. What is known is that it initially was to entail twelve merchant ships, then in Iceland, sailing at twelve-hour intervals (roughly equivalent to 200 miles distance between sailings) from October 29 to November 2, 1942, with British and American ships alternating departures. At the last moment, the Russian ship SS *Dekabrist* was added, bringing the total to thirteen ships.

No escorts were provided for the individual ships, but the trawlers *Cape Palliser*, *Northern Pride*, *Northern Spray*, and *St. Elstan* were spaced along the route from Iceland, while *Cape Argona*, *Cape Mariato*, and *St. Kenan* were sailed from Murmansk to cover the eastern end of the passage. In addition, two submarines, HM submarine *Tuna* and the Dutch *O-15*, were ordered to provide protection for ships sailing between October 23 and November 9.

The first ships, *Richard H. Alvey* and *Empire Galliard*, sailed on October 29 without being spotted by the Germans. These were followed by *Dekabrist* (Russian) and *John Walker* and *Empire Gilbert* (British) on October 30; *John H. B. Latrobe* (U.S.) and *Chulmleigh* (British) on October 31; *Hugh Williamson* (U.S.) and *Empire Sky* (British) on November 1; *William Clark* (U.S.) and *Empire Scott* (British) on November 2; and, finally, the last two British ships, *Daldorch* on November 3 and *Briarwood* on November 4.

Of the thirteen ships, three (*John H. B. Latrobe*, *Briarwood*, and *Daldorch*) returned to Iceland, five completed their voyages (*Empire Galliard*, *Hugh Williamson*, *Richard H. Alvey*, *Empire Scott*, and *John Walker*), and five were sunk (*Chulmleigh*, *Dekabrist*, *Empire Gilbert*, *Empire Sky*, and *William Clark*). For the crews of *Chulmleigh* and *Dekabrist*, their tales of survival are epics of suffering and endurance. For the five crews whose luck ran out, their stories also endure.

At 0118 hours on November 2, 1942, *Empire Gilbert* (Master William Williams) was hit on the port side by two torpedoes from *U-586* (Kapitänleutnant Dietrich von der Esch). She sank within two minutes, southwest of Jan Mayen. The U-boat had chased the ship for about two hours but missed with a first spread of two torpedoes at 0017 hours, only to hit a minute later. Within thirty minutes, the Germans arrived at the sinking position and rescued two men who were sitting on a beam, floating in the icy water. Von der Esch tried to question six survivors on a raft but received no answer, so he took gunner Douglas Meadows as prisoner aboard. The Germans took good care of their prisoners and landed them at Skjomen Fjord, Norway, on November 5. However, the master, forty-six crewmembers, and seventeen gunners aboard *Empire Gilbert* were lost.

The crew of *Empire Gilbert* was typical of a British merchantman in time of war. The merchant navy part of her crew tended to come from one area of the United Kingdom, though not exclusively. In this case it was from Tyneside in northeast England. The large complement of Defensively Equipped Merchant Ship (DEMS) gunners came from all over the country. There was a strong element of experienced men in all departments, together with many who were only in their first few years of seafaring.

Twenty-one-year-old Eric Aisthorpe was a quiet, conscientious lad. During his youth, he learned to play the harmonica and the accordion very well. He was looking forward to seeing more of the world when he joined *Empire Gilbert* early in September 1942. But apart from a short visit to Iceland, he would see no more of the world before he lost his life.

Two other young men, John Stewart and Alex Souter, grew up only a few doors from each other in Lossiemouth, a small town in Scotland. Inseparable friends, they shared good times as well as bad. The bond between the two was as strong as ever when they both signed on *Empire Gilbert* in early September 1942.

Bombardier Arthur Hopkins of the Maritime Royal Artillery had already completed five wartime voyages in merchant ships: two to Canada, one to the United States, one to Freetown, and then to the Middle East on a troopship, sailing around the Cape of Good Hope. After joining *Empire Gilbert*, Hopkins said the voyage from England to Iceland was uneventful.

Empire Gilbert sailed as ship number five from Hvalfjödur on October 30 and remained undetected for about two days until a German aircraft found them on November 1. The plane did not attack, instead flying around, well out of anti-aircraft range, making signals to base. Bombardier Hopkins was on watch when, at 2200 hours, he spotted a U-boat running parallel to them on the port side. He raised the alarm, and the ship was brought to action stations immediately. Soon afterward, though, a torpedo hit *Empire Gilbert* on the port side, sinking her. There was no time for lifeboats to be lowered. Only three men survived.

Bombardier Hopkins and those around him were forced to jump into the icy sea. In the frigid November waters of the Arctic Ocean, it would have taken only minutes for most of them to succumb. Though Hopkins recalled hearing men shouting in the darkness around him while he was still in the water, as Harry Hutson described in *Arctic Interlude*, Hopkins remembered little else about the event until being rescued by a U-boat. There, he found two of his shipmates also on board.

Ralph Urwin also signed on *Empire Gilbert* in early September 1942. Just seventeen years old, he signed on as deck boy, as did three other seventeen-year-olds: Thomas Stobbs, George Carey, and Ronald Birch.

After *Empire Gilbert* sank, like Hopkins, Urwin remembered little until he awoke on board the submarine and found himself being rubbed down by the German crew to try to bring warmth and circulation back to his numb limbs.

The third survivor was also a DEMS gunner: twenty-year-old Army gunner Douglas Meadows of Gloucester.

In mid-December 1942, Urwin's mother received a letter from the ship's managers, Turner Brightman & Co., telling her that the *Empire Gilbert* was overdue and must be presumed lost with all hands. It was not until March 1943 that Mrs. Urwin received a letter through the Red Cross from her son, saying that he was well but a prisoner of war.

The day after *Empire Gilbert* was sunk, *William Clark* (Master Walter Edmund Elian) left the safety of Hvalfjödur, sandwiched between *Empire Sky* and *Empire Scott*. The passage from Hvalfjödur to the North Cape of Iceland was uneventful. No warships were seen, though one or two white lights were observed in the distance from time to time, most likely from small Icelandic fishing vessels. Soon after leaving

North Cape on November 2, a British Catalina aircraft buzzed them and then flew off. Hutson notes that, if it was an RAF aircraft, then it likely was from 330 (Norwegian) Squadron, RAF, based at Akureyri, or one of the long-range Catalinas of No. 210 Squadron, based at Sullum Voe in the Shetlands. The American VP-94 Squadron of the U.S. Navy was based at Reykjavik and also flew Catalinas.

By the morning of the November 4, *William Clark*, an American Liberty ship, was in the vicinity of Jan Mayen. At 1333 hours on November 4, she was hit on the port side amidships by one of three torpedoes from *U-354* (Kapitänleutnant Karl-Heinz Herbschleb) off Jan Mayen Island. The torpedo struck in the engine room, disabling the engine, flooding the room, and killing the five men on watch below.

No one aboard *William Clark* had seen anything suspicious before the attack. No one saw any signs of the submarine or the first torpedo. Seven lookouts had been on duty at the time: one in the crow's nest, two in the bows, two on the flying bridge, and two on the after gun platform.

The surviving sixty-six crewmen, officers, and naval armed guards of *William Clark* abandoned ship in three lifeboats after the hit. The U-boat missed the ship with a torpedo at 1400 hours, but hit her ten minutes later with a *coup de grâce* on the starboard side amidships. She broke in two forward of the midship house and sank in a few minutes.

The three boats got together, and the motor lifeboat (No. 1), under the charge of Elian attempted to tow the other two, but because of the danger of swamping, he ordered the lines cast off. Elian told the other two boats he was going to try to sail to Iceland so that he could send help to them. This boat with the master and twenty-two other men was never seen again, presumed to have been swamped with all hands lost.

First Mate William F. Goldsmith was in charge of No. 2 boat. On the strength of the briefing before sailing from Hvalfjödur and the fact that a distress message had been sent, he decided to stay in the vicinity, for the time being at least. The remaining two boats drifted apart. After three days and two nights of suffering through brutal, unrelenting Arctic weather, rescuers finally arrived.

The telegraphists of *St. Elstan*, which also had sailed with PQ-16, had received the distress call from *William Clark* and knew she was astern of their own position. The vessel was turned round and steamed at full speed toward the given position. She searched for several days before Able Seaman Anstey, a Newfoundlander who was on look-out aft, sighted the flare sent up by Goldsmith's lifeboat astern of the trawler. After some confusion over the bearing, the trawler steamed off at full speed on the correct course to find the boat. Approaching quietly and smoothly, *St. Elstan* was almost alongside the lifeboat before most of the occupants realized it.

The long and cold days and nights of searching for the survivors of the *William Clark* were made up for by the sheer joy displayed by those rescued. The lifeboat had drifted roughly 20 miles from the given position during the day of November 7. Quickly taking the twenty-six men on board, *St. Elstan* was under orders to continue her patrol until all of the independently sailing merchant ships were clear of her area. Thus, it was not until November 17 that she landed the survivors at Reykjavik.

HMS *Cape Palliser* picked up No. 3 lifeboat and its fifteen survivors and two dead crewmembers—the second mate and a utility man—on November 12. All the survivors in this boat were near death when rescued, and a Navy gunner among them died shortly after being rescued. Two of the survivors lost their legs due to exposure. All of the survivors were landed at Akureyri, Iceland.

Eighteen-year-old Anthony Spinazzola had joined the SS *William Clark* in August 1942, in New York, after having already served as an Armed Guard gunner on board SS *James Gunn* and SS *Valley Forge*. He recalled the events in the Arctic:

My boat station was with the Chief Mate's crew while my duty station was aft on the 4.5-inch gun, 12 to 4 watch. November 4th was a calm morning and we were about to sit down to chow when the torpedo hit directly amidships, right into the engine room, just below the crew's mess hall on the port side. We all rushed out to the port side passageway but the outer door was jammed shut. We went over to the starboard side passageway and had to pass the engine room hatchway by this route. I remember looking down as we passed but I could see nothing but steam, fire and smoke. I did not think anyone down there could have survived that explosion.

I made my way to my boat station, stopping to pick up some extra warm clothing on the way. The Chief Mate's boat had been destroyed by the explosion and the other port lifeboat was hanging by one of its falls. We crossed to the starboard side but both these boats were already full so we went back to the port side.

The Chief Mate organized us into getting this boat into the water. The greatest danger was from the water being continuously washed in and out of the hole in the ship's side made by the torpedo. We managed to get the boat launched and to heave on the line fastened to its stern. This kept us clear of the yawning hole. We had to row with all our might when we cast off, but we made it clear of the ship. All three boats came together and the Master said he was going to use his motor to try and reach Iceland to get help for us all.

The Second Mate hoisted his sail and also left. Mr. Goldsmith, however, decided to wait near the scene to see if rescue came. We did not see the submarine at all. The weather got worse and I do not know how we managed to stay afloat. Morale slumped rapidly as the weather deteriorated. We had seen a Catalina while we were in the boat but there was still no sign of rescue. I remember being suddenly engulfed by a bright ray of light which frequently disappeared below the wave tops. We did not know then if it was a rescue ship or a submarine. Fortunately it turned out to be HMS St. Elstan and the Captain was warning us to keep clear of the propeller.

Soon we were all on board the rescue ship and all her crew did everything they could to make us comfortable. Some of us had frozen feet and hands. I cannot remember how long we were on board, but we searched for other survivors, unsuccessfully. When we reached Reykjavik we said our farewells to the rescue ship crew and were taken by ambulance to the Quonset hut hospital. I was there for a month before being taken back to the States on board the USS Polaris. *I was sent to Brooklyn Naval Hospital for two months until my frozen feet got better and then I returned to sea until the war ended.*

I spent all my remaining sea-time in warmer climates!

The final death toll for the *William Clark* was thirty-one men: four officers, fourteen crewmen, and thirteen armed guards.

While *Empire Gilbert* and *William Clark* were unsuccessfully fending off attack, *Empire Sky* was dealing with troubles of her own. At 2224 hours on November 6, *Empire Sky* (Master Thomas Morley) was torpedoed and sunk by *U-625* (Kapitänleutnant Hans Benker) south of Spitzbergen, Norway. The master and forty-one crewmembers were lost, as were eighteen DEMS gunners (ten from the 4th Regiment Maritime Artillery and eight from the Royal Navy).

Only a year old at the time of this sailing, *Empire Sky*, a British cargo steamer, likely was the first victim of *U-625* (Kapitänleutnant Hans Benker) when she was listed as missing as of November 14, 1942. British records show her as sunk off Murmansk, cause unknown, with no survivors from her crew of sixty. Most historians agree that the missing ship almost certainly was *Empire Sky*, as no other missing vessel was unaccounted for in this northern area at the time.

Empire Sky had loaded at Hull, England, during August and September 1942, and two teenage boys from nearby Grimsby joined her there. Victor James Jennings, sixteen years old, signed on as mess room boy. The second youngest of ten children, Jennings was a quiet boy, who, after leaving school, had begun work at a local cycle shop until he had joined the merchant navy in 1941. After working on *Empire Sky* for about two weeks, he was given permission to sign off and did so. He told his family that he had seen rats on board and that he considered *Empire Sky* an unlucky ship. This action saved Jennings's young life—for a time. But his luck would not hold. He signed on the SS *Almenara*, a much smaller ship than *Empire Sky*. He sailed in this vessel on his seventeenth birthday, bound for the Mediterranean. The vessel was mined off Taranto on September 20, 1943, and Jennings died in the tragedy.

George Rhodes was the other teenager who had signed on *Empire Sky* at Hull. He had signed on as cabin boy. Like Jennings, Rhodes, too, came from a large family His father, Bill, was a ship's carpenter. This left his mother, Ethel May, to bring up the family on her own while his father was at sea. Rhodes's first job upon leaving school was on a farm, but his heart was not in it. There was salt water in his blood, and so in 1940 he joined the merchant navy as a cabin boy. He had already been shipwrecked off Australia and had two years sea time under his belt when he signed on *Empire Sky*. He decided to stay with the ship when Jennings signed off. This decision was to cost him his life.

Sergeant Edward Edgar Stoackley joined *Empire Sky* at this time, too. He was the senior Army gunner on board. He enlisted in the Royal Artillery before the outbreak of war, and early in 1941 volunteered for duty as an anti-aircraft gunner on merchant ships.

During the last week of October 1942, *Empire Sky* was in Hvalfjödur. Three men, including two firefighters, were discharged there. Fireman James Carr, thirty-nine years old, signed on as one of the replacements for this fateful voyage. The other two firemen also joined *Empire Sky* at Hvalfjödur shortly before she sailed on her fateful journey: Robert Hall and John Murray.

The only records regarding the loss of *Empire Sky* are from the log of *U-625*. The entry for November 6 shows that after attacking the stranded SS *Chulmleigh*, the U-boat set off to return to her designated patrol area. An hour later, she dived to reload her torpedo tubes and while submerged the sound operator detected propeller noises on a bearing of 150 degrees true at 1830 hours. The U-boat surfaced ten minutes later and set off at high speed on this bearing, looking for the contact.

Fifty minutes later, the lookouts on the U-boat could see a dark shadow off the port bow. It was a large merchant ship, steering an easterly course at about 9 knots. The U-boat rapidly gained on the ship and overtook her to get into a suitable attack position. By 2000 hours, *U-625* was beginning her run in. At 2014, she fired two torpedoes. Both missed.

U-625 increased speed to get ahead of the merchantman, and once again Benker maneuvered his submarine in a favorable position to attack. He waited half an hour as the sky grew bright with shimmering waves of light from the Aurora Borealis. Benker intended his next attack to be from close range in order not to give *Empire Sky* any time to avoid action, should she spot his torpedoes running toward her. Meanwhile, the forward torpedo tubes had been reloaded, and Benker ordered Tubes 1 and 2 to stand by. At 2224 hours, he then ordered them to be fired. One hit the bow. The other struck just aft of the midship's superstructure. Benker wrote in the logbook:

> The ship is listing to starboard then to port. The bows sink deeper. Transmits a radio message, name of ship not recognized. Boats are lowered. Astern is an aircraft on a catapult were fitted with a fighter on a catapult which straddled the foc'sle head, not the stern. [None of the ships taking part in this operation were CAM ships.] On deck aircraft are lashed and there are large boxes. On the bow and stern there are guns. Ship has six holds. Estimate 6,500 tons. Ship now stopped.
>
> Fire torpedo from tube five (stern tube), hit after thirty-five seconds. Ship explodes in a great detonation, night is brightened to daylight, a fire column rises in the sky, wreckage splashes around in the water, which seems to boil. Many splinters hit our boat. Only a short time later, smoke marks the scene of the disaster. The lifeboats have also disappeared. Return to patrol area.

Late in 1942, George Rhodes's mother was informed that her son was missing. The terrible uncertainty of his fate remained a burden for her until February 1946, when she received a letter from the ship's managers. The letter said that a postwar examination of German records indicated that *Empire Sky* had been sunk by a U-boat and that none of the crew survived.

On October 31, *Chulmleigh* left Hvalfjödur for North Russia, carrying a cargo of government stores. The weather was overcast, and heavy snowstorms made it difficult to fix positions. A snowstorm was raging, and visibility was very poor. Master Daniel M. Williams had made good progress, when at 2300 on November 5, his ship struck a reef. The *Chulmleigh*, stuck firmly amidships on the reef, with her stern almost out of the water. She was so much down by the bows that the foredeck was almost awash and the captain was afraid the swell then running would break her back. A wireless message was issued, and after an hour and a half the men were ordered to the boats.

The captain remained on board with Chief Officer E. J. Fenn and Second Engineer Richard A. Middlemiss. The numbing cold so affected the men in the boats that they seemed incapable of action. The master at length got *Chulmleigh*'s engines started, but the ship only settled more down by the head. Finally she hogged amidships. The engines were stopped for fear that the ship would break in two. A further wireless message was sent, and by 0400 hours, *Chulmleigh* had been abandoned. The boats seemed to be in a horseshoe-shaped lagoon, with heavy seas running and breakers all around; the boats were kept alongside the ship, as otherwise they would have been crushed on the reef.

At the first sign of daylight on November 5, the fifty-eight men in three boats moved off toward an opening in the lagoon. Almost at once, five Ju-88s flew over the ship at masthead height and scored two direct hits with their bombs. A column of black smoke rose high into the air, but the *Chulmleigh* did not catch fire. Williams decided to make for the nearest settlement, which he calculated to be about 150 miles away.

At 1558 hours on November 6, *U-625* torpedoed the stranded *Chulmleigh* and completed the destruction of the vessel with gunfire. Later, the wreck was again bombed by a Ju-88.

The following account, based on the report by Williams and Third Officer David F. Clark, conveys a graphic illustration of the appalling hardships suffered by the survivors.

The men of the *Chulmleigh*, struggling to remain connected in three lifeboats, could not easily keep together. One of the boats was in dangerous condition and was soon abandoned, its crew divided between the two remaining seaworthy boats. They proceeded along the Spitzbergen coast, which was visible during the few hours of twilight that relieved the otherwise perpetual darkness. A gale blew up on November 8, but on November 9, the two boats turned toward the shore and regained contact with each other. Captain Williams's boat had a serviceable motor, and it was agreed that he should go on ahead to the settlement to fetch help. It was very cold, and a lot of water was shipped; the wind froze the sails, and the crew's clothing became rigid with frost and ice.

The night of November 9/10 was so severe that the steward became delirious and died. On the afternoon of November 10, some huts at the entrance to a fjord were sighted, but as Williams and his crew were making toward them, the motor froze up and could not be restarted. Without the motor helping them, the wind and current made it impossible to make landfall, and the boats drifted out to sea, losing sight of land.

At about 0200 the next day, after several hours among the reefs, they were suddenly washed up on the beach, where a heavy sea broke over the party and the master regained consciousness at the shock. By good fortune, they found several wooden huts within 20 yards; two of the crew had died in the boat and another died on the beach, but the survivors managed to reach the huts, although the youngest among the crew had to be carried.

They at once fell fast asleep. In the morning, the twenty-three men who remained from the original ship's company of fifty-eight moved into one of the larger huts. This proved to be quite habitable; it had a small coal stove, and there was enough wood and coal to make a good fire. Although no trees were in sight, there was plenty of driftwood and a great many old boxes they could burn. "After we had slept that first night," Clark recalled, "we all felt a little better."

> We collected what was left of the lifeboat's rations and at once made ourselves hot drinks, coffee and Horlicks, melting the snow for water. This revived us considerably and we became terribly hungry. We also found some tins of corned beef and biscuits in one of the huts, so we managed very well.
>
> As long as we had food for tomorrow our morale remained good. Captain Williams encouraged us to take about two hours' exercise each day, but after a time most of us suffered so much from frostbitten feet that it was impossible. Feet and hands became gangrenous and I became very ill.

After a few days on land, Captain Williams recovered enough to take charge. Most of the men had swollen hands and feet and could do very little, but the four Army gunners were hardly affected. One man in particular, only 4 feet 11 inches tall, was phenomenally tough; the captain said of the gunners that they "looked after us all, nursing the men who were ill, going out to collect firewood, and generally running things."

Clark and Lance-Sergeant R. A. Peyer made two attempts during their first few days on land to reach the settlement, but the intervening country was barren and strewn with rocks. Deep ravines and great stretches of snow and ice were further hindrances to the explorers, who had to turn back and arrived back at the huts completely exhausted.

During the first week, thirteen more men died from frostbite, gangrene, and exposure. "They seemed to give up hope," said Williams, "and then died; but I believed right to the end that we would come through."

Expeditions of any kind were never easy. The men had only a few hours of twilight during which to work, and visibility often was reduced to 10 yards. Another sortie, in a northeasterly direction up the fjord, revealed a small hut in which there was a sack of flour and some tins of corned beef and cocoa. This was brought back, and the flour, mixed with water and cooked in the form of small cakes, kept the party alive for another three or four weeks. There were dozens of boxes of matches in their hut, and with the petrol from the lifeboat's tank they managed to keep two Primus stoves working. They had hot drinks three times a day; and when the coffee and cocoa ran out, they made do with hot water. They also found some tins of whale-blubber preserved in oil; this sustained them for another five or six days, and they also drank the boiled oil.

A second attempt to reach the settlement was unsuccessful, and toward the end of December, the situation was becoming desperate. According to the master's statement:

> By now the Third Officer and an Able Seaman were suffering badly from gangrene, as were several of the others; their feet and hands were discharging and the smell was awful. Another man died on Christmas Eve. I therefore decided to make a final attempt to get help, or die in the effort.

When they were halfway to the settlement, Williams's two companions broke down. They could not go on. So they turned back, and upon reaching the hut, all three collapsed. On January 2, 1943, one of the gunners went out to collect firewood; almost at once he came rushing back in a state of complete terror. Captain Williams could get nothing out of him, and the nine men still alive could think only that they were about to be set upon by polar bears. Luckily, it was nothing more fearsome than two hunters who were on a trapping expedition wearing white furs. They took word of the survivors' plight to the settlement, and a rescue party was sent with sleighs.

"We were all in a pretty bad condition," said Captain Williams, "as we had ceased to have the energy to exercise ourselves. Our clothes were soaked with pus from gangrenous limbs and gave off a horrible stench."

After two months in bed, Williams and the remaining survivors were allowed to get up. They spent most of their time learning to ski. This pastime provides an ironical footnote to the long story of endurance, as Williams noted: "There had been a pair of skis in the hut, and if only we had known how to use them we could probably have got help much sooner."

At 2000 on January 4, the survivors reached the settlement, where they stayed until June 10, 1943. The survivors eventually boarded the cruisers HMS *Bermuda* (Captain T. H. Back, RN) and HMS *Cumberland* (Captain A. H. Maxwell-Hyslop, RN) and landed at Thurso, Scotland, on June 15, 1943. The master, three crewmembers, and nine gunners survived. However, thirty crewmembers and nine six gunners were lost, many to gangrenous infections brought on by frostbite. Their ordeal lasted 217 days.

SS *Dekabrist* of Odessa, under the command of Captain Stephen Polukarpovic Belyev, had already survived two convoys: PQ-6 in late 1941 and QP-5 in early 1942. Now, in autumn 1942, she loaded her cargo in the United States and sailed in convoy to Iceland, originally intended to be part of convoy PQ-19.

Dekabrist was located on November 4 by Junkers Ju-88s from Norway. She was attacked several times with bombs and torpedoes and then strafed with machine guns. *Dekabrist*'s gunners drove off all of the attacks, leaving the ship undamaged.

The ship was attacked again just after midnight, this time by three aircraft, soon followed by five more. The final aircraft made its attack when one well-aimed torpedo struck the vessel in the bows. The Russian crew struggled all day to keep the water at bay, expecting more attacks to come, but no other aircraft found them.

By 2000 hours, it was obvious to Captain Belyev that the water was gaining on them at an ever-increasing rate. The vessel was going to sink. Belyev ordered the crew to abandon ship once she was well down by the head and the foredeck was awash. A final distress message was transmitted soon after midnight on November 5, giving their position as 7530N 2710E.

All four of *Dekabrist*'s lifeboats were launched safely, well stocked with food and other supplies. Once the boats were safely in the water, the captain ordered the crew to stand off the vessel but to remain in the vicinity in the hope that rescue would come to them from one of the two submarines. *Dekabrist* was east of Spitzbergen when she was attacked, and the trawlers were much further to the south and west.

None of the submarines arrived in time to save the *Dekabrist*. Soon after dawn, another flight of German aircraft found her and sent her to the bottom of the Arctic Ocean. While the crew watched the vessel sink, a thick blanket of fog developed, and the four lifeboats soon lost sight of each other. A few hours later, the fog lifted and the survivors in the captain's boat saw land and a hut on Hope Island to the east of Spitzbergen.

People were running along the beach, waving frantically. One of the other lifeboats came into view, too, and they closed on each other. Under the command of Third Mate Treticyn, this boat confirmed the sight of human habitation. Treticyn's boat managed to land safely through the surf, but Captain Belyev's boat could not make it through the breakers. The crew was not strong enough to prevent her broaching and so the captain stood off the beach, his men totally exhausted. Belyev and his crew never again caught sight of Treticyn or of any survivor from his boat.

After failing to land with Treticyn, Belyev's boat drifted further north with the wind for another four days before the weather changed and they began to drift south again. The crew was in a very bad way, unable to assist themselves. On November 14, nine days after they abandoned the *Dekabrist*, they spotted land (Hope Island, southeast of Spitzbergen). A few hours later, they found themselves washed up onto the beach. All nineteen survivors reached the shore before the next wave smashed the boat.

The men had no idea where they were. They were weak from hunger and dehydration. The conditions in the lifeboat had been very bad indeed. There was only four ounces of water per person a day early on after the sinking, but this soon had to be cut in half and finally there was only enough water to wet their tongues. Food was more plentiful, but without water, the men found it difficult to eat because of swollen tongues and cracked lips.

The ship's doctor, Nadejda Matvevna Natilich, had brought the ship's cat with her into the lifeboat, and more than once it was suggested that the pet should be killed and used as food. Natilich, however, strongly resisted this, and the cat was reprieved after long and heated discussions.

Four lifeboats had left *Dekabrist*. The crew numbered around eighty, about twenty people per boat. The reports of Belyev and Natilich quote a total figure of nineteen survivors in this boat. By the time they reached the beach, the survivors from Belyev's boat could barely walk. Miraculously, no one drowned when the boat was smashed by the pounding surf.

Once ashore, the survivors set to work. The sails were recovered from the lifeboat, and the fittest among them erected a makeshift tent. Two small parties were organized from the fittest men to search for better shelter, one going south, the other, led by Belyev, heading north.

Belyev's group located a seal hunters' hut. The rotting hut was in poor condition, large holes dotting the walls. The floor was covered in ice. But with an ancient stove and some bunks, it was better than their makeshift tent. Not long after reaching the hut, the weather deteriorated to hurricane-force winds and blizzard conditions. Before long, snow several feet thick covered the hut.

The survivors made a rough chimney from wet wooden boards and this worked well—until the boards dried out and caught fire. As soon as the weather moderated sufficiently, they dug themselves out and everyone went back to find the tent, three men, the doctor, and the cat. They eventually located the tent, but all the men had died from exposure. They were left where they had died.

It was at first thought that the doctor was dead, too; as there was no reaction from her, but the cat was still alive and kept close to its mistress. Able seaman Vasiley Nichalovich Borodin investigated further and realized that Natilich, although close to death, was still alive—barely. Every effort was made to revive her. About three days later, she was taken to the northern hut. Not long after, Soviet Navy seaman Kamenskji became gravely ill and died, most likely from pneumonia. He was soon followed in death by seaman Nicholas F. Ivanov.

The survivors soon established a routine, the fittest making daily forages for firewood, others melting snow and boiling water for treating victims who suffered from gangrene. Scouting the shoreline for goods that had been washed up proved fruitful as they frequently found a keg of butter, a sack of flour, and other valuable items of food, all of which helped to sustain them throughout the long winter and spring months. The hut itself also contained meager supplies of flour and butter, as well as an ancient shotgun (though only a few cartridges).

One evening after settling in for the night, an enormous polar bear pounded open the flimsy door of the hut. Belyev kept his head and picked up the loaded shotgun, not knowing for sure whether it would fire correctly or explode in his face. He pointed it in the general direction of the bear and pulled the trigger. There was a tremendous explosion, and the bear fell mortally wounded. The crew made the most of its quarry. Its body was skinned for the fur, the meat used for food, and the less savory parts for baiting fox traps.

On Saturday, 1 May 1943, almost six months after the Russian survivors had first set foot on Hope Island, a Heinkel He-115 seaplane from Banak in Northern Norway, flown by Luftwaffe pilot R. Schutze, had been ordered to overfly the island just in case the Allies had put ashore a weather station during the winter. The aircrew was amazed to see the figure of a man against the snowy white background. The German pilot cautiously flew lower on his second run. He could see the castaway beckoning him to land. Instead, the pilot climbed and then sent a signal to its base reporting the incident. The reply ordered the aircraft not to attempt to land but to return to base immediately and make a full report.

German intelligence officers concluded that there could be only two possible explanations for human presence on Hope Island: Either the man was indeed a member of an Allied weather party and the beckoning had been a deliberate ploy, or he was a shipwrecked mariner who had somehow managed to reach the island. The Germans knew that they had sunk ships in the vicinity during the past few months, but they found it difficult to believe that any man could have survived without assistance.

This, however, gives rise to even more questions. If the hut had been occupied, presumably by shipwrecked mariners, then which ship were they from? What happened to them? Had they tried to reach safety in their lifeboat?

Other aircraft were sent to the island, and one reported finding a wooden hut, most likely constructed before the war by seal hunters. The aircraft also reported seeing not one but three castaways, one of whom was almost certainly a woman. None of the survivors had made any attempt to hide from the aircraft—quite the reverse: They all seemed happy to have been discovered, and all waved excitedly. When the aircraft returned and the crew was debriefed, the German authorities decided that they had no other choice than to order a U-boat to make a landing on the island to discover exactly what was going on.

On July 24, 1943, *U-703* (Oberleutnant zur See Joachim Brunner) was ordered to make a thorough search of Hope Island, take off the survivors if indeed they were shipwrecked mariners, and destroy the hut if it was, or had been, used as a weather station.

U-703 reached Hope Island the next day. The U-boat circumnavigated the island at a discreet distance while several members of the crew scanned the barren snow-covered rock with powerful binoculars. They found no signs of human habitation. Brunner decided to take a closer look. On the second run, a keen-eyed lookout spotted a wooden hut. A shore party was made ready while other members of the crew inflated a rubber dinghy, checked the 88-mm deck gun, and made it ready for immediate action. Light machine guns were mounted on the conning tower and small arms, grenades, and ammunition for the shore party were checked. A small, well-armed group were put into the dinghy and paddled to the shore.

The group approached the hut with caution, not knowing exactly what to expect. After bursting through the door, they discovered the hut was empty, although there were signs that it had been recently occupied. They soon found a second hut, and once again the shore party of four men under the command of Leutnant zur See Heinz Schlott went ashore.

Once the shore party was in position surrounding the tiny refuge, they signaled the submarine and a warning shot from the 88-mm deck gun on the U-boat was fired. This brought forth a solitary figure, hands crossed behind his head in sign of surrender. The shore party advanced and eventually found that no one else was inside the hut to pose a threat.

Inside the shelter they found an old revolver, ammunition, a few meager rations, old newspapers, and animal skins. They discovered the foul-smelling castaway was Russian. Although he could not speak any German, he could speak a few words of English. The Germans soon discovered it was Belyev.

Captain Belyev told his rescuers that he would be more than pleased to guide them to the survivors who were living in other huts. He was taken back to *U-703*, where he showed Brunner where the other huts were situated. The first hut was found easily. It was empty when investigated, though it, too, showed definite signs of having been occupied quite recently. The shore party was again recovered, and *U-703* set off for the next position.

By that afternoon, the third hut was sighted, and a few short bursts of light machine gun fire were used to attract attention before deciding whether to put men ashore. The gunfire immediately brought three people from the hut. Two seemed quite fit, but the third was obviously seriously ill or injured. Captain Belyev used the megaphone to instruct the people to come out to the U-boat in the small boat that could be seen on the shoreline.

The two fit survivors placed the sick man in the boat and then rowed out to *U-703*. Brunner and his crew were surprised to find that one of the fit survivors was a woman.

While the Russians were on board *U-703* being questioned and given food, clothing, and facilities to wash, a small landing party went ashore to examine the survivors' hut and its contents. When they returned they reported that the hut was indeed only a refuge. There was no sign of weather or radio equipment.

Brunner decided that because he still had to lay another weather buoy and because accommodation on the U-boat was limited, he would take only the Russian captain with him. The others would be left behind. Brunner ordered his crew to assemble a survival kit from the U-boat's stores while he explained to Belyev what he proposed to do.

When Captain Belyev translated this to his compatriots, their disappointment was obvious, but they accepted the fact that they had no choice. They were sent ashore with the survival kit, which contained medical supplies, vitamin tablets, food, clothes, diesel oil, matches, cigarettes, and tools. The U-boat crew gathered firewood from the shore and brought it to the hut.

U-703 set off again for Narvik, arriving on August 3 without further incident. Belyev was almost in tears as he shook hands with every member of the submarine's crew before being taken away under a Navy guard.

On her next patrol, *U-703* received a signal ordering her to return to Hope Island. Aircraft had reported seeing at least two people still alive, nine months after they had first reached the island. The message indicated that the middle hut seemed to be their base. Brunner was ordered to bring everyone off the island.

When *U-703* arrived, the shore party found only two survivors in the hut, the woman and, amazingly, the man who previously had been so ill. The third survivor also was still alive, living in a separate hut further away along the shore. After bringing the doctor and the man aboard the U-boat, *U-703* then made her way to the more remote second hut. The lone Russian, Lobanov, came out of the hut, crawling on his hands and knees to meet the landing party.

Lobanov was placed in the rubber dinghy by the four Germans, and they set off to paddle back to the submarine. They soon ran into difficulties in the choppy water and found they could make no headway against the surf. Brunner brought the submarine closer and managed to float a line to the exhausted dinghy crew. They retrieved the line and made it secure, and *U-703* went slowly astern, pulling the dinghy and its occupants through the turbulence and alongside.

The rescue had come too late for Lobanov. He died a few hours later and was buried at sea with a formal ceremony. The two remaining Russians,

Borodin and Natilich, were put ashore at Harstad, Norway, on October 9, 1943, almost eleven months after first being marooned. Seventy-seven of their comrades had died as a result of the sinking of the *Dekabrist*, lost to the enemy and to the even deadlier Arctic.

As the eastbound ships fought their way through storms, ice, and the patrolling Germans, eight Soviet ships sailed westward between October 29 and November 25. Eighteen additional Soviet ships ran the gauntlet, the last one sailing on January 24, 1943. All but three of these arrived safely.

The first lost was the hard fighting *Donbass* (M. I. Pavlova, Master), which had survived PQ-17 in summer 1942 and rescued fifty-two survivors from the *Daniel Morgan*. On November 7, *Donbass* ran into a Kriegsmarine battle group consisting of the heavy cruiser *Admiral Hipper* and the 5th Destroyer Flotilla (*Z-27*, *Z-30*, *Friedrich Eckoldt*, and *Richard Beitzen*). After an unequal battle against *Z-27*, she was sunk, and forty-nine of her crew were killed. Pavlova and fifteen crewmembers were taken prisoner. The other two losses were cargo ships *Krasny Partizan* (Captain A. F. Belov) and *Ufa* (Captain L. I. Patrikeev), both sunk by *U-255* in late January 1943.

Krasnoe Znamya left the Kola Inlet on January 26. She sent a message later that day that German aircraft were attacking, but then contact was lost. According to U-boat records, at 1100 hours on January 26, *U-255* sank an iced-up steamer with two torpedoes west of the Bear Island. The ship had just escaped from the chasing *U-625* (Kapitänleutnant Hans Benker) when it was torpedoed by *U-255*. *U-255* surfaced after the attack and tried to question the survivors who had taken refuge in a lifeboat, but they only spoke Russian, which the Germans could not understand and the U-boat left without taking any prisoners. No distress message was heard by shore stations or any ships, and the survivors were never found. *Krasnoe Znamya*'s captain Belov and fifty crewmen were lost.

Ufa had set out from the Kola Inlet a day earlier, on January 25. At 0547 hours on January 29, *U-255* fired a torpedo at a steamer, identified as a Myronich-class freighter, which was located south of Bear Island in the Barents Sea and observed it sinking by the bow twenty-five minutes after being hit. Two torpedoes had missed at 0231 and 0233 hours, possibly passing underneath the vessel. When the U-boat surfaced after five hours, they still found survivors at the sinking position and tried to question them, but they only spoke Russian. Once again, there is no record of a distress message being sent and, like *Krasnoe Znamya*, *Ufa*'s captain and thirty-eight of her crew were never found.

The loss rate of eight out of thirty-nine unescorted ships that ultimately sailed as part of Operation *FB* was significantly better than that of the heavily guarded convoys. But all loss is relative. We'll never know what hell most of the survivors went through before dying or how their families suffered not knowing, often for years, what had happened to their loved ones. Regardless of the personal tragedies, Operation *FB* with its 20 percent casualty rate, was considered by the British Admiralty, militarily and logistically, a success.

The last PQ/QP convoy series was QP-15, which sailed from Arkhangelsk on November 17 consisting of twenty-eight ships with Captain W. C. Meek as commodore. Protection was provided by the anti-aircraft ship *Ulster Queen*, five minesweepers, four corvettes, and the Soviet destroyers *Baku* and *Sokrushitelnyy*.

A gale sprung up on November 20, and by the time QP-15 reached the vicinity of Bear Island, it was badly scattered. Ted Balaam, a British telegraphist on board one of the escort ships, wrote graphically about what happened when the gale hit QP-15:

> *A story regarding QP15, a convoy in which our Russian allies lost ships in tragic circumstances.* London (Flag), *with* Suffolk, *A.A. ship* Ulster Queen, *5 minesweepers, 4 corvettes, one trawler, destroyers* Onslaught *and* Orwell, *Russian destroyers* Baku *and* Sokrushitelnyy, *left Arkhangelsk with 28 ships formed into a convoy. More destroyers, two flotillas, had been promised as an enemy cypher had been decyphered by the Admiralty under the "Ultra" system informing Admiral Hamilton that German surface craft, including* Hipper *and attendant destroyers, had express orders to proceed and destroy QP15 and escorts.*
>
> *However, after leaving port we ran into what developed into a hurricane, and within no time at all convoy lines were broken. The close escort screen was fighting to stay afloat. When* Suffolk *could be seen, her four screws became visible before plunging into the depths again.* London, *since the 1939 refit, rolled even at anchor and was going over to 45°, then 50°.*
>
> *The height of the swell was measured and the seas running were eighty feet. A little later the anemometer screamed and took off, the graph in the plot came off the paper and ceased, the last reading was 110 mph.*

The wind and sea increased, as did the icing up, suddenly we went over to 70°, everyone wedged themselves into something as we listened above the wind to hear the crashing of crockery, and many unidentified items moving. To our relief we came upright again and slewed to Port to receive a huge wave which did not break until it reached "B" Turret and all but drowned us. As we surfaced we were horrified to see Baku *listing badly and her entire bridge went over the side.*

We tried with the largest signal lamp to tell her to go home and tried to find Sokrushitelnyy *to tell her the same. On the crest of an eighty-foot wave we saw her in a 'Vee' shape and tragically watched as she broke in half amidships and foundered, with all aboard we feared.*

The only consolation was that the weather kept the aircraft grounded and Hipper *in harbour, not that they could have done much in the prevailing conditions and with the convoy completely scattered and fighting damage.*

At 1430 hours on November 20, *Sokrushitelnyy* was hit by a large wave, tearing off her stern and sinking her within ten minutes, killing six men. Other destroyers managed to take off 191 men, but thirty of them were lost during the rescue effort. At 1530, the other destroyers in the convoy began to leave due to a lack of fuel, leaving a crew of thirteen to man *Sokrushitelnyy*. She was not seen again.

The storm kept the Luftwaffe at bay, but it didn't deter the U-boats. Two of them struck the badly scattered convoy on November 23. *U-625* (Oberleutnant zur See Hans Benker) was the first, sinking the British freighter *Goolistan* (Master William Thomson) at 0145. Second was the Soviet motor merchant *Kuznets Lesov* (Master V. A. Tsibulkin), when *U-601* (Kapitänleutnant Peter-Ottmar Grau) fired a spread of four torpedoes, one of which hit home. *Kuznets Lesov* sank in four minutes. Neither ship's crews, totaling eighty-two men, survived.

The battered remnants of QP-15 began arriving at Loch Ewe on November 30. The last limped in four days later. With its arrival, the PQ/QP convoys passed into history.

CHAPTER 9

GERMAN GÖTTERDÄMMERUNG
December 1942–May 1945

B etween December 1942 and March 1943, the Axis Powers' (Germany, Italy, and Japan) tide of success reached its high-water mark and began turning in the Allies' favor. In North Africa, the British Eighth Army had pushed the German Afrika Corps a thousand miles westward. At the western end of North Africa, Anglo-American forces, firmly in control of Morocco and Algeria, were slugging eastward through Tunisia. The Allies encircled and then defeated their foes on May 16.

In Russia, Soviet Red Army troops fought bloody house-to-house battles for control of Stalingrad and, during its winter offensive, surrounded and captured 300,000 German Army troops that had threatened the city. On the other side of the world, U.S. soldiers and Marines slowly eliminated Japanese forces on Guadalcanal, the first step in driving the marauders out of the Pacific. Guadalcanal was secured on February 9, 1943, six months after the Marines landed on August 7, 1942.

In the Atlantic, U-boats still reigned supreme through the bitter winter months, wreaking havoc among almost every convoy they encountered. They were finally fought to a standstill and their dominance broken at the end of March, following three months of cataclysmic convoy battles.

As these battles raged, the British Admiralty resumed regular convoys, sailing in mid-December to the Soviet Union. There were several changes in these new convoys. The most important was replacing the PQ and QP with the randomly chosen designations "JW" for eastbound convoys and "RA" for the westbound ones. This was done in a futile attempt to confuse German Intelligence. Another significant change was that the eastbound convoys would sail from Loch Ewe instead of Reykjavik. What hadn't changed, though, was the heavy force of escorts accompanying the convoys.

The first of the dual eastbound convoys to sail from Loch Ewe was JW-51A with sixteen ships on December 15, 1942, escorted by seven fleet destroyers and four smaller vessels. It was a quiet passage, and all the ships arrived safely off the Kola Inlet just five days later, on December 20.

The second, JW-51B consisting of fourteen ships, left on December 20, escorted by six fleet destroyers (*Onslow*, with Captain R. St. V. Sherbrooke, senior officer of the Escort Force, *Obedient*, *Orwell*, *Obdurate*, *Oribi*, and *Achates*), the corvettes *Rhododendron* and *Hyderabad*, the minesweeper *Bramble*, and the trawlers *Vizalma* and *Northern Gem*. Distant cover was provided by the battleship *Anson*, flying the flag of Vice Admiral Sir Bruce Fraser, with the 8-inch-gun cruiser *Cumberland* and three destroyers, which sailed a few days later from Akureyri on the north coast of Iceland, on December 26.

For the first six days, the convoy's passage was uneventful. Then, on December 26, when the convoy was half way between Jan Mayen and Bear Island, a great gale overtook it. The five ships of the port wing column and the trawler *Vizalma* lost touch with the convoy. The next afternoon, the minesweeper *Bramble* (Commander H. T. Rust) was detached to look for the missing merchantmen. Three of the merchantmen rejoined the convoy the next day. The fourth, *Chester Valley*, and *Vizalma* found each other and proceeded independently to Murmansk. The fifth lost ship, *Ballot*, reached the Kola Inlet two days after the rest of the convoy, only to be wrecked afterward.

By the morning of December 31, the storm had abated, the wind had dropped to a mild breeze, the sea was slight with no swell, and the sky was overcast with occasional snow squalls. But the masts, rigging, and upper works of all the ships were coated with ice.

Unknown to Captain Sherbrooke was that on the previous day, U-354 had sighted and reported the convoy, which she described as comprising six to ten ships steaming eastward at 12 knots and weakly escorted. After receiving this report, Admiral Erich Raeder immediately issued orders for a force consisting of *Lützow, Hipper* (flagship for Vice Admiral Oskar Kummetz), and six destroyers to sail as soon as possible to attack the convoy. Operational command was to be exercised by the Flag Officer Northern Waters, Admiral Klüber, at Narvik. Tactical command was vested in Vice Admiral Kummetz.

Kummetz's instructions included the destruction of the convoy and avoidance of action with superior forces. No time was to be wasted rescuing enemy crews, and enemy ships were to be prevented from rescuing their comrades. The capture of a few merchant ship captains for interrogation—or even the capture of a single ship—was desirable. He was informed of where the convoy would be on the night of December 30/31 and that it was steering east at between 7 and 12 knots.

While the Germans were searching for the convoy, they found the corvette *Bramble*, returning from a search for stragglers. *Hipper* opened fire and badly damaged the little corvette. Later, the destroyer *Eckholdt* finished her off. Eight officers and 113 ratings were lost. The loss went unnoticed by the British until after the battle.

Sydney Parkins, a signalman on board HMS *Jamaica*, wrote about what was to be called the Battle of the Barents Sea:

This is roughly what happened on New Year's Eve 1942. A German Naval Force sailed from Altenfjord and split into two sections, the heavy cruiser Hipper *and three destroyers in one, and the battle cruiser* Lützow *and three destroyers in the other. They would attack Convoy JW51B from different directions. To locate the convoy in quite poor visibility, each section was deployed some distance apart to widen the search area. The* Hipper *was the first to find the convoy.*

Captain Sherbrooke on Onslow *was in command of the convoy escort. When* Hipper *was sighted,* Achates *made smoke to obscure the convoy, which enabled* Obedient, Orwell, *and* Onslow *to feign a torpedo attack by emerging from the smoke screen, advance toward the* Hipper, *and retreat into the smoke again, after which they attacked from a different direction. This was repeated several times without firing torpedoes, thus maintaining the threat.*

The Onslow *received a direct hit and sustained heavy casualties, including Captain Sherbrooke, who received a severe facial injury.* Onslow *retired from the action, leaving* Obedient *in command. Although* Achates *was also in a crippled state, she continued to make smoke. This small destroyer force out-maneuvered* Hipper *for a considerable time, thus preventing it from attacking the convoy and allowing the* Sheffield *and* Jamaica *to arrive on the scene.*

The cruisers under the command of Admiral Burnett closed the convoy at more than 30 knots and achieved complete surprise. They opened up with their six-inch guns and almost immediately scored direct hits. The Hipper *retired after sustaining damage and casualties, a six-inch shell entering her boiler room and another setting her hanger on fire. The German destroyer* Eckholdt *appeared on the scene and, mistaking the British cruisers for German ships, steered straight toward them. She was literally blown out of the water.*

The Lützow *then made a challenge with the aim apparently of protecting the* Hipper, *abandoning the operation, and making for base.* Sheffield *and* Jamaica *then broke off the engagement in order to cover the convoy, whose escort had been badly depleted. The trawler* Northern Gem *picked up the survivors of the* Achates, *which eventually sank. The fate of the minesweeper* Bramble *remained unknown, but it was assumed she was sunk by a German destroyer when searching for convoy stragglers.*

Captain Sherbrooke of the badly damaged Onslow *survived and was awarded the Victoria Cross, but spent the rest of his life with only one eye. The following signal was made by C. in C. H.F. (Commander in Chief Home Fleet—Admiral Tovey):—"To CS 10, 'Sheffield,' 'Jamaica,' Capt. D 'Onslow' (R), Escorts of Russian Convoy. Your defence of the convoy was most gallant. The boldness of your action was entirely responsible for the safe conduct of the ships under your escort, a feat of which you may all be proud."*

JW-51B completed its voyage without further trouble from either the sea or the Germans.

Succeeding eastbound convoys JW-52 and JW-53 totaling forty-two ships completed their voyages without loss, as did westbound convoy RA-51 with its fourteen ships. All three convoys endured Luftwaffe attacks and, although the ships got away cleanly, the attackers weren't so lucky.

The German air attacks always followed the same pattern. First, reconnaissance planes sighted the convoy, followed shortly by the arrival of bombers and torpedo planes. But the pilots had a tougher time in winter than they did during summer's long sunlit days. Shorter days allowed for no waste of time and no errors in navigation. Often flying toward their targets in storms and snow squalls, the crews were lucky to even catch sight of the ships. Wind buffeted them on their approach flight, which could knock them off target during the attack's crucial final seconds. A dozen aircraft took off on January 24 to attack convoy JW-52, but only three reached the convoy. In the midst of a squall and facing an almost solid wall of anti-aircraft fire, they pressed home their attack. All three were shot down.

The small, eleven-ship convoy RA-52 sailed from Kola Inlet on January 29, 1943. Despite the usual bad weather, it was smooth sailing until *U-255* (Kapitänleutnant Reinhart Reche) struck on February 3. In broad daylight, Reche fired two torpedoes at the freighter *Greylock*, one of which hit aft, sealing the ship's doom. The ten officers, twenty-six crewmembers, twenty-five armed guards, and nine passengers, including three survivors from *Ballot*, all abandoned ship safely in four lifeboats. Most were picked up quickly by HMS *Lady Madeleine* and HMS *Northern Wave*, while four crewmembers were picked up by HMS *Harrier*.

So far, the season's JW and RA convoys avoided the large losses experienced by their PQ and QP predecessors. But RA-53 wasn't so lucky. Sailing from the Kola Inlet on March 1, the convoy's thirty merchant ships were guarded by thirty-one escorts, including three cruisers and eleven destroyers. The relative peace and quiet lasted four days. At 0924 hours on March 5, Reche's *U-255* slipped through the escort screen and fired a three-torpedo spread, scoring a fatal blow on the *Executive* and damaging the *Richard Bland*. *Executive*'s sixty-man crew hastily abandoned ship without orders and were soon rescued, but not before nine men had died. Fortunately for *Richard Bland*, the torpedo passed through the ship without exploding, leaving 8-foot-wide holes on either side of the ship.

A dozen He-111 dive bombers arrived at 1430 hours, but none of them could penetrate the ack-ack barrage. Undeterred, the Luftwaffe tried several more times during the few remaining daylight hours, though with the same lack of success.

Having beaten off one enemy, RA-53 met another challenge for which there was no defense: an Arctic winter storm. The Liberty ship *J. L. M. Curry* was smashed by the heavy seas on March 7. The crews of the other ships saw to their horror a colossal wave lift her up and break her in two. Her crew was rescued, but the convoy was scattered. Twenty-two vessels arrived together at Loch Ewe and then four more in succession. Two others never made it to safety.

Having survived one torpedo from *U-255*, *Richard Bland* succumbed to another one fired by the same U-boat on March 10. Thirty-two of her crew were lost; the remaining thirty-five rescued.

The *Puerto Rican*, an American merchant ship, straggling far behind, was torpedoed and sunk on March 9 by *U-586* (Kapitänleutnant Dietrich von der Esch). Severe weather and ice had rendered three of the ship's four lifeboats frozen and useless. When the fourth one hit the water, its stern boatfall tackle could not be released due to the ice, and it capsized. Eight men swam to a cork life raft, and six later transferred to a larger raft.

From a crew of sixty-two, only eight managed to reach the raft. All except one of them were swept away by the waves or perished in the cold. The sole survivor, August Wallenhaupt, twenty-six years old, was picked up on March 12 by a British destroyer, half crazed and nearly dead. The military doctors at Reykjavik could not understand how he had survived. Both his legs had to be amputated at the knee, as were all the fingers on his right hand and all but the index finger and thumb on his left hand.

Wallenhaupt's story began on a stormy winter night in the Arctic Ocean, just 400 miles off the north coast of Iceland. The *Puerto Rican* was in convoy when she left a Russian port, but for two days the freighter had been alone, cut off from the convoy and the rest of the world by radio silence. The temperature was 30 degrees below zero and the water was 21 degrees above zero—just 11 degrees below freezing. The entire ship was caked with ice.

Wallenhaupt was asleep in his quarters when *U-586*'s torpedo struck at 2200 hours, instantly awakening him. Right away, he knew what had happened: He'd been torpedoed before. Wallenhaupt took time to dress warmly. He slipped on his rubber lifesaving suit, put on his life jacket over the suit, and donned a knee-length woolen seaman's coat with a hood to protect his head.

He went out to his position at No. 4 boat and found other members of the crew trying to free the lifeboats from the ice. They rammed the boats with their shoulders, but "it was like ramming your shoulder against the Empire State Building and expecting it to fall." The boat finally worked loose and was lowered into the water. Wallenhaupt feared that the lifeboat would capsize because of the heavy ice on the falls, which would make it impossible to release the lines.

But he didn't have time to lose: the *Puerto Rican* was sinking fast. He threw himself out of the boat and tried to get clear of the sinking ship. Just four feet from the side of the freighter, he remained afloat with little effort because she generated little suction as she went down.

Wallenhaupt spied a small doughnut raft just a short distance away. It was impossible to swim to it, but the heavy seas brought the raft to him and he climbed aboard. Within ten minutes, he'd pulled seven men aboard the tiny raft.

At some point during his ordeal, Wallenhaupt noticed that he'd lost his heavy fur-lined gloves. His hands were getting numb. In fact, all the men's hands were beginning to freeze, and they tried to warm them by holding them over the automatic flare light on the raft. Just then, a large wooden raft floated by. Wallenhaupt grabbed it and secured the two rafts together. The party, now numbering eight men, split up, five of them crawling over to the wooden raft. Two seamen, however, were sitting motionless in the doughnut raft. They could not be revived.

Wallenhaupt moved to join the men on the other raft but found that he no longer had control over his legs. The other men helped him crawl aboard, and they all huddled together in the center of the raft. Thirty-foot seas pitched the raft unmercifully. Soon the heavy seas, breaking wildly over the tiny craft, encapsulated them in a sheet of ice. A huge wave washed one of the men overboard. One man went mad. All of them prayed.

Their prayers did little good. By daybreak the next morning, one of the survivors had vanished into the icy seas. Wallenhaupt watched helplessly as a third seaman also went over the side.

The other man on the raft was lying on his stomach, his head bare and iced over. Wallenhaupt couldn't budge him: He had become frozen stuck to the bottom of the raft.

Wallenhaupt had been on the raft thirty-six hours without food or drink. He tried to quench his thirst by lapping up some snow with his tongue. He lay on the pitching raft beside his frozen shipmate, drifting in and out of consciousness as the seas washed over him. Shortly before daybreak on the third day, he heard voices. He opened his eyes and looked around in the darkness but saw nothing. The mysterious voices were unrelenting, he prayed aloud to drown out the sound.

Near dark, the voices became stronger. "Hello, there! Hello, there!"

Wallenhaupt said his prayers more loudly. Suddenly he felt a violent bump against the side of the raft: it was a destroyer. The men on the deck of the warship broke into cheers when they saw him move.

He was carried into the ship's sickbay and given a hot cup of Bovril (a salty meat extract), a few sips of water, and a shot of morphine. His hands and feet were wrapped in ice-cold towels. Although safe, he was in pain, his hands swollen to three times their normal size and white with frost.

Wallenhaupt was taken ashore at an Iceland port and transferred to a U.S. transport. In the transport's sickbay, they wrapped his legs in cotton and hoisted them on pulleys. Morphine was injected at four-hour intervals. That, along with frequent injections of blood plasma and intravenous feeding, was just about the only thing that kept him alive.

He was taken to a hospital (which caught fire while Wallenhaupt was there). Just two days later, he contracted pneumonia and pleurisy. But that wasn't the worst of his troubles: his legs and fingers, ruined by frostbite, were amputated.

RA-53 was the last convoy to sail that spring because the longer days brought increased Luftwaffe activity. The British Admiralty suspended sailing convoys until November 1943 for other operational reasons as well, including the invasions of Sicily in July (Operation *Husky*) and at Salerno, also in Italy, in September (Operation *Avalanche*). In addition, with the German defeat in North Africa, the Allies regained control of the Mediterranean Sea. This meant that supplies for the Soviets could be sent through the Suez Canal and to ports on the Persian Gulf, a longer, but significantly safer route. With the opening of the Mediterranean, the Germans permanently transferred several Luftwaffe torpedo and dive-bomber squadrons from Norway to southern France to counter this new threat. Coincidently, many of the British Home Fleet escorts provided coverage and faced their old Luftwaffe opponents from up north.

Although Allied merchant ships and the Royal Navy were out of the battle for seven months, the German and Soviet naval forces fought relentlessly from the north coast of Norway eastward into the Kara Sea and half way to Siberia. The most significant encounter was Operation *Wunderland II*.

Between August 1 and October 3, the Kriegsmarine ran Operation *Wunderland II* against the Siberian sea route. The first action actually took place on July 27, when *U-255* (Oberleutnant zur See Erich Harms) sank the Soviet survey ship *Akademik Shokalski*. The U-boat was on its way to establish a weather station near Sporyy Navolok on the northeast coast of Novaya Zemlya. While the station was being constructed, the U-boat refueled a BV-138 flying boat on August 4. This aircraft spent the following week reconnoitering the area as far as the Vilkitsky Strait in preparation for operations against Soviet convoys by the Viking wolf pack U-boat group, comprising *U-302*, *U-354*, and *U-711*, and by the cruiser *Lützow* standing ready in Altenfjord.

No convoys were sighted. When the flying boat was no longer available, a second operation from September 4 to September 6 with *U-255* and *U-601* produced no results. Three weeks later, on August 21, *U-354* sighted a convoy off Port Dikson and followed it eastward, but wasn't able to reach attack position. *U-255* and *U-601* were followed by *U-354* and *U-302* during the last week of August in the western Siberian Sea. They damaged the steamer *Petrovski* (3,771 tons) and sank the *Dikson*.

From August 13 to September 25, 1943, U-boats of the Dachs wolf pack carried out mining operations in the Kara Sea: *U-625* east of the Yugor Strait; *U-639* off the Ob Estuary; *U-960* east of the Matochkin Strait, where *U-711* was hunting in vain; *U-636* off Dikson; *U-629* off Amderma; *U-601*, which had been out patrolling; and U-*960* off Dikson. On September 18 and 24, *U-711* shelled the wireless Russian telegraph stations at Pravdy and Blagopoluchiya.

At the end of September *U-703*, *U-601*, and *U-960* relieved the boats of the Viking group. On September 30, they located the Soviet four-ship convoy VA-18 coming from the east escorted by the minelayer *Murman* and the minesweeper trawlers *T-31*, *T-63*, and *T-42*. *U-960* sank the freighter *Arkhangelsk* near the Sergeya Kirova Islands but missed the *Mossovet*. The next day, *U-703* sank the *Sergei Kirov*. *U-601* missed the *Murman* and was in turn shelled by her. *U-960* sank the escort *T-42* but missed *A. Andreev*. After these attacks, the U-boats returned to their Norwegian bases, declaring the operation a success.

The German U-boats had dealt a heavy blow to navigation in the western Arctic. So much so that Soviet authorities decided to leave fifteen transport vessels wintering in Port Dikson.

On November 15, 1943, the fall's first convoy, JW-54A, set out from Loch Ewe with eighteen ships, followed by JW-54B's fourteen ships seven days later. These two and the first half of December's convoys, JW-55A, all made it safely to Russia, as did the one returning convoy, RA-51, despite attacks by U-boats and aircraft.

The commander in chief of the Kriegsmarine, Gross Admiral Karl Dönitz, who had replaced Admiral Raeder on January 30, 1943, came under increasing pressure to sanction a sortie by his remaining heavy surface ships. An opportunity presented itself at Christmastime, as it became apparent that outbound convoy JW-55B and homeward-bound convoy RA-55A would pass relatively close to one another as they rounded the North Cape of Norway, only a short passage from the Kriegsmarine base at Langefjord. On December 25, the battleship *Scharnhorst* (Captain Fritz Hintze) with the destroyers Z-29, Z-30, Z-33, Z-34, and Z-38 left Norway's Altenfjord under the overall command of Konteradmiral Erich Bey.

British intelligence intercepted and decoded messages about the German plan. To counter the Kriegsmarine threat, the British assigned Force 2 composed of the battleship *Duke of York*, light cruiser *Jamaica*, and four destroyers—the Norwegian *Stord*, and the British *Scorpion*, *Saumarez*, and *Savage*—under the command of Admiral Sir Bruce Fraser to escort convoy JW-55B. Force 1 commanded by Vice Admiral Robert Burnett in his flagship HMS *Belfast* with the cruisers *Norfolk* and *Sheffield* would cover westbound RA-55A.

At 0755 hours on December 26, Bey ordered the 4th Destroyers Flotilla to search for the convoy, placing each destroyer five miles from each other while *Scharnhorst* went on a southwest course, later turning to the west-northwest. Partly as a consequence of this and of poorly transmitted and executed orders, *Scharnhorst* and the destroyers lost contact with each other.

Forty minutes later, *Norfolk*'s radar picked up *Scharnhorst* at a distance of 16 miles. *Belfast* also picked up the contact, and along with *Sheffield*, they headed for the lone German ship. For Admiral Burnett and his senior officers, this was the opportunity they had been waiting for, and they accepted it calmly. When the cruisers closed to within 6 miles, they launched the opening salvos of what was to become the Battle of North Cape.

Belfast's crew described the battle in their diaries, journals, and interviews. *Belfast* Captain Frederick Parham was among those who recalled the battle:

> On the evening of Christmas Day 1943 we had a warning from the Admiralty that it was believed that the Scharnhorst *was probably putting to sea and we were ordered to push on ahead ... and to cover another convoy which was on its way out from England and was about halfway to Murmansk. I remember very well having a long discussion with my Admiral ... in the Charthouse about what we should do ... that I think finished at about midnight.*

The news about the approaching *Scharnhorst* was met with mixed emotions. On the lower deck, the information that the German battleship was at sea was greeted with a mixture of apprehension and disbelief. Bob Shrimpton, known as "Ping" by virtue of his role as *Belfast*'s ASDIC operator, thought that it was all "a load of rubbish." In the engine room, however, Lieutenant Charles Simpson, *Belfast*'s torpedo officer, remembered more of a sense of calm and reserve:

Nobody showed any apprehension ... after all this was the job for which we'd trained, in some cases for twenty years. This was it. You now relied upon the skill of the gunners to sink the enemy before he sunk you. This was where interdepartmental co-operation was seen at its most intense. We got the gunners to the position they desired as fast as we could.

Since the Christmas Day announcement that *Scharnhorst* had put to sea, *Belfast's* crew was at their defense (combat action) stations. Larry Fursland was part of the engine room staff and recalled how the day passed: silent, tense, everybody waiting. Finally, on the day after Christmas, St. Stephen's Day, the storm broke. Fursland recalled that:

Then came Boxing Day, St. Stephen's Day, I remember as only yesterday, twenty to nine in the morning that's 0845 Navy time, "Action Stations," bugle. The Padre (chaplain) gave a short service of prayer and we all had to go to our action stations ... well my place was down the port diesel, and that's where I went down and that's where I stayed for twelve hours ... Chief ERA came down and started up the diesels and left me. I was clamped up each side, watertight doors, and just a hatch to go down.

While Burnett's 10th Cruiser Squadron screened the vulnerable merchant ships, Admiral Fraser, in the battleship HMS *Duke of York*, with the cruiser HMS *Jamaica* and four destroyers, set sail to deploy to the south, between *Scharnhorst* and her base in Norway. The trap was set. If Fraser's *Duke of York* could bring *Scharnhorst* to action, she would enjoy an overwhelming superiority in firepower, with her 14-inch guns out-ranging and out-punching *Scharnhorst's* smaller 11-inch guns.

At 0730 on the morning of Boxing Day (December 26), the British superiority in numbers further increased when Bey's destroyers were detached to search for the convoy. They failed to make contact and, being notoriously bad sea boats (in part due to their oversized 5.9-inch gun turrets), they were ordered home as the weather worsened.

By this stage, JW-55B was 50 miles south of Bear Island, as the Germans headed north to intercept. Meanwhile, Admiral Fraser was 200 miles away to the southwest, and Admiral Burnett's cruisers were approaching the convoy from the east.

First contact took place just before 0900 hours on December 26 when *Belfast* detected *Scharnhorst* by radar, heading south only 30 miles east of the convoy. HMS *Norfolk* engaged and hit the German battlecruiser, followed by *Belfast* and *Sheffield*. Crucially during this action, *Norfolk* disabled

Scharnhorst's main fire control radar, leaving her almost blind. She turned north and away, still trying to circle Burnett's force and reach the convoy.

Belfast had never fired a full broadside before, and some of the effects were unanticipated. Alone down at his action station on the port diesel generator, Fursland was faced with a problem: the vibration from the first broadside knocked out the two circulating pumps that cooled it. Without the generator, two triple 6-inch turrets—half *Belfast*'s armament—would be out of action.

Acting quickly, Fursland diverted a fire main along the passageway above his position and down through the hatch. Without any tools, he connected it to the generator with his bare hands, bypassing the disabled pumps, and circulated salt water from the main through the generator for twelve hours. He was completely alone.

The first broadside had caused another problem on the bridge, where the armored door of the plot room had been blown off by the shockwave from the *Belfast*'s own after turrets. For Seaman George Burridge, the destruction had a silver lining: "for the rest of the battle we [were] literally able to see what was going on first hand!"

Admiral Burnett was faced with possibly the most significant decision of his career, as Captain Parham later recalled:

> The Scharnhorst *turned north and made away at high speed, and this is where* my *Admiral, Burnett, had to make his really big decision, and I am absolutely convinced it was the right one. Which was that he was not to follow the* Scharnhorst ... *because we couldn't possibly have kept up. The weather was so bad that she would have probably outstripped us and would merely have got round us and probably back on to the convoy. And so my Admiral's decision was to fall back on the convoy and wait and see, I remember him saying to me "I'll bet she'll come again."*

Burnett was absolutely correct. *Scharnhorst* returned to the convoy, only to find the 10th Cruiser Squadron once more in her path. Contact was regained at noon, and all three cruisers opened fire. During a twenty-minute firefight, *Scharnhorst* was hit again, and *Norfolk* was badly damaged by the battleship's 11-inch shells.

The German ship fled south, away from the convoy in an attempt to return to Norway. This time, Burnett shadowed by radar. With *Norfolk* disabled and *Sheffield* suffering from engine problems, *Belfast* was at one point pursuing her formidable adversary alone. Burridge was rather less than impressed by this development:

I recall Admiral Burnett coming on and saying that we were at the moment alone and we were going to engage the Scharnhorst, which frightened the life out of everybody! … [The atmosphere] was as tense as it could be, because we knew we were in real danger then.

Shrimpton was also painfully aware of just how dangerous this period was: "We had to do a cat and mouse game with it … if she had turned towards us and opened fire with those massive gun turrets of hers she would have blown us out of the water."

Brian Butler, another gunner confined with twenty-six other men in one of the ship's 6-inch turrets, recalled how "During lulls in the action, you'd sit there with your eyes closed. There was no way you could sleep. It was cold in the turret, bitterly cold in the turret."

Admiral Fraser in *Duke of York* was to the south-southwest, ideally placed to cut off *Scharnhorst*'s retreat. Fraser made radar contact soon after 1600 hours at a range of 22 miles and closed in. At 1650 hours, *Belfast* illuminated *Scharnhorst* with star shell. Burnett's cruisers engaged from one side and *Duke of York* and *Jamaica* from the other.

Duke of York succeeded in hitting *Scharnhorst* with her first salvo and swiftly began to inflict severe damage. Shrimpton, his ASDIC unusable in the frantic high-speed maneuvering of a surface action, witnessed the death blows.

Once the Duke of York *got in there, with those tremendous guns, it was horrendous to watch … they just smashed the thing to pieces … it was just one blaze from one end to the other … You could see these flashes in the darkness coming through and you could watch the fall of shot as it lit up … we closed as close as possible so that we could open fire on it … her guns kept firing, just before she went down.*

Scharnhorst's forward 11-inch turret Anton was put out of action early, jammed to starboard with guns in the elevated position. Turret Bruno, the remaining forward turret, soon followed when an outbreak of fire forced the crew to flood it to avoid a catastrophic explosion. At 1708 hours, a 14-inch shell hit *Scharnhorst*'s aircraft hangar aft of turret Caesar, starting another fire.

At 1725 hours, Admiral Bey signaled his high command, informing them that heavy surface forces had surrounded *Scharnhorst*. At this stage, the chance of escape was still good, as *Scharnhorst*'s superior speed still enabled her to gradually increase the range. Her greatest chance came at 1824 hours, when a lucky shot severed the connection for *Duke of York*'s main fire control radar, forcing her to cease fire. A young officer, Lieutenant Bates, recognizing the urgency of the situation, climbed the mast and reconnected the radar.

By this stage, unbeknownst to the British, *Scharnhorst* was already lost. A shell from *Duke of York*'s last salvo had penetrated No. 1 boiler room and severed a steam pipe. *Scharnhorst*'s only advantage slipped away from her as her speed dropped to 10 knots. Bey sent his last signal to his superiors: "We shall fight to the last shell." But the end was near. According to eyewitnesses, *Scharnhorst* was on fire from stem to stern.

As soon as Fraser recognized what had happened, he seized his chance and ordered his destroyers to close in to point-blank range and attack with torpedoes. Crewmembers reported seeing the destroyers approaching at high speed, a comforting sight.

HMS *Saumarez* paid the price for this daring attack. *Scharnhorst* was mortally wounded, but she still had teeth, and a German shell smashed into the flimsy director control tower of the destroyer, killing eleven men.

Seaman Eric Parry was aboard *Scorpion* when ordered to attack the *Scharnhorst* with torpedoes:

> *I could hear the orders from the captain to various officers so it became obvious we were close to the enemy. I thought at one time we were going right alongside as we seemed to be looking down the muzzles of* Scharnhorst*'s armament.*
>
> *Our captain was calm with his orders—the S class destroyers being encouraged to attack on their own with torpedoes.* Savage *and* Saumarez *were on the battle cruiser's port quarter,* Scorpion *and* Stord *on the starboard. We closed at a range of 2,000 yards:* Scharnhorst *could have blown us out of the water. I could hear the torpedo officer calling off the fish as they fired, swinging away we fired all eight and heard them running towards* Scharnhorst*, two hits were reported. Gunner (T) reported to bridge "all torpedoes fired."*
>
> *The captain replied: "Good, let's get the hell out of here."*
>
> *As we turned away we could hear muffled explosions. The S force attack over,* Virago, Jamaica *and* Belfast *followed by* Musketeer *and* Matchless *went in. By now* Scharnhorst *was a dead duck. About 1930 I saw this once magnificent battlecruiser go down by the bows with her screws still turning as she rolled over and sank.*

Four torpedoes found their targets, leaving *Scharnhorst* dead in the water and a sitting target as *Duke of York* and the cruisers opened fire again. At 1928 hours, *Duke of York* ceased fire for the last time, having expended nearly five hundred 14-inch shells. Further torpedo attacks followed, although by now *Scharnhorst*'s captain had given the order to abandon ship.

At 1945 hours, *Belfast* was ordered in to deliver the *coup de grâce* to *Scharnhorst* with Lieutenant Andy Palmer's torpedoes. Years later, he described the moment:

> *In that very last stage she was a very clear point of fire because she was on fire ... she was a mass of flames all the way along the ship ... we closed a bit [but] Bob wouldn't go closer than 6,000 yards, at the beginning of this last phase,* Scharnhorst *was firing an occasional gun and Bob wasn't going to take the cruisers in any closer than 6,000 yards ... we swung the ship and fired the starboard torpedoes and I said to Captain Parham, "Swing her back the other way and we'll fire the other salvo" but by the time we got the ship swinging somehow or other the* Norfolk *had crept up ... and I would have torpedoed her so I had to say "I'm sorry she's fouled the range" so we turned round and then when we turned round and when we turned back again the flames had gone out and she's sunk ... I was so certain that we'd got a hit that I had a swastika painted on to that particular tube.*

In fact, as *Belfast* turned, a tremendous explosion ripped through the German ship, probably originating from her forward magazines. She rapidly began to settle, and at 1948 hours, as Lieutenant Palmer fired, her radar blip vanished, followed by a series of muffled underwater explosions.

The initial reaction aboard *Belfast* was one of elation, but as the full enormity of loss of life became apparent, that elation was soon replaced by more somber feelings. All that could be seen were a pitifully small number of red lifejacket lights, each representing a man fighting for his life in the oil-covered water. Seaman Jack Wright was conscious that, when all was said and done, the Germans were just "sailors like ourselves."

Shrimpton remembered a moment of dead silence. "I think a lot of people were thinking there's a hell of a lot of men on there the same as us, youngsters, families, wives, kids, and they're in that water. I think that was a subduing effect."

Seaman Eric Parry recalled picking up survivors:

In company with Matchless *we were ordered to move in as close as possible and pick up survivors. Being stopped, the ASDIC crew were sweeping the area in case U-boats were about. We were now attempting to rescue the poor bloody crew of the* Scharnhorst, *what few were left, as few survived. The survivors were drenched in oil and half dead with cold, and swallowing fuel, some were injured.*

One of them, a very "arrogant Nazi," seemed to want to die rather than become a prisoner of war. Whilst hanging on to the scrambling net over the ship's side he refused all help from me and my mates, but we finally pulled him aboard where he still struggled and was very arrogant and defiant. He was dragged on deck but refused to sit. He fell down and started to cry. I went over to him, pulled him to his feet, at the same time receiving a blow to the chest. Stripping most of the oily clothing from the young seaman, he was only 19, known as "Hans," we discovered a shoulder wound which was bandaged with a handkerchief.

The next day the survivors were transferred to the Duke of York. *As the "arrogant Nazi" left he walked over to me, put his hand on my shoulder, stood for a moment and smiled, shook my hand vigorously and then got into the boat. Opening my hand I found an oily, soggy photograph. I never saw him again but was proud to have known him. A German sailor, some poor mother's son who, in a small way, was saved from the cold Arctic waters of the North Cape.*

Boy Seaman David Jones, aged seventeen, added his recollections of the battle:

It was only when the Scharnhorst *caught fire and was burning; you could see it on the horizon. At that time I was on P2 twin 4-inch gun ... and we had a port at the front of the gun shield, open, and I had my head out there looking and I could see it.*

We could see the tracers and things like that, we couldn't actually see the ships because it was pitch dark ... that time of year there was just a couple of hours of daylight at noon.

About thirty odd survivors out of about 2,000. I sometimes think of them, particularly about Christmas and say a little prayer for them. I'm not a religious person but I think of them sometimes.

Just thirty-six survivors were rescued before the British ships were ordered to vacate the area due to the danger of attack by U-boats. The death toll was 1,927 men, many left on board *Scharnhorst*, as well as several hundred who perished in the water.

As a consequence, the command to abandon rescue operations has become the source of some controversy in recent years, but the U-boat danger was very real. Rear Admiral Bey had received a signal at 1911 hours stating that all U-boats and aircraft in the area were being deployed to assist *Scharnhorst*. But in the frozen waters of the Arctic, it was highly unlikely that any of the *Scharnhorst* men would have survived more than a few minutes waiting for rescue.

British dead numbered eighteen from *Norfolk* and *Saumarez*. This was bad, but the completeness of the victory could not be denied. As the triumphant *Belfast* made her way to Murmansk, Captain Parham ordered "spice the main brace," and extra rum was distributed to all. In Murmansk, eighteen-year-old Oscar de Ville was faced with the reality of battle, as the victorious destroyers, cheered by all the ships in the harbor, tied up alongside and their casualties were brought across *Belfast*'s decks to the waiting ambulances on shore:

> *We went back to Kola ... there was a small assembly of ships, some damaged, and I think the experience [I] had there that I remember the most was being detailed to be one of a hospital party to take some of the wounded to a hospital locally, which meant helping them across the decks of destroyers onto land ... and that was quite a harrowing thing at 18 to be doing. I thought they were very very brave guys—one felt very bad about leaving them in a hospital in a one-off village like Kola ... goodness knows how good it was.*

Fraser's forces entered the Kola Inlet in triumph, although not without genuine regard for an enemy they believed had fought bravely in very unfavorable circumstances. In a moving ceremony aboard *Duke of York*, the German survivors were assembled and the flagship's officers somberly saluted them, after which Admiral Fraser paid tribute to the courage and determination of the enemy ship and her crew. Privately he later told his officers: "I hope that if any of you are ever called upon to lead a ship into action against an opponent many times superior you will command your ship as gallantly as *Scharnhorst* was commanded today."

The ship's company was aware of the importance of their achievement. With the destruction of *Scharnhorst*, any hopes the Germans had of mounting a serious surface threat to the Arctic convoys disappeared. Palmer summed up the victory later: "We'd been waiting for this opportunity for a couple of years and we knew that once the *Scharnhorst* was eliminated the real threat to arctic convoys would be removed ... we returned to Scapa and great jubilation."

Although the Kriegsmarine's large ships were no longer a threat, the U-boats were still a force to be reckoned with. New types of torpedoes were being added to their arsenal, making them even more deadly to merchant ships and escorts.

The first was the FAT (*Federapparat Torpedo*), which came into service in late 1942. Instead of running a straight course after being fired, a FAT followed a preprogrammed wandering course with regular 180-degree turns. Convoy JW-56A would be the first Arctic convoy to encounter U-boats with FATs.

The *Zaunkönig* (German for "Wren" and designated as "GNAT" by the Allies) was introduced in autumn 1943. Designed to be an escort-killer, it worked by locking onto the loudest propellor noise after a run of 400 meters from its launch. Its one drawback was that the loudest noise often proved to be the U-boat itself.

Another innovation was the snorkel, which, when raised to the surface, allowed a U-boat to recharge its batteries without surfacing. A low-lying camouflaged float attached to the snorkel was all that betrayed the U-boat's presence. It was almost invisible to the eye and no radar could detect it.

JW-56A, a twenty-ship convoy, sailed from Loch Ewe on January 12, 1944, heavily escorted by the cruisers HMS *Brunswick* and *Kent* in addition to destroyers *Hardy* (SOE), *Inconstant, Obdurate, Offa, Savage, Venus, Vigilant, Virago*, and the Norwegian *Stord*. Three days later, the convoy ran into heavy weather off the Faroe Islands, and many of the ships set off for Akureyri, Iceland, where they took shelter until January 21. After clearing Iceland and setting course once more for the Kola Inlet, the convoy's troubles were far from over. Waiting for the rich merchant ship targets was a line of ten U-boats.

Penelope Barker was the first victim, falling to *U-278* (Kapitänleutnant Joachim Franze) leaving sixteen dead and fifty-six survivors to be picked up by *Savage* on January 25. The British destroyer *Obdurate* (Lieutenant Commander C. E. L. Sclater, DSO and Bar, RN) was damaged by a GNAT from *U-360* (Kapitänleutnant Klaus-Helmuth Becker) and left the convoy. The next day *Andrew G. Curtin* was sunk by *U-716* (Oberleutnant Hans Dunkelberg) this time with three dead; sixty-eight survivors were picked up by *Inconstant*.

The final blow that day was struck by again by *U-360*, which damaged *Fort Bellingham*. The wounded ship fell behind the convoy and later that same day was sunk by *U-957* (Oberleutnant Gerd Schaar). Master James Ninian Maley, Convoy Commodore Commander I. W.

Whitehorn, RN, four naval staff members, twenty-two crewmembers, and seven gunners were picked up by HMS *Offa* (Lieutenant Commander R. F. Leonard, RN) and landed at Murmansk. Two crewmembers were taken prisoner by *U-957*. Eighteen crewmembers, sixteen gunners, and two naval staff members were lost. In less than a day, U-boats had destroyed 15 percent of the convoy, fifty-five men, and tons of valuable war supplies in addition to eliminating one of the escorts as an effective weapon.

U-278 struck again with a GNAT on January 30. The destroyer HMS *Hardy* was severely damaged and had to be sunk by HMS *Venus*.

HMS *Mahratta* as part of the escort for JW-57 was the next warship felled by a GNAT. JW-57, consisting of forty-two merchant ships, two tankers that doubled as oilers, and the rescue ship *Copeland*, all under the command of Commodore R. D. Binks aboard *Fort Romaine*, departed Loch Ewe on February 20, 1944. In addition, three Soviet-manned coastal minesweepers and three patrol craft were being delivered to the Soviet Northern Fleet.

The corvettes *Bluebell*, *Camellia*, *Lotus*, and *Rhododendron* provided close escort, along with a local escort of *Burdock* and *Dianella*, also corvettes. Also joining were two Western Approaches support groups, one under Commander Ismay J. Tyson in *Keppel* with *Beagle*, *Boadicea*, and *Walker*. The second support group, under Commander Louis B. A. Majendie, had two frigates, *Byron* and *Strule*, in addition to destroyers *Wanderer* and *Watchman*. Rounding out the escort force was the escort carrier HMS *Chaser*. Distant cover forces were commanded by Vice Admiral Irwin G. Glennie in the cruiser *Black Prince*. With him were the cruisers *Berwick* and *Jamaica* and the Polish light cruiser *Dragon*, as well as a destroyer screen including *Mahratta* (Lieutenant Commander Eric A. F. Drought, DSC, RN).

Lying in wait were eight U-boats of the Werewolf wolf pack.

On February 23, HMS *Chaser* flew off her F6F Wildcat aircraft to chase an FW-200 Condor shadowing the convoy. *Chaser*'s aircraft also flew patrols around the convoy and located several U-boats in the area. They were almost immediately detected by a Swordfish patrol, whereupon Commander Tyson's *Keppel* depth charged and sank *U-713* (Oberleutnant Henri Gosejacob) with its fifty-man crew.

Two days later, a long-range PBY Catalina from 210 Squadron RAF flew above the convoy and attacked the trailing *U-601* (Oberleutnant Otto Hansen), sinking the boat along with the fifty-one men on board. So far U-boats hadn't got close enough to attack thanks to the air patrols, but flight ops ended at dusk, leaving the ships vulnerable to the U-boat's night surface attack tactic.

On HMS *Wanderer*'s bridge, there was a certain amount of criticism from Lieutenant Commander Reginald F. Whinney about Vice Admiral Glennie's plan for night screening positions of the convoy. In the prevailing rough seas, the convoy was thought to be even more vulnerable than usual to a stern attack, but only *Mahratta* and one other destroyer had been assigned to cover this vulnerable sector. Whinney's misgivings were proved justified.

On the evening of February 25, Whinney received a message from one of the destroyers calling up the flagship on radio telephone: "Have been hit by a torpedo, aft, and am stopped." Soon after he heard another message: "Have been hit amidships by a second torpedo."

A GNAT from *U-990* had struck *Mahratta* at 2055 hours. The destroyer exploded and sank within minutes. HMS *Impulsive* (Lieutenant Commander P. Bekenn, RN) and *Wanderer* quickly arrived on the scene to pick up survivors. *Wanderer*'s antiquated guns illuminated the scene with star shell so they could search for survivors. Only sixteen men were recovered from the freezing waters; the commander, ten officers, and 209 ratings lost their lives.

Noel Simon was on board *Chaser* during the convoy and later wrote about what happened when the ships reached Murmansk:

> On arrival in Murmansk, the survivors were transferred to Chaser for the passage home. I talked to a group of Mahratta ratings—none of the officers had survived—who told me of the heroism of their doctor. Having managed to climb onto one of the few Carley floats to have come through the sinking, he set about hauling the others aboard. The float soon became overcrowded.
>
> Remarking almost casually, "There's not enough room for us all," the doctor slipped over the side into the sea and was never seen again.
>
> The straightforward manner in which the survivors recounted this event, and the admiration and affection with which they spoke of their doctor—whose name (oddly enough) none of them knew—made a deep impression upon me.
>
> Not until months later, and then quite by chance, did I discover that Mahratta's doctor was none other than Peter McRae, a contemporary of mine at school. As a boy he had been one of the most delightful and gifted of people. A good all-rounder, successful in all he undertook, yet completely unassuming. I remember him as an exceptionally fine rugger player—certainly the most outstanding fly-half in the school during my time there.

Several years after the war, a proposal was made that his self-sacrifice should be recognized by a suitable award but, sadly, the Admiralty did not concur.

The succeeding convoys, RA-57, JW-58, RA-58, and RA-59 totaling 161 ships, only lost one merchant ship: *Empire Tourist* from RA-57. After RA-59 arrived in Loch Ewe on May 6, 1944, the British Admiralty again halted the convoys until mid-August. Although the large Allied convoys had ceased, a constant flow of small Soviet convoys and single ship sailings continued to work their way through the eastern Arctic.

Freed of the need to fight the large convoys, the Germans turned their attention to disrupting this traffic. It was during this time that one of the most tragic events of the Arctic sea war occurred, when *Marina Raskova* (the former U.S. freighter *Ironclad*) under command of Captain V. A. Demidov, was sunk on August 12, 1944.

On August 8, *Marina Raskova* put to sea with a load of general cargo and 354 passengers, including 116 women and 24 children, as part of convoy BD-5. She was accompanied by three escort trawlers, T-*114*, T-*116*, and T-*118*, with escort commander Captain of 1st Rank A. W. Shmelev. By order of Shmelev, the trawlers protected the transport with a half circle, ahead and to the left and right of *Marina Raskova*.

Among the crew on *Marina Raskova* was twenty-year-old Claudia Mihajlovna Nekrasov, who had just finished a course at the Arkhangelsk Medical Institute. The diploma of doctor of general medicine was nestled in a small suitcase among her simple belongings. Nekrasov lodged with two girls aboard *Marina Raskova*: medical assistant Shuru Galstuhovu and doctor Revekku (years later, Nekrasov no longer remembers her surname). Both were young and cheerful. Revekku was twenty-four, and Galstuhovu had only recently turned eighteen.

On the evening of August 12, 1944, Nekrasov conducted First Aid lessons with crew. It was the first time she had led a class, and she was a little worried. To make a good impression upon her listeners, she wore her best dress and shoes. She recalled the events of the voyage in her somewhat broken English:

Suddenly a blow shook the vessel. Doors swung open, boxes flew off tables, heaps of medicine vials scattered on the deck. I was flung away from a door, at falling painfully and was kicked by something.

Limping, I headed out in a corridor only to find it filling with water. She ran out on deck and was drenched from above [by] the cold stream of sea water.

Children and adults rushed about on deck, searching for rescue. Shouts were heard:

"Torpedo!"

"Boat!!"

"We're sinking, help!"

Panic became ripe. And in the sea new explosion thundered ...

On the bridge of T-118, Shmelev and the commander of a trawler, Captain Lieutenant Kuptsov, heard the explosion. Although sonar did not find any hint of U-boats nearby, messages received from Dikson asserted that they prowled somewhere nearby.

Shmelev ordered a course change to close in on White Island, 60 miles away, where he hoped shallow depths will not allow submarines to steal up to an escort.

Then at 2151 hours, the trawler's hull shuddered from the deaf explosion distributed behind the stern. Having turned back, Shmelev with Kuptsov had seen Marina Raskova's *right side foamy in the water and wreathed in smoke.*

With a rage Shmelev punched on gunwale.

"It seems it was a mine," he signaled the other ships.

"Typically for not contact mine," he thought.

"Ask Marina Raskova *how they're doing."*

Raskova replied: "I have a hole on the starboard side."

"Let's go to their aid," Shmelev ordered. "Have 116 and 114 there too."

As T-118 rushed off to the transport, she was torpedoed in the stern and a minute later began to plunge quickly into the sea.

This explosion also was heard on Marina Raskova.

Marina Raskova's *Captain Victor Alexandrovich Demidov and crew quickly put things in order on a deck, calmed the frightened people and stopped the beginnings of panic.*

"Women and children—forward!"

On Marina Raskova, *the first boats had been loaded with children and women. Only then did the other passengers begin to abandon ship.*

On a deck the senior assistant to Captain P. I. Menynutkin with group of sailors tried to get a patch under a hole. Unfortunately, all efforts of crew to rescue a vessel were vain. Having tilted to starboard, Marina Raskova *slowly plunged into the sea.*

Boats from T-116 and T-114 began rescuing passengers and seamen from Marina Raskova *and the sinking trawler T-118. T-114's boats picked up all the women and children from the steamship. In total on this small craft were over two hundred persons.*

After the explosion, the trawler T-118 with the torn-off stern held on the surface of 27 minutes, then its depth charges, which had rolled down from the racks, exploded and the flagship disappeared.

Without sparing any effort, seamen struggled to keep their ship afloat, but the outcome was inevitable.

Shmelev, who was onboard T-114 after the destruction of his ship, analyzed both explosions and not finding any suspicious underwater noises, concluded that the escort has got on a minefield and no submarine was nearby.

But it was.

Six thousand yards away from DB-5, *U-365's* commander, Oberleutnant Heinz Eckelmann, carefully raised his periscope, looking for the next victim. Meanwhile, the commander of T-*114*, Captain Lieutenant I. O. Panasjuk, started rescuing passengers of *Marina Raskova* and stopped his antisubmarine search. The weather began to worsen, but rescue operations went ahead at full speed. The evacuation of passengers, and then of the vessel's crew, went smoothly. During these dramatic and dangerous hours, the seamen of the steamship *Marina Raskova* showed the best human qualities: courage, selflessness, and readiness to offer themselves for the sake of the lives of others.

Nekrasov did not consider herself as the weak woman among the valiant men aboard *Marina Raskova*. When it came time for her to abandon ship, she did the same as the crewmembers, leaving the vessel with them. She also helped the other women into the lifeboats and handed them the children who were on board.

Claudia Mihajlovna Nekrasov continued her story:

Suddenly the trawler T-114 was rocked by a deafening explosion. A high water column and smoke shot up, ship fragments, and when the smoke has dissipated, only the bow part of the trawler was seen. In three minutes it turned over and disappeared.

Horror captured all who observed this picture. On the lost trawler were over two hundred persons rescued from Marina Raskova *and trawler T-118 and most terribly, 136 of them were women and small children.*

Shaken by the awful tragedy played before their eyes, passengers noticed at once that their little craft has ceased to move. T-116 had chopped off the towline and at full speed left the scene.

The commander of a trawler Captain Lieutenant V. A. Babanov, at last understood that the escort was exposed to attacks of the submarine or submarines and was afraid for life the 186 survivors he had on board and the life of his ship.

Shortly after T-116 disappeared behind the horizon, at two fifteen. A double explosion shook the sky and the sea: fascist pirates had finished Marina Raskova.

When the steamship disappeared from a surface from sea depths, the submarine slowly emerged. The boat passed by the overflowed boats, heading west after the surviving trawler.

In a stormy sea remained more than 150 persons. Except for the kugas [small boats] there were three whaleboats, several lifeboats, and a boat from the lost trawler T-114.

It is difficult to describe sufferings of these people. Semi-undressed, hungry, tormented by thirst, doused by ice splashes, and penetrated by a gale, they behaved differently in these hours and days of heart-rending experiences. The general misfortune is a litmus piece of paper that showed sincere qualities of everyone. Here was heroism and cowardice, selflessness and egoism, hope and despair, struggle and capitulation.

The high call of duty and courage was shown by such people as the senior technician-lieutenant M. P. Makarovsky, the captain purser. S. Rashev, the third assistant to the captain of a steamship Marina Raskova I. D. Vondruhov, chief petty officer N. I. Alekseev, engineer Malinin, captain Voevodkin, science officer Kuharev, nurse Galstuhova, and others.

For more than twenty days, searches by the people scattered across Kara Sea which have endured tragedy at White island proceeded. In them participated seven ships of the Belomorsky military flotilla, eight seaplanes, field men, and polar explorers on island White Island and peninsula Yamal.

When still hundred miles from White Island, we were found out by a seaplane piloted by Captain S. V. Sokola, and it happened that after almost in three weeks of drift only fourteen persons were still alive.

Samples of courage and heroism was shown by the pilots. Unprecedented, the feat was made by Lieutenant Colonel M. I. Kozlov. So overloaded with rescued people, the aircraft couldn't take off. The pilot, Matvej Ilyich, used it as a boat for twelve hours on a raging sea among the huge waves ready the entire fifty to the White Island.

Remember the names of those who risked their lives, tearing the survivors from the icy grip of death. These were military pilots Kozlov, Sokol, Fedukov, Khotulev, Evdokimov, Ruban, Belikov and their comrades. Looking for crews of warships involved, DO-203, BO-2W, MO-501, T-60, T-61, T-116, and T-117. Vice Admiral S. Kucherov, commander of the White Sea Flotilla, personally led the search and rescue effort.

The boat with *Marina Raskova*'s captain V. A. Demidovym, First Lieutenant P. I. Menyputkinym, the second assistant to captain A. A. Kazimirom, the fourth assistant N. A. Vaganov, A. N. Volochkovym, the assistant to the captain V. I. Vennikovym's military gunners, and four rank-and-file members of crew, whose names it was not possible to establish, completely disappeared in the cold open spaces of Kara Sea.

At the end of August at Rogozin's Cape on White Island, a boat with twenty bodies was found. It proved impossible to identify individuals or which ship the boat was from, so all were buried in a communal grave on this far polar island.

Claudia Mihajlovna Nekrasov's grief was enduring:

> *For about a month I had still nightmares connected with memoirs on torpedoing. I could not see relatives of victims on* Marina Raskova *which, having learnt that I survived, came in hope of learning about destiny of the relatives. What could I tell them?*

Of all the losses suffered at sea in the Arctic regions during World War II, this was the greatest single loss of life and, perhaps, the greatest tragedy. On board *Marina Raskova* and the two minesweepers were 618 people. Sailors and airmen rescued 256 people. The 362 dead included all of the children.

On August 15, 1944, JW-59 with thirty-three ships left Loch Ewe for the Kola Inlet. This was the beginning of the end for the Arctic Convoys.

Although on the defensive in the air, on land, and at sea, Wehrmacht forces continued fighting tenaciously. After the destruction of its surface units, Kriegsmarine U-boats continued to strike in the Atlantic and Arctic. For boats operating in the Atlantic, each mission meant almost certain death from Allied hunter-killer groups, which were often built around escort carriers or radar-equipped long-range aircraft that flew day and night in all weather. With the loss of their bases in France's Atlantic coast after the D-Day landings in June, the boats stationed there transferred to Norway, operating against the Arctic convoys with occasional forays west to the British coast.

A FEW FINAL WORDS

Sixteen convoys sailed between August 1944 and April 1945. U-boats claimed seven merchant ships and four Royal Navy escorts. Three of the escorts, HMS *Bluebell*, *Lapwing*, and *Goodall*, were lost in the final nine weeks of the war.

Although World War II in Europe ended on May 8, the last convoy, RA-67, sailed from the Kola Inlet for the River Clyde on May 31, 1945. The convoy had to contend with the ice barrier and leftover drifting mines, and it was deemed prudent to sail one more convoy. Then it was over, the convoy system was dismantled, and, except for the tragedy of PQ-17, the memories of the Arctic Convoys were overshadowed by other World War II events.

Between August 1941 and May 1945, seventy-seven Arctic convoys sailed the Arctic Ocean, not including Operation *FB*, which totaled roughly 1,400 merchant ships. Of these, 104 were sunk and 829 lives were lost. It cost the British Royal Navy eighteen warships with 1,944 of their crews. The German toll was five war ships, thirty-one U-boats, and an unknown number of aircraft and dead. The Soviets lost at least twenty-nine other merchant ships as part of the Arctic Convoys as well as an uncounted number of warships, aircraft, and casualties. Although these numbers pale in comparison to the losses sustained in the Battle of the Atlantic or to millions of men, women, and children killed during the Great Patriotic War and throughout the world, the losses still reverberate.

Regardless of the comparison, Arctic Convoys were proportionately the deadliest for ships and crews of any in the war. Yet the sacrifices brought on by these convoys have been largely ignored or forgotten in Europe and America, except for a few isolated locations in England and Scotland. The Russians remember and have raised monuments honoring all those who fought regardless of nationality. Even there, though, memories are fading as veterans of the war die. So it remains for us in later generations to remember their sacrifices.

So long as we live, they too shall live,

for they are now a part of us,

as we remember them.

—R. B. Gittelsohn

RESOURCES

T he research material and stories used for this book came from a variety of sources. Many of the books and publications are out of print and their authors have passed on.

BOOKS (BY LANGUAGE)

English

Blond, Georges. *Ordeal Below Zero*. Mayflower-Dell: London, 1956.

Brookes, Ewart. *The Gates of Hell: The Terrible Story of the Arctic Convoys in the Second World War*. Arrow Books Ltd.: London, 1962.

Carse, Robert. *A Cold Corner of Hell: The Story of the Murmansk Convoys 1941–45*. Doubleday & Company, Inc.: Garden City, New Jersey, 1969.

Campbell, Ian and Macintyre, Donald. *The Kola Run: A Record of Arctic Convoys 1941–1945*. Futura Publications Limited: London, 1958.

Churchill, Winston S. *The Grand Alliance*. Houghton Mifflin Company: Boston, 1950.

Clifford, Kenneth J., Lieutenant Colonel USMCR, Ed. *The United States Marines in Iceland, 1941–1942*. Historical Division Headquarters, U. S. Marine Corps: Washington, D.C., 1970.

Donovan, James A., Colonel, U.S. Marine Corps (Ret). *Outpost in the North Atlantic: Marines in the Defense of Iceland*. "Marines in World War II Commemorative Series." Marine Corps Historical Center: Washington, D.C., 1991.

Evans, George H. *Through the Corridors of Hell*. Formac Publishing Company Limited: Antigonish, Nova Scotia, Canada, 1980.

Fairchild, Byron. *Command Decisions*. Center of Military History, Department of the Army: Washington, D.C., 2000.

Griffith, Hubert. *R.A.F. in Russia*. Hammond, Hammond and Company, Ltd.: London, 1942.

Hague, Arnold. *The Allied Convoy System 1939–1945: Its Organization Defense and Operation*. Naval Institute Press: Annapolis, Maryland, 2000.

Haynes, John L. *Frozen Fury: The Murmansk Run of Convoy PQ-13*. PublishAmerica: Baltimore, Maryland, 2010.

Hazell, Martin. *Poles Apart: Polish Naval Memories of World War II*. South West Maritime Society: Exeter, England, 2007.

Hughes, Robert. *Flagship to Murmansk*. Futura Publications Limited: London, 1956.

Hutson, Harry C. *Arctic Interlude: Independent to North Russia*. Merriman Press: Bennington, Vermont, 1997.

Llewellyn-Jones, Malcolm, Ed. *The Royal Navy and the Arctic Convoys: A Naval Staff History*. Routledge: Abingdon, England, 2007.

Lund, Paul and Ludlam, Harry. *Trawlers Go to War*. New English Library: London, 1972.

Mansergh, Audrey, Ed. *With the Red Fleet: The War Memories of the Late Arseni G. Golovko*. Putnam: London, 1965.

Moore, Arthur R. *A Careless Word ... A Needless Sinking*. American Merchant Marine Museum: Kings Point, New York, 1983.

Morison, Samuel Eliot. *History of United States Operations in World War II, Volume I: The Battle of the Atlantic, 1939–1943*. Little, Brown and Company: Boston, 1975.

Mills, Morris O. *Convoy PQ-13: Unlucky for Some*. Bernard Durnford Publishing: West Sussex, England, 2000.

Naval Historical Center. *The Official Chronology of the U.S. Navy in World War II*. Washington, D.C., 1993.

Ogden, Graeme. *My Sea Lady: The Story of HMS Lady Madeleine*. Hutchinson of London: London, 1963.

Pearce, Frank. *Last Call for HMS Edinburgh*. William Collins Sons & Co. Ltd.: London, 1982.

Raebel, Geoffrey W. *The Royal Australian Air Force in Russia—1942*. Australian Military History Publications: Loftus, New South Wales, Australia, 1997.

Reminick, Gerald. *No Surrender: True Stories of the U.S. Naval Armed Guard in World War II*. The Glencannon Press: Palo Alto, California, 2004.

Rohwer, J. and Hümmelchen, G. *Chronology of the War at Sea 1939–1945* (2 volumes). Arco Publishing Company, Inc.: New York, 1973.

Ruegg, Bob and Hague, Arnold. *Convoys to Russia: Allied Convoys and Naval Surface Operations in Arctic Waters 1941–1945*. World Ship Society: Kendal, England, 1992.

Rutter, Owen. *Red Ensign: A History of Convoy*. Robert Hale Limited: London, 1943.

Schofield, B. B. *The Russian Convoys: Heroes of the Murmansk Run—Allied Seaman Who Fought Stukas, Nazi Subs and Frozen Arctic Seas in WWII*. Ballantine Books: New York, 1967.

Tye, Chris E. *The Real Cold War*. Delco Creative Services Ltd.: Rochester, England, 1994.

U.S. Department of State. *Peace and War: United States Foreign Policy, 1931–1941*. (Publication 1983.) U.S. Government Printing Office: Washington, D.C., 1943.

Woodman, Richard. *Arctic Convoys 1941–1945*. Pen & Sword Maritime: Barnsley, England, 2004.

Polish

Borowski, Michael. *Memories*. Naval Museum: Gdynia, Poland, 2007.

Boruciński, Henryk. *W Lodach I Ogniu [In Fire and Ice]*. Krajawa Angencja Wydawnicza: Poland, 1975.

Russian

Alexandrov, J. E., Ed. *Polar Convoy: Memoirs of Participants Anniversary Collection for the 60th Anniversary of Great Victory from Dateastvo Island*. Island Publishing: St. Petersburg, Russia, 2005.

Blinov, Vladimir, Ed. *Trips of Fire: Murmansk Shipping Company in the Great Patriotic War*. Murmansk Shipping Company, Murmansk Book Press: Murmansk, Russia, 2005.

Bitsnob, B. M., Ed. *Murmansk Shipping Company in the Great Patriotic War*. Murmansk Publishers: Murmansk, Russia, 2005.

Dremliug, Valentine V. *War Years in the Arctic*. Federal State Institution "Seaport Authority." Big Port of St. Petersburg, Russia, 2010.

Grishanov, V. V. (Chairman). *Arctic Allied Escorts 1941–1945: Report on the First International Conference of the Brotherhood of Northern Escorts*. St. Petersburg, Russia, 2000.

Ilyin, V. N., Editor-in-chief. *Fleet in Victory: All-Russian Socially-Scientific Readings (on May, 19–20th, 2004)*. Administration of the Arkhangelsk Region, Department of Information and Public Relations: Arkhangelsk, Russia, 2004.

Lifshits, Anatoly L. *Sea and on Land*. St. Petersburg, Russia, 2005–07.

Platonov, A. V. *War in the Arctic Seas 1941–1945: Protection of Domestic Maritime Transportation*. NIKA: St. Petersburg, Russia, 2010.

Somkin, Alexander. *We Remember You*. Publishing House "Homeland Lomonosov": Arkhangelsk, Russia, 1995.

PUBLICATIONS

"1941–1945: The Arctic Lookout." *The Russian Convoy Club Official Magazine*. Bob Allan, Ed. Articles selected from issues including Nos. 5, 6, and 29–37.

"Army Air Forces in World War II." Edited by Wesley Frank Craven and James Lea Cate. Office of Air Force History: Washington, D.C., 1983.

"Dictionary of American Naval Aviation Squadrons, Volume 2: The History of VP, VPB, VP(H) and VP(AM) Squadrons." Department of The Navy, Naval Historical Center: Washington, D.C., 2000.

"Guarding the United States and Its Outposts." *Stetson Conn*, Rose C. Engelman, and Byron Fairchild. Center of Military History, United States Army: Fort Lesley J. McNair, Washington, D.C., 1964.

"It Will Remain in Memory Forever" (Russian). Gymnasium 9: Arkhangelsk, Russia, 2009.

"Northern Light Murmansk—Archangel." Official Publication of the
    North Russia Club. Articles selected from issues including Nos.
    15, 23, 47, and 50.
"The Pointer, USN Armed Guard WWII Veterans." Charles A. Lloyd, Ed.
    Articles selected from issues published between 1997 and 2011.
"Polar Convoys 1941–1945" (Russian). Galea Print: St. Petersburg,
    Russia, 1999.

UNPUBLISHED WORKS

Hewitt, Nick. *"Guns in the Night:" HMS Belfast and the Battle of North Cape,
    26 December 1943.*
Matte, Joseph, U.S. Coast Guard. Personal log from the USS *Ingham* (CG).

WEB SITES

"All World Wars:" http://allworldwars.com/Operation-Wunder-
    land-1942.html
"Feldgrau:" http://www.feldgrau.com/code.html
"Soviet Merchant Ship Losses:" http://www.shipsnostalgia.com/guides/
    Soviet_Merchant_Marine_Losses_in_WW2
"U-Boat.net:" http://www.uboat.net
"U.S. Navy Patrol Squadrons:" http://www.vpnavy.com/vpnavy_library_
    donated.html
"War Sailors:" http://www.warsailors.com/convoys/arctic.html

ABOUT THE AUTHOR

Mike Walling grew up in East Brunswick, New Jersey, the oldest of five boys. His parents, Don and Jean Walling, both served in World War II, Don as a meteorologist assigned to the U.S. Air Army Air Force 9th Air Force tactical fighter squadrons in Europe, Jean as a Navy WAVE officer in Boston and Vero Beach, Florida.

After graduating from Montclair State College with a B.A. in Biology, Mike served in the U.S. Coast Guard for six years as a commissioned officer and a senior petty officer. Most of his sea-going experience was in the North Atlantic and included two trips to the Arctic. His assignments included buoy tending, search and rescue missions, drug and fisheries law enforcement, and oceanographic operations. As part of the Boarding Party and Prize Crew on two cutters, he participated in the seizures of a Panamanian drug-runner and a Cuban fishing boat.

Mike's first book, *Bloodstained Sea: The U.S. Coast Guard in the Battle of the Atlantic 1941–1945*, was published by International Marine, a division of McGraw-Hill, and received critical acclaim by reviewers and veterans. The Naval Order of the United States honored him with its 2005 Samuel Eliot Morison Award for Naval Literature. *Bloodstained Sea* is now available through Cutter Publishing (www.cutterpublishing.com).

In conjunction with Flat Hammock Press, he published a new edition of *Sinbad of the Coast Guard*, the adventurous, true story of the USCGC

Campbell's mascot, whose exploits during World War II became legend. Appropriately, Sinbad's story was told by a fellow member of the Coast Guard, Chief George F. Foley, Jr., while the fine pictures were drawn by the outstanding Coast Guard Reserve artist, George Gray.

His book *In the Event of a Water Landing* tells for the first time the full stories of the Bermuda Sky Queen and Sovereign of the Skies rescues, the only two completely successful open ocean ditchings in Commercial Aviation history. These two stories encompass many facets of ditchings: bad weather, engine failure, horrific sea conditions, and indomitable courage in the face of death. Between these two are tales of other ditchings, as well as the journey we humans have undertaken from the beginning of transoceanic flight to today.

Mike's first novel, *Choke Points* (Cutter Publishing, 2009), addresses the real threats to Maritime and Port Security. It's the first of a ten-book Fletcher Saga series spanning 250 years.

In different venue, Mike produced a new version of the old song "I'd Like to Find the Guy Who Named the Coast Guard," originally written and recorded by Paul Yacich and the Coast Guard Band in 1945. The music has been lost, but working with Alison Freemen, this wonderfully humorous tune has been given a new lease on life and updated with three verses reflecting today's Coast Guard global missions.

He has spent more than fifty years collecting stories from veterans from World War II, Korea, Vietnam, and Iraq, as well as those of pilots, merchant seaman, and civilian personnel with NATO and EUFOR in Sarajevo. His research has included visits to London; Sarajevo; Baska Voda, Croatia; Halifax, Nova Scotia; St. John's, Newfoundland; New Orleans; and St. Petersburg, Arkhangelsk, and Murmansk, Russia.

Mike and his wife, Mary, live in Hudson, Massachusetts. He can be reached through his web site: www.mikewalling.com.

INDEX